STEAMBOAT YESTERDAYS

ON CASCO BAY

The Steamboat Era in Maine's Calendar Island Region

~Capt. Wm. J. Frappier

BIRDS EYE VIEW OF CASCO BAY: PORTLAND, MAINE AND SURROUNDINGS.

STEAMBOAT YESTERDAYS
ON CASCO BAY
The Steamboat Era in Maine's Calendar Island Region

CAPTAIN WILLIAM J. FRAPPIER

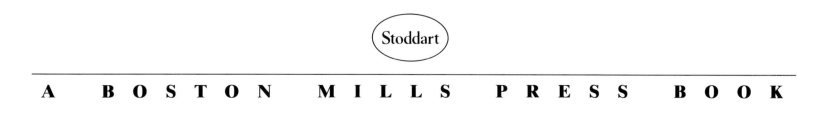

Stoddart

A BOSTON MILLS PRESS BOOK

Canadian Cataloguing in Publication Data

Frappier, William
    Steamboat yesterdays: the steamboat era in
Maine's Calendar Islands region

Includes bibliographical references and index.
ISBN 1-55046-086-2

1. Steamboats — Maine — Calendar Islands Region —
History — Pictorial works.   2. Steam-navigation —
Maine — Calendar Islands Region — History —
Pictorial works.   3. Calendar Islands Region (Maine)
— History — Pictorial works.   I. Title.

VK24.M2F73   1993   387.2'044   C93-093620-5

Design by Gillian Stead
Edited by Gordon Turner
Typography by Justified Type Inc., Guelph, Ontario
Printed in Canada by Friesen Printers

First published in 1993 by
Stoddart Publishing Company Limited
34 Lesmill Road
Toronto, Canada
M3B 2T6
(416) 445-3333

A BOSTON MILLS PRESS BOOK
The Boston Mills Press
132 Main Street
Erin, Ontario
N0B 1T0
(519) 833-2407

Winners of the
Heritage Canada
Communications Award

American Association
for State and Local History
Award Winner

*To my grandfather, Augustus P. Johnson of Bailey Island,
whose many fond remembrances of the old island steamers spurred me
to compile this book about them before the chasm of
passing time erased all chance,*

Augustus P. Johnson of Bailey Island.
Author's Collection

*and also to Judy, Kristin, and Billy, for all the lonely months and
many miles of ocean that came between us, and those times a
secluded writing desk seemed equally as distant.*

TABLE OF CONTENTS

Preface   8
Introduction   9

PART I

The Principal Island Steamboat Lines: Early Horizons and Bygone Zeniths

CHAPTER 1   Beginnings: Early Days of Steam on Casco Bay   13

CHAPTER 2   Rise of the Casco Bay Steamboat Company: A Time of Kindred Companies   21

CHAPTER 3   Steamboats to the Eastern Isles: The Harpswell Boats   39

CHAPTER 4   Days of Glory and Fruits of Expansion   47

CHAPTER 5   Bold Triumphs and More Misadventures: The Seeds of Decline   61

CHAPTER 6   Casco Bay & Harpswell Lines: Brightest Moments and Fleeting Fortunes   75

CHAPTER 7   Casco Bay & Harpswell Lines: Darkest Hours— The Route to Oblivion   93

PART II

The Independent Island Lines

CHAPTER 8   The Inner Bay Awakens to Steam   109

CHAPTER 9   Routes of the Rivals: The Long and Short of Bay Opposition Lines   121

CHAPTER 10   More Routes of the Rivals: Greenwood Shuttles to Gurnet Gambits   135

CHAPTER 11   Lesser Lines: Some Leftover Remnants and Steamers of the Evening   149

CHAPTER 12   Steamboat Courses into Limbo and More Steamboats East of Harpswell   159

APPENDIX A   Steamboat Data/Log: A Table of Vessel Particulars   167

APPENDIX B   Fleeting Bygones: Other Steamboating Events Remembered   177

APPENDIX C   Wayward Steamboats: A Compendium of Prior or Later Histories of Island Steamers off Casco Bay   181

Bibliography   187
Acknowledgments   191
Index   193

PREFACE

Among my earliest memories of the steamboat era in Maine, I still recall vividly a bright June morning on Bailey Island during the summer of 1946. A sizable emerald in scenic Casco Bay, the island was still served by steamboat on a daily year-round mail contract schedule. On this Saturday, a crowd of Bailey's resident and summer population had turned out at Mackerel Cove landing to await the noonday arrival of the *Aucocisco*, steaming in from Portland with mail, freight, and passengers.

At age four, I was mainly concerned with hopping over the heavy wharf timbers, attempting to dodge the cracks, while my mother tried valiantly to hold me in check. Finally tiring of this, I followed the distant gaze of others past the end of the large and weathered old fishhouse. Toward the far end of Abner's Point, beyond which the broad cove opens into Merriconeag Sound and the blue-green expanse of the bay, there suddenly appeared what I imagined to be the biggest boat anywhere!

Decks crowded with people, flags flying, an occasional cloud of black smoke rising from a tall silver-and-black-topped smokestack, the *Aucocisco* steamed gracefully around the entrance buoy and into the cove. A billowing geyser of white steam erupted from around that stack, and seconds later the sound of her whistle filled the air, announcing her approach for miles around. In minutes, amid the clang of maneuvering bells, the creak of ancient wharf pilings, and the dull thump of mooring lines onto weatherworn planking, the *Auco* eased her way into the slip before us.

Towering majestically over us at high water, with boat deck and pilot house well above our heads, the steamer held me spellbound. Hardly less impressive was her captain, a tall, distinguished-looking gentleman in full uniform, who, during the next few summers, was to become the image of everything I wanted to be.

Even though the faithful old *Aucocisco* has gone the way of most American coastal passenger steamers, the emotional impact made by this first sight of a steamboat and her captain is still larger than life in my memory. As fortune had it, my generation was to watch the dying days of steamboating. The last active coal-burner documented at Portland paddled her aged way among the islands until autumn 1959, then two idle years later blew her final solemn parting blasts to the rockbound coast of Maine.

The following chapters relate the tale of an era. Thanks to the experiences and recollections of many local folk who once worked aboard or close by the island boats and knew them in an intimate way, definitive biographies of the steamers are interwoven with vignettes of steamboating personalities and running histories of the steamboat companies. Their steamers provided a necessity of life—reliable transportation for the ocean-borne patchwork of islands stretching north and east of Portland, Maine's largest seaport city.

Many less prominent steamboat companies and steamers plying among the 136 accountable islands have left a fascinating story of their own. The earlier enterprises were frequently unsung and are all but forgotten now. Year by year the chances of reconstructing a comprehensive history of their operation have grown dimmer. On the other hand, some of the later independent and opposition lines survived into the 1920s and 1930s. Indeed, several rival vessels joined the unified Casco Bay Lines fleet and figured prominently in that firm's later history, even into fairly recent times.

As to Portland Harbor ferryboats, these less glamorous steamcraft were far fewer in number and seldom operated outside the harbor limits, but I felt that their story was worth telling here.

In all, 126 powered island and harbor ferry vessels, 98 of them coal-fired steamboats, have plied the waters of Casco Bay (a more relaxed interpretation that included additional gasoline and diesel-powered craft would easily turn up several more). The trade which so busily engaged them all rendered service to upwards of 98 wharf landings, operated over time by as many as 45 companies.

For those who knew and remember any island steamers and personalities presented here in picture and story, I hope this work will be a source of pleasurable nostalgia. In equal measure I hope that those readers who are unfamiliar with Casco Bay steamboat lore will find the book an enjoyable and informative experience.

INTRODUCTION

Steam navigation, as it existed for nearly a century and a half along the rocky shorelines of Casco Bay, Maine, and among its storied islands, is the focus of this volume. Sorely neglected, but not totally forgotten in the decades since its demise, the story of the Casco Bay steamboat fleet reveals it to have been a microcosm reflecting an age of steam navigation growth and fervor, not only in Maine, New England, or the East Coast, but indeed on all of America's coasts and waterways.

Of the once-complex pattern of steamboat routes traversing Casco Bay, a certain amount of the original mileage is still operated with successor diesel-powered ferries. The reader of *Steamboat Yesterdays* could actually opt to relive today the steamboating experience, with some active imagination, of course. For those unable to do this, I intend to offer a journey back in time, digestible in easy doses, perhaps over several evenings beside a cozy fireplace—an ideal spot to visualize and remember when similar but larger fires roared in fireboxes under hundreds and thousands of steam boilers, great and small, to create a force that literally moved the world, ashore and afloat.

According to *United States Coast Pilot 1—Atlantic Coast—Eastport to Cape Cod*:

Casco Bay is a very extensive area between Cape Small and Cape Elizabeth, a distance of 17.8 miles. Between these two capes the bay extends up into the land an average of about 12 miles. The number of islands in Casco Bay is 136, and very many are fertile and under cultivation, and nearly all are inhabited. Nearly every large island extends northeast and southwest, which is the general course of the bay and of all rivers and coves contained within its limits.

This up-to-date description does not differ seriously from the studied observations of the seventeenth-century explorer Captain John Smith, who recalled that "Westward of Kennebec is the country of Aucocisco, in the bottom of a deep bay full of many great isles, which divides it into many great harbors." The Abenaki Indian word *Aucocisco*, translated as "a resting place," has long since become corrupted to Casco. Within this bay it has been said that the islands were as numerous as the days in a year. Not true, said the state and federal governments, but such accounting long ago became legendary; hence the still popularly applied nickname "Calendar Islands." In fact, an April 1992 report compiled by computer programming under the federally-funded Casco Bay Estuary Project not only supported the 365-island count of yore, but went on to reveal a total of 763 islands and ledges appearing at mean high water.

The bay is known not only for its islands but for its headland peninsulas. The one on which the city of Portland is built extends seaward between Fore River and Back Cove and was once the site of an Indian settlement known as Machigonne. To the eastward, the peninsula of Harpswell stretches its fingers some eight miles into the sea, flanked by an even longer chain of islands, known from the mainland point of Gurnet to seaward as Great Island (Great Sebascodegan), Orrs Island (Little Sebascodegan), and Bailey Island, today reached by a long, winding, unique, granite cribstone bridge. Nearer Portland and the western shore, or foreside, are located other chains of important islands. One group, consisting of Great Chebeague, Long, Great and Little Diamond, Peaks, and also remote Cliff Island, is still the domain of public ferryage today.

Offering many safe havens to sailing vessels in centuries past, Casco Bay's relatively protected waters slowly encouraged early nineteenth-century experiments with the newfangled steamboat. Fifteen years after Robert Fulton's successful Hudson River experiments, island steamboating on the bay got off to an abortive start, but then ended abruptly. Coastwise steamboat operations, stemming from their New York origin, developed rapidly, however, attracting investors for routes of considerable distance.

By the 1830s, coastwise lines flourished between Boston and Portland, Bath, Gardiner, Hallowell, Penobscot Bay, and Penobscot River ports to Bangor. Between 1823 and 1845, neither local interest nor travel-conscious residents or vacationers in sufficient numbers existed to justify the formation of steamboat companies within the confines of Casco Bay.

Ironically, the average number of passengers traveling nightly on the early Boston-Portland line vessels had reached about 225 in prime season, realizing over an eight-week period gross receipts of $34,000, a hefty sum in those days.

When local steamboating did gain a firm toehold, island living became far less of a struggle for bare existence. For everyone, it became more tenable, more eventful—even more sophisticated for the affluent. Long before the automobile became popular, many Casco Bay islands had been transformed by the threading courses of the steamboats into scenes of brisk social life. At the turn of the century, for example, Peaks Island had a famous amusement park, as well as the Greenwood Opera House, the first summer theater in America. Cushing Island boasted the Ottawa House, a seasonal mecca for up to 300 guests, many of them Canadians, prior to the fire which destroyed it, for the second, and last, time in 1917.

Scores of other wooden Victorian summer hotels existed, with wide verandas and ever-present rocking chairs or porch swings to accommodate the legions of transient "rusticators" or regular summertime boarders. There was, of course, no shortage of distinguished summer resident families, such as the Curtises, Roots, Thaxters, Hales, Wishes, and Hayses, with heads of each household ranging from railroad presidents to publishers of sheet music, magazines, and newspapers, all ensconced in rambling, weathered-shingle cottages on their favorite island.

To us, the surviving accounts of their summer evening promenades in elegant attire, to meet the island arrivals of such steamers as the *Forest City*, *Emita*, or *Aucocisco*, represent a social lifestyle gone forever. It is part of an American steamboat heritage which can be savored and relived to the full in the pages that follow.

∽

The names of several islands and other places located in the Casco Bay region were formerly spelled in the possessive form. Over time, government agencies such as the old U.S. Post Office Department and the former U.S. Coast & Geodetic Survey added confusion through rigidly prescribed postmarks and garbled geographic place names on government charts, some of the latter based on misinformation of long standing, which sometimes misconstrued local traditional practice and common usage.

The contemporary names of these islands or localities have been used throughout *Steamboat Yesterdays*, except in quotations, which retain original spellings. A representative list follows, with the older form in parentheses: Bailey Island (Bailey's Island); Bustins Island (Bustin's Island); Cushing Island (Cushing's Island); Great Island (Great Sebascodegan Island); Haskell Island (Haskell's Island); Littlejohn Island (Littlejohn's Island); Merriconeag Sound (Merryconeag Sound); Orrs Island (Orr's Island).

PART I

THE PRINCIPAL ISLAND STEAMBOAT LINES
EARLY HORIZONS AND BYGONE ZENITHS

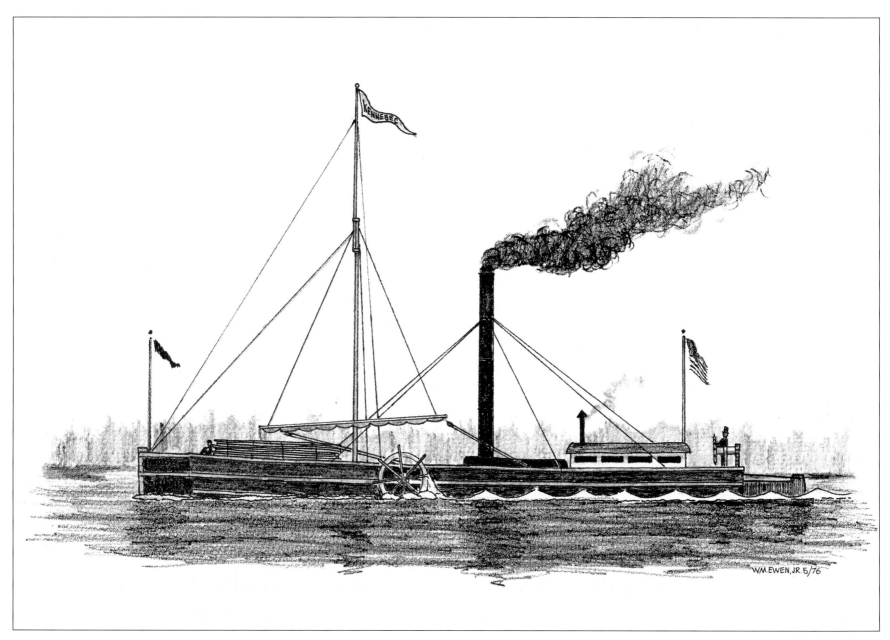

Captain Seward Porter's vision gave Casco Bay its first island steamboat, the Kennebec, *in 1822. Built for Kennebec River use, her limitations there brought her to Portland where she found wide acceptance in island service.* William H. Ewen, Jr.

CHAPTER 1

BEGINNINGS
THE EARLY DAYS OF STEAM ON CASCO BAY

Kennebec, *Experiment*, *Antelope*, *Casco*, and *Favorite*

In the early decades of the nineteenth century, a new and different type of watercraft emerged along the shores of America's coastal bays and rivers. Primitive compared to their successors, these first "steamboats" were mechanically contrived in a number of ways, but all were propelled by the generation of live steam under pressure in a boiler. Most boilers were low-pressure and of the fire-tube type, mounted either on deck or in the hold. Many awkward first attempts at steam navigation went unnoticed, and what local records still survive indicate that both developers and financial backers went unrewarded for their pioneering courage.

Most notable among coastal Maine efforts were the ventures of Captain Seward Porter, one of 11 sons of a prominent Freeport family. Young Seward rose early in life to the command of sailing vessels before he and his brother Samuel became shipowners in the Caribbean and coastwise trades. Perhaps the best known of their sailing vessels, the privateering 222-ton topsail schooner *Dash*, built by master shipwright Brewer in 1813 at Porter's Landing, Freeport, became legendary following her loss in early 1815, when she vanished without a trace, supposedly in the vicinity of Georges Bank. Allegedly, the disappearance of the *Dash* caused poet John Greenleaf Whittier to set the story down in his familiar work "The Dead Ship of Harpswell."

Some six years after the sinking of the *Dash*, Captain Porter's attention focused on the fledgling marvel of steam power, and he tried his hand at operating a steam sawmill at Bath. The mill was not profitable and he quickly left this business; however, his experience with the mill machinery had encouraged him toward the use of steam power to propel a vessel. He determined to make good on the earlier experiments he had heard about elsewhere in the United States and Europe.

On May 13, 1822, Captain Porter caused a considerable local stir by launching the steamboat *Kennebec*, with which he intended to open a passenger and freight service between Bath and Hallowell on the Kennebec River. This endeavor also failed; the *Kennebec* was too underpowered to stem river currents. Undaunted, Porter immediately took her to Portland, where he proposed to run seasonal excursions among the Casco Bay islands.

Starting out as a small, flat-bottomed gundelow, the *Kennebec* had been fitted with a sharp prow and raised sides to give her more freeboard. A crude double-oblique beam engine was mounted to power her two large open-air side paddle wheels. She was subject to some harsh criticism by islanders, and the large open paddle wheels with their protruding paddle boards, as well as the tall stack and flagpoles, quickly earned her the derisive nickname of the "Horned Hog." However, the little steamboat soon came to be appreciated. A crossing on the *Kennebec* from Portland to the nearer harbor islands was far more relaxing than rowing and much more dependable than a sailing passage subject to capricious bay breezes.

The enthusiasm of people who traveled on the *Kennebec* was not dampened even when the wheezing engine would stall on "dead center"—sometimes as many as five or six times on each trip—and all hands would have to pry it over with hand spikes. If this failed, crew—and passengers, if necessary—had to step onto the paddle boards on each of the side wheels to make it turn off the center. On fine clear days, when "chabacco" boats and other sailing vessels found themselves becalmed, the "Horned Hog" did a highly impressive business, scuttling neatly, if noisily, back and forth between the city and the islands with loads of freight and scores of contented passengers.

These daily trips apparently went unadvertised in the local press, probably because service was usually irregular. The *Kennebec*'s first notice in a Portland newspaper was an advertisement in the *Eastern Argus* of August 13, 1822:

The steamboat *Kennebec* will leave Union Wharf at 4 o'clock, Wednesday morning for North Yarmouth to spend the day. Will return on Thursday to take passengers to the islands as usual. If required, will stop at Week's Wharf to receive and land passengers. Will also, should sufficient number of passengers apply, go to the

[North Yarmouth Academy] commencement the day preceding and also the day of commencement. For tickets apply to Mr. A.W. Tinkham's Store.

The *Kennebec* prompted Louis Pease, a Portland constable, bank messenger, and local versifier of the time, to compose these lines:

A fig for all your clumsy craft,
Your pleasure boats and packets
The steamboat lands you safe and soon,
At Mansfield's, Trott's and Brackett's.
And down below they keep the stuff,
and everything is handy;
My jolly boys, I'll tell you what,
That steamboat is a dandy.

However, on days when an unfavorable tide or wind opposed the *Kennebec*'s path, her limitations became painfully apparent. Countless delays caused by the elements showed her to be capable of little more than fair-weather service on the island route. Tradition has it that whenever the wind was nor'west, she was obliged to lay over at Peaks Island—sometimes for almost a week—before a wind shift allowed her to return to Union Wharf. Whether the *Kennebec* operated for more than two seasons is open to question. Beyond a doubt, the harbor ice of winter would have been more than she could have handled, so it is safe to assume that she never ran after the early days of autumn.

Meanwhile, Captain Porter had purchased from New York the most substantial steamer seen in Maine up to that time. When he proudly entered Portland Harbor on July 7, 1823, with the sidewheeler *Patent*, he was now embarked on a much more successful endeavor in coastwise operation.

For many years, no other steam venture warranted local excitement or attention in the press. In 1848, however, a second island steamboat, the *Experiment*, actually showed up at Portland while headed for Boston in command of her inventor, Captain Ebenezer Beard. Powered by a boiler and two small steam engines, the 61-ton craft was driven by Beard's own invention, one screw propeller for each engine. Built by Deacon Follansbee on the Kennebec River at Pittston and fitted out by Beard at Kimball's Wharf in Bath, the *Experiment* ran on Casco Bay for one entire summer, taking excursion parties to the islands.

When this random island service proved less popular than he had expected, Captain Beard worked out a more exclusive service for the 1849 season. He thus began a twice-daily run between Portland and a Cape

The premier effort of Horatio Cook to link the islands with the "Forest City" by steam was the sidewheeler Antelope. *Her design established the styling and appearance of many local steamboats yet to come.* William H. Ewen, Jr.

Cottage wharf, on Mondays, Wednesdays, and Fridays, and as often as traffic demanded on Sundays. The one-way fare of 12½ cents and a commitment to Sunday travelers, flying in the face of reason and Sabbath-day abstention commonly practiced into the 1880s, might explain why business was abysmal, and Beard felt to be a lunatic. A reportedly disgruntled Beard, tired of a sometimes imperious public, then resumed his long-delayed voyage to Boston in search of better recognition for his design, engineering—and perhaps business—prowess.

In 1850, Horatio G. Cook, Jr., a Portland-born machinist and boatbuilder of some stature by the age of 35, built his first notable steamcraft and christened her *Antelope*, a name chosen in anticipation of the new vessel's expected swift performance against oar and sail power. She ran for two seasons between Portland and Peaks Island—and very successfully, it is said. As with many earlier steamboats on the nation's bays, lakes, and rivers, little is known of her today. A sidewheeler, she was 55 feet long with an 8-foot beam and a depth of 2.5 feet. Despite

The Casco *exceeded the* Antelope *in size, capacity and performance. She ran successfully until her engine and boiler were required for the new* Favorite. *Following a lay-up and the installation of a new steam plant, she made a striking comeback.* William H. Ewen, Jr.

Finest of her kind on Casco Bay prior to the War Between the States, the Favorite *had only a brief career before falling into U.S. Government hands. Transformed into a Union gunboat, she never returned to Maine waters.* William H. Ewen, Jr.

her low rating of 3 horsepower, the *Antelope* could carry about 100 passengers; her success in service soon encouraged Cook to expand his steamboat ventures.

In 1852, Cook's second steamer, the *Casco*, was launched to replace the smaller *Antelope* on the Peaks Island run. She was in many ways an improvement over her predecessor, being 75 feet long, with a 12-foot beam and a 4-foot depth of hold. Also a sidewheeler, the *Casco's* horizontal engine had two 12-inch cylinders and a 2-foot stroke. Because of her larger passenger capacity, she greatly improved communication with the mainland, and in her first incarnation ran continuously to Peaks and Cushing Islands for nine years. Her greatest claim to fame came on October 20, 1860. Crowded to capacity, she steamed along as unofficial escort to a royal barge on which the youthful Prince of Wales, later King Edward VII of England, concluded a North American tour before boarding his British flagship amid the cannon salutes from warships of two nations.

With better service and larger profits in mind, Horatio Cook joined forces with Captain Cyrus F. Sands in the winter of 1860. They collaborated on construction of the steamer *Favorite*, a sidewheeler of 96 tons that

could carry 400 passengers. The *Casco* was laid up and her trustworthy steam plant was installed in the new boat, which was ready for launching early in 1861. The *Favorite* was well named, for she proved popular with the island people. By today's safety standards, her length of 100 feet with only a 14-foot beam and a 6-foot depth might be seriously questioned in terms of stability, but geared up at a 3 to 1 ratio, her boiler and engine provided adequate power, and no recorded problem ever beset her on Casco Bay.

By 1863, the Civil War had caused a dramatic decline in the local island tourist business, which had built up steadily since 1850 when William Jones opened the first summer hotel on Peaks Island. Ownership of the *Favorite* had passed to Ross & Sturdivant, prominent Portland shipping agents, and she was chartered by the government and converted to a light gunboat. Accounts of her later years are blurred with the passage of time. One version has her lost off the Carolina coast, the result of a "torpedo" (mine) explosion aboard during the war. Another places her back in commercial service at Boston, re-engined as a screw-propelled steamer and finally destroyed by fire.

Meanwhile, to care for the decreased tourist traffic in 1863, Cook and Sands installed another engine in the empty hull of the idle *Casco* and brought her out to make do on the island line until war's end and the arrival of better times. By the spring of 1864, however, the entry of a new steamer, the *Gazelle*, relegated her to spare boat on the Peaks Island run.

The return to peace, and preservation of the Union, brought an expected upturn in summer trade in 1866, and the 300-passenger *Casco* re-entered full-time service, opening a new Cook and Sands route from Portland to South Freeport. This endeavor did not last, but the *Casco* remained in local registry until 1869, when she was finally beached and cut up for salvage.

The Passenger Towboats and Early Opposition Lines

Tiger, Uncle Sam, Warrior, Island Queen, Gipsy Queen, Clinton, Teazer, and *Lily*

In the mid-1880s, Portland Harbor boasted a number of steam towboats that were much lighter and far less powerful than today's tugboats. They were scant-looking affairs and justified their existence by towing large sailing vessels to and from the open sea under confined harbor and river conditions, where clumsier craft could not maneuver well. Scows also had to be towed from place to place and potable water hauled to fill the tanks of sea-going ships at anchorage. In addition to their regular towboat duties, these small boats found another, more unusual, purpose. Each summer the myriad harbor and bay islands, with their cool salt-air breezes and uncrowded expanses, would beckon to excursionists, and here were the little steamers to take them there. An extra open deck or canopy and a few settees were all that the passengers required. Simply outfitted in this way, many steam towboats came to ply the island waters during the summer season, still towing on the side whenever such business offered and, of course, throughout the off-season.

The towboat *Tiger*, built at Philadelphia in 1852 for William Willard, was one of the most popular of these little vessels and holds the distinction of having been the first steam tug in Portland Harbor. Her owner was also first to explore the option of passenger excursions. In the beginning, he accomplished this by loading crowds of day-trippers onto the barge *Comfort* and then towing her with either the *Tiger* or the larger *Uncle Sam*, built in 1855.

The *Tiger*, *Portland Harbor's first steam towboat, participated in the island passenger and excursion trades by towing the tourist-oriented people-only barge* Comfort. *The* Tiger *was also said to be an early part-time passenger steamer among the islands.* Willis H. Ballard

The *Tiger* soon gained passenger-boat status in her own right after being equipped for a pioneering run between Portland and Harpswell, touching at Diamond Cove on Great Diamond Island. The *Brunswick Telegraph* of April 28, 1855, stated: "Harpswell is a charming place of resort, and we dare say Capt. Willard and his associates will reap a fair reward for their enterprise, in affording this new facility to pleasure resort." The *Tiger's* success was to last barely two seasons. Beginning in 1856, the Willard operation was undermined by competition from the Oxnard Line.

Both the *Uncle Sam* and *Tiger* subsequently became towboats of the Randall & McAllister Company, the former disappearing from the Register in the late 1870s. The *Tiger* even managed to gain local fame by assisting the hastily enlisted large coastwise steamships *Chesapeake* and *Forest City*, as they dashed to intercept Lt. C.W. Read's Confederate Navy spy force aboard the seized Union cutter *Caleb Cushing* on June 27, 1863. The three steamcraft caught the government sailing cutter off the Cod Ledges, setting the soldiers, sailors and Portland volunteers to freeing the *Cushing's* detained officers and crew and capturing the Confederates. Cook and Sands's steamer *Casco*, though not widely heralded in accounts of the affair, had made a special trip to Fort Preble, there loading soldiers and arms for transfer to the larger steamships involved.

With the appearance in late 1863 of the passenger towboat *Warrior*, the handwriting was already on the wall, and by 1871 the *Warrior*'s owner, J.S. Winslow & Co., had placed in service the new passenger steamboat *Magnet*, built that year at Deering. Being light of machinery and tonnage, the *Magnet* was a fast boat. She quickly garnered popularity on various island routes, and in 1873 passed into the hands of John B. Curtis, an influential name in early Casco Bay steamboat circles, who had made a fortune, first in spruce gum and later in "Oh Boy" chewing gum. Curtis had been known as the "Spruce Gum King" before shrewdly seizing upon gum chicle and paraffin in the infancy of their importance and using them to monopolize the United States chewing gum market. His "Oh Boy" gum was chewed by every American president from Lincoln to Wilson, and even by youthful early 1900s fictional hero Frank Merriwell whenever his adventures called for feats of daring. Almost immediately, the *Magnet* locked horns in fierce competition with another equally good steamboat, Captain C. Howard Knowlton's *Tourist*, also built at Portland in 1871.

Although rivalry between these competing passenger steamboats diminished greatly the inter-island meanderings of dawdling passenger towboats, the latter concept took another decade in dying out altogether. In fact, the formative years of the two major island steamer lines began with still other passenger towboats, as related in later chapters.

Other early lines of opposition vessels running to the Portland Harbor islands included the short-lived operations of William Oxnard, as well as those involving two former Kennebec River sternwheel steamboats. Captain Oxnard built his sidewheeler *Island Queen* at Portland in 1856. From there he began a run to Brackett's Landing, on the site of the later Forest City Landing at Peaks Island, thence across the bay to Harpswell before returning the boat to her Portland berth. The *Queen* ran only three seasons before she was gutted by fire and abandoned in 1859, but the owner did manage to salvage her boiler and engine for reconditioning, and promptly built a larger boat in which to install them. Christened *Gipsy Queen*, the new steamer was too large for her second-hand steam plant and had barely enough power to get her by on the run. The Oxnard Line consequently went out of business in the middle of the 1859 summer season, and the *Gipsy* Queen was retired.

At the same time, Cyrus Sturdivant and his associates opted to begin operating another scheduled boat. Their sternwheeler, the *Clinton*, built by John Carter at Gardiner in 1851, was first used as a replacement boat on Captain Nathaniel Kimball's Kennebec River passenger and freight line. Chartered hurriedly for Peaks Island service at considerable monetary risk,

the *Clinton* entered service quite late in the summer and did poorly for the remainder of the season. Since her operators lacked the funds for another try, their shallow-draft "wheelbarrow boat" did not run again locally.

Subsequently, the sternwheeler *Teazer* was brought around from the Kennebec to run between Portland and Scott's Landing on Peaks Island. Built in 1853 for Captain Kimball, the *Teazer* became third in a series of boats connecting Augusta with the Boothbay region, where many upper Kennebec citizens spent the summer. When the *Teazer* proved too large to clear the new Arrowsic Bridge drawspan easily, she was taken off that route and operated instead from Augusta to Hunnewell's Point at the river entrance. But she was too big for the patronage on this run, so Captain Kimball evidently decided that he and Captain Charles H. Beck could sail the *Teazer* into Portland Harbor and take a great portion of the seasonal trade away from local operators. This was a sad mistake, for in spite of her added service to Cape Cottage wharf and admittedly impressive proportions by bay island standards, after only one season in competition, the *Teazer* retired in defeat. Last of the "wheelbarrow" type to hail from Portland, she added a mournful benediction for the sternwheel steamboat on Casco Bay.

Next to enter the fray was the screw steamer *Lily*, built in 1868 as a towboat and later converted to a modest passenger vessel. After opening a Kennebec River line between Augusta and Boothbay Harbor, she was replaced by a newer vessel. It was on the *Lily* that veteran Captain Alfred S. Oliver, a native of Georgetown, Maine, first ran to the Casco Bay islands in 1870. The 38-year-old skipper had acquired his nautical experience by steamboating on the Sacramento River in California, after journeying west to seek his fortune in 1850. Back home in Maine, occupied with only a marginal towboat business, Captain Oliver plunged into a Peaks Island passenger run as a summer sideline. His dream of a successful and independent island line died, however, with the destruction of the *Lily* by fire after only one season.

The Peaks Island Steamboat Company

Gazelle (later *Forest City*) and *Express*

With the ambition and optimism that seemed to characterize all their efforts, Horatio Cook and Captain Cyrus Sands reached the climax of their steamboating enterprise by constructing their largest sidewheeler, the *Gazelle*, during the winter of 1864-65. Like the *Favorite* before her, she was extremely slender of beam for her length and was considered by critics to be unsafe; however, her legal capacity was 800 passengers. Captain Sands himself served as her master until 1880, while Cook was her engineer for some years, finally stepping ashore after training his fireman, Francis M. Foote, to succeed him. Later, a father- and-son team was formed when Lendall G. Foote became fireman, his wages paying for the board charged in his father's house.

The pattern of island steamer travel on the bay continued to expand, and in 1871 a group of Peaks Island residents, including William T. Jones, proprietor of the popular Union House, and members of the Libby and Trefethen families, formed the Peaks Island Steamboat Company. Through islander subscriptions, this company acquired the Philadelphia-built screw steamer *Express*, a towboat with added passenger cabin, and engaged Captain Alfred S. Oliver to command her. The new year-round line ran in opposition to the *Gazelle* for two seasons, with neither boat doing enough business to warrant the effort. Consequently, by 1873, the Peaks Island Steamboat Company easily absorbed the *Gazelle*.

Thereafter the steamers continued to maintain regular stops at both Peaks Island wharves, namely Evergreen and Scott's (later Jones) Landings, also making a single daily landing near the western end of Long Island. The Hog Islands, renamed the Diamond Islands in the 1870s, received less frequent service. At this period, the *Express* was used to advantage for towing duties during the off-season, but through each summer made eight round trips daily to the nearer islands, while the *Gazelle* made five. One or the other was used for two round trips on Sundays, and both made frequent excursion runs, some as far east as Harpswell.

The popular *Gazelle* had always rendered good service to the bay islands, and was perhaps overdue for a bout with misfortune, to be shared by Captain Sands, her kindly old skipper. On August 9, 1873, a fire ignited in a pile of excelsior at Galt's Wharf, Portland, blazed quickly out of control, spreading to Atlantic Wharf and Cromwell Line's coastal steamship *Dirigo*. Then sweeping toward the New York steamer sheds, the raging inferno engulfed the steamships *Carlotta* and *Montreal*. The crews of these vessels were aboard and managed to cast off from the piers, leaving the burning craft to drift helplessly out toward the harbor breakwater as the waters off the piers filled with swimmers escaping doomed ships.

Between Atlantic and Franklin wharves, efforts to get the coastwise steamers *Chesapeake*, *Falmouth*, *Chase*, and Portland Steam Packet's big sidewheeler *Forest City* clear of the fire were successful, but the conflagration destroyed all buildings on both Galt's and Atlantic wharves.

The *Gazelle*, meanwhile, was bound in from the islands with a crowd of passengers, and Captain Sands, approaching the breakwater, soon encountered the drifting vessels. Frantic cries for help rang out as he attempted to steer the safest course among the burning ships. The few panic-stricken crew members still aboard them began to leap into harbor waters, where five drowned and many were injured before help arrived. Sands, however, could think only of the danger of bringing his loaded steamer close to the flaming hulks, and fearful for the safety of everyone aboard the *Gazelle*, he continued on past the distressed ships to his own pier.

As the *Gazelle* continued inbound, the outbound *Express*, Captain Oliver at the helm, had just swung off from her Portland landing. When he sensed the gravity of the situation, he redocked and unloaded, then pulled away and made for the fiery ships. Captain Sands soon followed with the *Gazelle*, but both steamers were too late to stem the death toll. Before returning to her own slip, the *Express* was at least able to take the smoldering *Montreal* in tow and beach the sidewheeler on the shore of Cushing Island.

Although Captain Sands's judgment in the matter was pronounced beyond criticism, the incident left him a broken man. When he retired five years afterward, with Captain Oliver succeeding him in command of the *Gazelle*, his acquaintances said that an abiding sadness clung to him like a shadow.

Later that same year, the *Gazelle* was nearly destroyed in another waterfront fire, but made her comeback enlarged and handsomely rebuilt, having been hauled out and carefully sawn in half, with a new 20-foot midship section inserted. The *Gazelle* was now 125 feet long, with an 8-foot depth, and in order to widen her deck area, hull sponsons had been added. In spite of all precautions, though, for her remaining years she often steamed with a slight list. After still further alterations that increased her capacity to 1,000 persons, the *Gazelle* was renamed and re-registered as *Forest City* on May 8, 1884. Gaudier now, with yellow paddleboxes and lifeboats offsetting her sparkling white hull, and tall red stack with yellow mid-band, she continued to operate for the Forest City Steamboat Company.

Her useful service on Casco Bay ended in April 1896, when the old paddler was sold by the second Casco Bay Steamboat Company to Heald & Roberts of Biddeford and steamed down the coast to her new home port of Saco. This new lease on life in Maine waters was short-lived, however; the *Forest City* was too large a vessel to operate profitably in the Saco River area, even during the summer months. Her final hailing port was Baltimore, Maryland, where she arrived in July 1897 to join an extensive array of harbor excursion steamers for her final years of service. There the one-time queen of Casco Bay, so skillfully guided and devotedly cared for by old Captain Sands and Engineer Foote, was abandoned to shipbreakers on September 11, 1902.

The arrival in Portland of the steamer *Express* under the banner of the newly formed Peaks Island Steamboat Company fulfilled a long-felt need for an all-season service. However, she was first and foremost a light towboat and not especially suited to her new tasks. Passengers complained that she was noisy and that her high-pressure steam exhaust rained endless spray on those who wished an open-air ride on the upper deck.

Disadvantages notwithstanding, the *Express*, along with the *Gazelle*, steamed usefully through the years under the successive house flags of the Peaks Island line (called Casco Bay Steamboat Company after 1878), the two Forest City Steamboat Companies, and finally the second Casco Bay Steamboat Company, which had evolved after 1887. Captain Oliver was transferred to the *Gazelle* in 1880 and was succeeded on the *Express* by Captain Granville Lowell, who remained for the last decade of her passenger service. These were placid years for the *Express*, marred only by a broken shaft that put her out of commission for a time in March 1883.

During the 1880s, the volume of steamboat passengers grew at an impressive but not surprising rate, considering the great number of summer hotels and boarding houses. On Peaks Island alone stood 21 establishments, ranging from the large Peaks Island House, Union House and Coronado Hotel down to the smaller transient guest homes and lodges; accommodations seemed at times to be unlimited. With a much smaller population, neighboring Long Island could still boast three major hostelries, the 150-room Granite Spring Hotel, and the smaller Dirigo House and Casco Bay House. On Cushing Island, the great Ottawa House could accommodate up to 250 guests at $3 and $4 per day.

By 1891, the fleet included a number of faster and more commodious steamboats, and the *Express* was withdrawn and sold for service between Portland and the Saco River. With her old cabin and house cut back considerably and closed in, she resembled more closely the classic small towboat.

The *Biddeford Daily Journal* of November 7, 1892, told a sad tale on page 3:

Saturday there were three tugs on the Saco River ready for service. Today there isn't one and a vessel that wants to come up river must sail up, as did [schooner] *A.J. Miller* this morning.

Two of the tugs, the *Express* and the *Willard Clapp*, which were tied up at the Factory Island wharf Saturday night are now resting on the bottom, their smokestacks just showing a few feet at high tide. The *Joseph Baker*, the other tug, experienced a mishap to her boiler last night, blowing a hole in her water leg, and was laid up today for repairs. . .The tide ran unusually low. . .and the two tugs which were tied up side by side, grounded and listed over in such a manner that they soon filled. . . .There were two men on board the *Express*, R.S. Andrews, the engineer, and Allie Oliver, the fireman. The steward, engineer, and fireman were aboard the *Clapp*. . .at about half past 3 [a.m.], Andrews was awakened by hearing water run in. He jumped up and landed in about three feet of water and then made for the door, arousing the others. The men worked hard to right the tugs but the tide was going out and they could not move them. The *Express* draws about 7½ feet and the *Clapp* about 8, and there is about 7 feet of water near the wharf at ordinary low tide.

Mr. Andrews says that the talk about the *Express* having sprung a leak and drawn the other tug down is all moonshine. The way they lie shows that both filled at the same time. A diver was sent from Portland and was expected out this afternoon to get chains around the hulls.

The *Journal* of November 9th reported:

The Tugs Afloat. . .the two tugs, *Willard Clapp* and *Express* which had been resting on the bottom of the river. . .were floated last night. . . .The *Clapp* was righted yesterday afternoon and when the tide went out last night one of the Biddeford [fire engine] steamers went to work pumping her out. . . .The *Express* had previously been righted and hauled upon the sand spit and when the tide ebbed, the water was readily siphoned and bailed out of her. . . .Both were steamed up today and the boilers and steam pipes found to be all right. The engines may need a little tinkering, but so far as can be told they are all right. The rail of the *Express* proved not to have been broken [as previously reported] and the *Clapp* is not damaged much, although her deck house was started. On the whole, the owners of the tugs may congratulate themselves on having got out of the scrape very fortunately.

Registered at Saco until 1900, *Express* was then purchased by New York Harbor interests and took leave of Maine waters, ending her active career with abandonment in 1911.

The Tourist Steamboat Line

Tourist, *Magnet*, and *Minnehaha*

Portland and the Casco Bay region had their share of entrepreneurs, many of whom tirelessly promoted interests that directly improved local steamboat services—and profits. One was Captain Charles Howard Knowlton, who opened the popular Greenwood Garden amusement park at Peaks Island in 1870, and in 1871 introduced the small steamer *Tourist* to supplement the amusement operation and carry city excursionists to his park.

Almost immediately the captain decided to vie with the Curtis steamer *Magnet* for a greater share of the overall tourist business. His move soon found both vessels making frequent stops at Diamond Island Landing, Diamond and Pleasant Coves, Ponce's Hotel Landing at Long Island, Little Chebeague, and almost any other island supply point that traffic warranted.

Evidently spurred by the strong position of the Knowlton interests, John B. Curtis, the prominent chewing gum magnate, who owned a harbor towboat fleet and the steam ferry *Josephine Hoey*, entered into association with Portland Harbor pilot Captain Benjamin J. Willard and Clark H. Barker. With the *Magnet*, they continued a stiff opposition to Captain Knowlton's line.

Since the Barker family controlled Custom House Wharf, terminus of both the *Tourist* and *Magnet*, Captain Knowlton sensed inevitable problems and agreed to negotiate; the energetic competition was wisely abated when the two seasonal lines united to form the Tourist Steamboat Line. All went well for this combine, except for a near-tragic sinking of the *Tourist* on August 15, 1878, following a scratch hit by the large coastwise liner *New York* within the dock area. No loss of life or serious injury occurred, and the little vessel was promptly raised and repaired.

The *Magnet*, first of the two "maverick" screw-propelled passenger steamers on the scene, also seemed to be the first to bow out of Casco Bay service. Her 1874 charter to Gardiner interests, for use by the Kennebec Steamboat Company, at first linked Gardiner with Hallowell and Augusta, but soon the expatriate Portland steamer, under Captain Anthony Sprague, served all the way to Bath, Boothbay, and the Boothbay Harbor islands. Back in Portland in 1875, though, the *Magnet* resumed passenger trade as a "Summer Steamer" with John B. Griffin, an influential Curtis associate, listed as owner. She remained a regular Tourist Line boat until 1879, when the *Minnehaha* arrived and forced her into spare-boat status. Soon sold, the *Magnet* odd-jobbed about Portland Harbor as a towboat until her abandonment in 1884. The *Tourist*, on the other hand, remained in service, but by 1882 had become outclassed in the islands trade and was sold to run on Passamaquoddy Bay. Registered at Eastport for the remainder of her active life, the *Tourist* was abandoned in 1885.

In 1879, under auspices of the Tourist Steamboat Line, Captain Knowlton brought out a third small steamer, the *Minnehaha*. Fresh from the pages of Henry Wadsworth Longfellow's *Song of Hiawatha*, the *Minnehaha*'s romanticized name translated as "laughing waters," and a statuette of that mythical Indian maiden adorned the top of the pilot house. Sharing in popularity with the other boats of the line, she ran for nearly a decade without mishap.

After 1882, the separate identity of the Tourist Line's "Summer Steamers" disappeared. The owners of the *Magnet*, *Tourist*, and *Minnehaha* had reorganized and were now better known as the first Forest City Steamboat Company. Of this trio, the *Minnehaha* alone continued to steam among the islands as a member of the growing bay fleet until in 1888 she, too, was sold and went to work as a Lamoine-Bar Harbor area ferry and workboat. Owned by the Rodgers Granite Company, she carried the firm's stone-cutting gang back and forth between Deer Isle and various quarries scattered about the waterway known as the Deer Island Thorofare. The *Minnehaha* had a notably long and useful career, hailing from Ellsworth through 1890 and Deer Isle between 1891 and 1914. In 1915, the owners altered the steamer's proud name to *Minnie*.

During her remaining years, the one-time Casco Bay steamboat hailed from New York by registry, although never actually leaving Penobscot Bay, and finally from Southwest Harbor until she was hauled up at Stonington and abandoned in 1926.

CHAPTER 2

RISE OF THE CASCO BAY STEAMBOAT COMPANY
A TIME OF KINDRED COMPANIES

Gazelle (later *Forest City*) and *Express*
Tourist, *Magnet*, and *Minnehaha*
Josephine Hoey and *Mary W. Libby*

In the early 1880s, the steamboat routes to the nearer harbor and bay islands came under the control of five influential businessmen, Curtis, Knowlton, Willard, Barker, and Griffin, although for some time the consortium of companies they owned continued to maintain the earmarks of independence.

An 1875 pen-and-ink sketch depicts the Cook and Sands steamer Gazelle *in her original rig. The perspective is from the (then) open outer end of Custom House Wharf, Portland.* Willis H. Ballard

In 1878 the Peaks Island Steamboat Company, which offered year-round service to the islands, changed its name to the first Casco Bay Steamboat Company and was purchased by Curtis and his colleagues, its fleet continuing to consist of the *Gazelle* and *Express*.

The same group, offering summer seasonal service to all the islands, operated as the Tourist Steamboat Line with the *Magnet*, *Tourist*, and *Minnehaha*, and this summer-only line became the first Forest City Steamboat Company in 1882. Finally, the small ferry shuttle steamers *Josephine Hoey* and *Mary W. Libby*, which ran from Custom House Wharf, comprised the fleet of the Portland & Cape Elizabeth Ferry Company, still a joint venture of the first Forest City Line officials and the Randall & McAllister Company.

Aiming for a single identity, these kindred companies reorganized in 1883, all properties and vessels of the former Casco Bay Steamboat Company and the former Forest City Steamboat Company being merged under the single banner of the second Forest City Steamboat Company. President and manager was Captain Benjamin Willard, while John B. Curtis became treasurer. The Portland & Cape Elizabeth Line (described later) meanwhile remained status quo until its sale two years later to the Peoples Ferry Company.

The Union Steamboat Company and Star Line

Cadet, *Emita*, and *Forest Queen*
Captain Chase's *General Bartlett* and *Florence*

After a few months of relative quiet, the directors of the second Forest City Steamboat Company awoke one morning to find themselves embroiled again in fierce competition. The year 1883 had seen the formation of another opposition line, the Union Steamboat Company. Backed largely by prominent officers of the Boston and New York coastal lines, the new company was indeed off to a prestigious start. Charles A.

The Express *was one of two Portland-based towboats involved in the wreck at Factory Island Wharf, Saco, on November 5, 1892. The slightly damaged ex-Casco Bay Steamboat Company vessel and the smaller* Willard Clapp *were soon raised and back in service.* McArthur Library, Biddeford

Last of the Knowlton "Tourist Line" steamers, the Minnehaha *appears as built, complete with a statuette of her little namesake Indian maiden adorning the wheelhouse roof.* Willis H. Ballard

Her career as a passenger boat over, the Express *rests at the Randall & McAllister coal pocket in 1899. The formerly lengthy passenger cabin and upper deck have been cut back and altered to meet the simpler needs of full-time towing.* Maine Historical Society

The Minnie *worked as a tender for the Rodgers Granite Corporation at Deer Isle. The new owners of the former* Minnehaha *had less need for cabin space and little use for Longfellow's poetically romantic name. For the balance of her lengthy career she remained registered as* Minnie. Willis H. Ballard, from Allie Ryan

Sparrow was named general manager and J. Melvin Carter became general agent. Delivering even more of a blow to the established line, Union Steamboat brought two fine vessels up from the Hudson River and initiated daily runs to the islands from Franklin Wharf.

The first of these latest rivals was the trim *Cadet*, a propeller boat built in 1879 at Newburgh, New York. Originally intended to become the private yacht of a prominent New York family, her plans were altered on the ways, and she was completed as an excursion steamer for service on the Hudson. There she remained for four years, operating to and from various landings between Newburgh and Albany. One of her frequent stops along the Hudson, the village of West Point, had prompted the steamer's name. During her earliest years on Casco Bay, the *Cadet* could easily be identified by the remains of her classic yacht bowsprit and raking stem, even though the bowsprit had been cut back to within a few feet of the stempost.

The second Union Steamboat Company vessel to enter service at Portland was the *Emita*. Built at Athens, New York, in 1880 for the Catskill Line, she was registered for a time in Albany, but came to Casco Bay to make her first run in June 1883.

The later but lamentable entry of Captain Charles G. Chase and his leased Boston-built Merrimack River steamer, the *General Bartlett*, into the island competition was an exercise in futility. Advertising four trips a day to the islands, Captain Chase waded in over his head by vying with three strong and resourceful steamboat companies, all with well-equipped vessels. The *General Bartlett* soon returned home to Haverhill and Newburyport.

Replacing her prosaic riverboat lines the next season, however, was the passenger towboat *Florence*, a much smaller 56-footer. Laid down on Boston ways, evidently soon after the *General Bartlett*'s losing struggle, she was better suited for local competition and able to tow on the side. The *Florence* ran daily to Cushing Island, Scott's and Trefethen's Landings at Peaks, and Ponce's Landing at Long Island.

Once the all-encompassing service of the second Forest City Steamboat Company had come to include Cushing Island, and with the well-organized Union Steamboat Company continuing its tidy opposition line, the *Florence* was badly outclassed. With defeat assured for their passenger service, the owners resorted strictly to towage work. Shortly after altering their business affairs, they sold the little passenger towboat and, as a unit of the Eastern Dredging Company, the *Florence* kept busy for a decade into the new century.

After its first season, the fortunes of the Union Steamboat Company began to take a rapid turn for the worse, and the *Emita* was laid up, leaving

An 1880s view of the Cadet *taken from another steamer with which it has paired for a special excursion among the islands. In close-steaming formation, up to three steamers could thus make use of one brass band like the one seen performing on the upper deck aft of the* Cadet's *tall stack.*
Warren N. Graffam Collection, from Captain Harold H. Cushing, Jr.

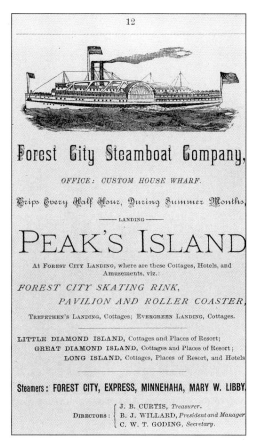

A timely amalgam of three earlier steamer lines is reflected in this advertisement of the first Forest City Steamboat Company.
Willis H. Ballard

The flat-bottomed General Bartlett, *built by the Atlantic Works at East Boston, found competition too well established when she arrived in Casco Bay and soon returned to the Merrimack River.* The Mariners Museum

In the Summer, trips are made every hour; in Winter, five round trips daily.

John B. Curtis *was one of the influential industrialists who controlled the first Casco Bay Steamboat Company. The Spruce Gum King also cornered the U.S. market as pioneer producer of chicle and paraffin chewing gum. Sometimes derisively known as "Gummy" Curtis by opponents, he showed more than a little vanity in allowing his countenance to grace a Casco Bay Line postcard. Clockwise from upper right are the* Forest City, Cadet, Forest Queen, *and* Emita. Philip H. Lee

The Peaks Island House *was long the leading summer hotel on the most populous Portland Harbor island. In its final incarnation, this famous inn was much larger and roomier, but less attractive in appearance.*
Warren N. Graffam Collection, from Hilda Cushing Dudley

The Ottawa House, *popular with Canadian visitors, made Cushing Island a tourist mecca until the hotel's destruction by fire in 1917.*
Warren N. Graffam Collection, from Hilda Cushing Dudley

With her running mate Cadet, *the able steamer* Emita *was the best that Union Steamboat Company could offer in the early 1880s. Her owners' fortunes diminished but the* Emita *had come to stay, eventually setting a record for total time in service which remains unbroken.* The Peabody Museum of Salem

A serene view, taken from the Peaks Island shore, shows the new steamer Forest Queen *leaving Forest City Landing on Diamond Island Roads at high water, bound for the next stop at Cushing Island.* The Peabody Museum of Salem

Star Line Steamboat Co.

Pass *J. Murchie, Prest.*

1886

Frontier St.b. Co.

UNTIL DECEMBER 31st, 1886, UNLESS OTHERWISE ORDERED,

UPON CONDITION THAT HE ASSUMES ALL RISK OF ACCIDENT AND DAMAGE TO PERSON AND PROPERTY.

52

PRESIDENT.

An 1886 pass, made out to the president of the Frontier Steamboat Company at Calais on the Maine-New Brunswick border, was signed by Star Line president Montgomery S. Gibson himself. David Crockett

only the *Cadet* to continue the schedule. By this time, too, the financial backers of the line, who at first had taken a rear seat to watch the proceedings, quickly took the helm and reorganized as the Star Line Steamboat Company. A concerted drive to increase revenues found the *Emita* chartered in May 1885 to the Boston, Winthrop and Shore Railroad, providing ferry service between Point Shirley Pier and Snow's Arch Wharf in Boston. Thereafter came an upward turn in the Maine business, and by 1886 both steamers were again operating from Portland's Franklin Wharf.

The year 1886 saw Star Line's optimistic plans incline toward the addition of a third steamer to compete better with the Forest City Line. On the builder's ways at Athens, New York, early in 1887, the new boat, which eventually became the *Forest Queen*, was proving quite costly for the dimming hopes and continued scanty revenues of the Star Line. The company had received most of its capital from the diverted coastal earnings of the owners, who found only diminishing returns. Because the Star Line seemed destined never to prosper by itself, its ownership and management, headed by Captain John F. Liscomb, made an offer of amalgamation with the Forest City Line that was eminently agreeable.

The Union Steamboat Company's Cadet *steams down Diamond Island Pass, probably in 1884. On the hill in the background is the old clubhouse of the prosperous Portland Club.* Maine Historical Society.

The Second Casco Bay Steamboat Company

Forest Queen, *Eldorado*, *Pilgrim*, *Verona*, *Merryconeag*, and *Venture*

With this consolidation, the former Star Line identity was soon completely eclipsed, and the resultant firm became officially the second Casco Bay Steamboat Company, with Preble House innkeeper Montgomery S. Gibson as president, Captain Liscomb as treasurer, and Charles W.T. Goding as secretary and general manager. The new "white elephant" steamer had been a key problem, best solved at last by merger, which allowed the reorganized firm to resume payments on construction of the *Forest Queen*.

When she finally arrived at Portland in July 1887, the *Queen* became the first steamboat to operate exclusively under the second Casco Bay Steamboat Company banner. Also the first local steamer equipped with a generator and outfitted with electric lighting throughout, the *Forest Queen* was an imposing sight, and passengers boarding her daily at Custom House Wharf soon formed a high opinion of this newest island steamboat.

Oddly enough, one of the greatest tests for the *Queen* was to take her away from Casco Bay environs. After barely five years of scheduled service to the bay islands, the tall-stacked steamer cast off from Custom House Wharf one Saturday morning in April 1892, and steamed straight for Penobscot Bay. In an astonishingly sudden move, the Casco Bay Line had leased her to the Fox Island & Rockland Steamboat Company until a new steamer could be constructed for the lessee's route from Rockland to Vinalhaven and Hurricane Islands.

Immediately upon arrival at Rockland, the *Forest Queen* entered into fierce competition with the steamer *Emmeline*, owned by the Frenchman's Bay Steamboat Company, which had used its slightly smaller boat, brought around from Lake Erie, in an effective battle against the plodding old steamer *Pioneer*. Once the speedier and more graceful *Queen* had replaced the *Pioneer*, however, the complexion of the contest quickly changed. The *Forest Queen* far outclassed the seedy-looking *Emmeline* and in short order attained a popularity with Penobscot Bay islanders rarely equalled before or since. She remained embroiled for three months in the Penobscot Bay steamboat rate war, with each company in turn trying to scuttle the other through dramatic steamer races and low-level "scalping" of freight rates and passenger fares. This northern adventure ended for the *Queen* on June 30, 1892, when the fine new steamer *Gov. Bodwell* was introduced. Thereupon the still-proud *Forest Queen*, hailed as "cock of the water" in the Penobscot region, returned once more to win the admiration of generations of summer residents and islanders on her Casco Bay home waters.

Now a member of the combined Casco Bay Steamboat Company fleet, the Cadet *sports a new and more modern bow. This type of stem was not likely to get hooked on island wharves as the troublesome old bowsprit and raked prow often did.* Maine Historical Society

The Casco Bay Steamboat Company's 1892 timetable opened up to reveal a detailed map of the company's various routes. Author's Collection.

An artistic photographer caught the Cadet's *departure over the picnic basket of some fortunate daytripper at Trefethen's Landing on a long ago summer day.*
Maine Historical Society

Proof that the old Casco Bay Steamboat Company was vitally concerned over its deteriorated fleet in the early 1890s is demonstrated in the reconstruction of the Emita's *bottom at South Portland.* Peter T. McLaughlin, from Warren N. Graffam

On Penobscot Bay, the *Forest Queen* had a tendency to roll badly during rougher sea passages over the open-water route from Rockland. Back on Casco Bay, however, the island runs were more sheltered and she always fared well. The *Queen* played a major role, in fact, in producing an outstanding 1892 season for the second Casco Bay Steamboat Company. By August 29, the line had carried over 300,000 passengers to and from the islands without a single accident.

The *Cadet* had kept busy on her scheduled rounds while the Union and Star Line managements had their brief escapade, but went over to the combined fleet to make the daily runs to lower Peaks and Long Islands. However, it soon became necessary to dispose of the stubby bowsprit after it had caught on and damaged too many wharves. Once freed of this bugbear, and sporting a more steamboat-like bow, the *Cadet* ran without further trouble or incident.

No doubt the most vivid event of the *Cadet*'s career came with the opening of the World's Columbian Exposition at Chicago in 1893. A coalition of Maine college groups hit upon a scheme to charter a Casco Bay Steamboat Company vessel and sail to Chicago and return, even though the trip might well consume the entire summer season. The students were in recess, and the plan had wealthy financing, so arrangements were completed and the *Cadet*, with her regular skipper, Captain John A. Fisher, was assigned the arduous task.

Before leaving Portland with her cargo of eager scholars, the low-slung steamer was specially refitted with a stubbier hinged smokestack for easier dismantling and lowering to clear the low bridges over the Erie Canal. The *Cadet* then ventured down the coast, stopping only for coaling and inclement weather. Seldom out of sight of land, she eventually transited Block Island and Long Island Sounds and New York Harbor. From there, the *Cadet* steamed familiar Hudson River waters to the Erie Canal, the trip through this waterway followed by a coaling stop at Buffalo on Lake Erie, a skirting voyage around that lake's southerly shore past Ashtabula, Cleveland, and Sandusky, across the connecting waterway past Detroit and out onto Lake Huron, where she hugged the westerly shore and sailed through the Straits of Mackinac. The gallant little vessel then coasted down the easterly shore of Lake Michigan and finally crossed to Chicago for the fair commemorating the 400th anniversary of Columbus's discovery of America. Far from Casco Bay, the *Cadet* was berthed close to the great Agricultural Building for a well-earned rest.

The wayfaring steamer finally returned to her home waters near summer's end, but much the worse for wear; a thorough overhaul and reconditioning at the South Portland marine railways were now essential. The *Cadet*'s tall smokestack, more conducive to good furnace draft, was

resurrected from its storage rack and remounted. Weeks later, Captain Fisher had the *Cadet* back on the local run, and a casual observer would have been hard pressed to believe that she had ever made such a fantastic voyage.

By the spring of 1894, the *Emita*'s tired white oak hull had begun showing the wear and tear caused by bucking the often severe winter harbor ice, but her popularity with management, crew and islanders came to her rescue. Soon she was trundled to the Portland Shipbuilding Company's leased South Portland marine yard and railways, where all the old hull planking below shelf and guards was stripped away. The exposed frames and keel were strengthened or renewed, and in a matter of weeks her hull was completely replanked. So much for the bottom work, but when the *Emita* re-entered service her ancient topsides were still no bargain to passengers.

All too soon, but perhaps not soon enough for island passengers who wanted something better, came the highly rated and comfortable new steamer *Eldorado* to take the *Cadet*'s place on Casco Bay. In the spring of 1896, the badly outclassed little steamer cruised out of Portland and down the coast, to be registered at Marblehead, Massachusetts, for the remainder of her days. For a while, she once again found herself a flagship, this time on the Boston and Marblehead Line. Now she made daily trips from Atlantic Avenue in Boston to the affluent and popular North Shore resort community between the headlands of Cape Ann and Nahant.

The line to Marblehead was a less than lucrative summer-only experiment by the Lynn & Nahant Steamboat Company, which made it necessary to lay up the *Cadet* or find other uses for her. When the year 1898 brought increased activity at the fortresses among the Boston Harbor islands, the firm seized on a golden opportunity and chartered the *Cadet* to the U.S. Army. With their steamer serving as a passenger and freight transport for the First Heavy Artillery Regiment at Fort Warren on Georges Island, her owners probably felt themselves fortunate.

On a chill and blustery April 28, 1898, however, luck ran out on the *Cadet*. Outbound with a cargo of 3,000 board feet of lumber, 15 barrels of bread, and other foodstuffs for the soldiers at Fort Warren, but apparently no passengers, her skipper chose to transit the Shirley Gut Channel, which in those days separated Deer Island from the Winthrop mainland.

The passage through the Gut nearly achieved, the *Cadet* left the lee of the land and instantly encountered stiff winds, heavy seas, and rolling ground swell so strong that she began to be set bodily sidewise, toward the entrance rocks. Fighting the wheel to steer clear, the captain saw his efforts failing and all hands felt the steamer grind onto the barely submerged rocks and rise abruptly only to pound down on them again and again. The *Cadet* rolled, pitched and yawed her way to destruction. One solid pounding came with such great impact, just as the steamer rolled down, that the upper deck broke from its supports. Torn clear of the main deck cabin, it was swept overboard and floated off through the Gut.

The steamer Forest City *(ex-*Gazelle*) in her waning years, was still flagship of the Casco Bay Line fleet. Her place as the bay's grand old lady was soon to be taken by the towering new* Pilgrim*, a mid-1890s import from Lake Erie.*
Maine Historical Society

The Boston Harbor patrol and boarding steamer *Guardian* and two steam tugs soon arrived on the scene, but could not venture close enough to the distressed steamboat to rescue the crew or to get out a towline. Severely battered and holed in a short time, her bottom timbers an increasingly broken and twisted shambles, the *Cadet* remained intact scarcely long enough to allow her crew to struggle shoreward and gain the safety the land offered. As it was, they barely escaped drowning, but no lives were lost. For the *Cadet*, the end came quickly. Before the wind and sea abated, the wreck broke up so completely that nothing could be salvaged.

The second Casco Bay Steamboat Company was beneficiary in the mid-1890s of ill-fortune that beset the Buffalo, New York, excursion firm of Sloan & Cowles. Overblown estimates of a surge in numbers of people thronging to get out on Lake Erie waters proved too optimistic, and glowing press sentiments were built mostly on hot air. Sloan & Cowles had banked on these calculations and had taken a thorough financial trouncing by the close of the 1895 season. The best of its fleet was for sale, featuring the great three-decked *Pilgrim* of 1891 and the smaller *Eldorado*, new in the spring of 1893.

The news carried from Erie's shores to the varnished second floor offices of the second Casco Bay Steamboat Company at Custom House Wharf. It must have seemed like music to the ears of John B. Curtis, recently promoted to president, and his officials, for the aged sidewheel steamer *Forest City* (ex-*Gazelle*) was tired indeed. There was concern, too, over the limited passenger accommodations of the smaller *Cadet*, in light of the ever-enlarging passenger business to and from the islands. Here was the answer to the problem of replacement vessels, at considerably below the cost of new construction, and owners and management lost no time in ''shuffling off to Buffalo'' to inspect the craft.

The Casco Bay Line purchased both the *Pilgrim* and *Eldorado*. Not long afterward, a convoy of three steamers began the lengthy trip to Casco Bay, via Lakes Erie and Ontario, the St. Lawrence River and Gulf, then around Cape Breton Island, down the Nova Scotia coastline and, finally, across the Gulf of Maine to Portland. The third vessel, the steamer *Island Belle*, purchased by Temple Brothers of Portland, was also destined to find a prominent place in local steamboat annals, of which more later.

Although the *Pilgrim*'s journey to Portland was skippered by Captain Ed Parsons, with Engineer Harry Ricker, a change of command in the early spring of 1896 saw Captain Alfred S. Oliver and Mate Safford Macomber transferred from the *Forest City* to the new flagship. Soon afterward, the faithful old sidewheeler was laid up for sale. The aging Captain Oliver, as senior master, remained in command of the *Pilgrim* until his retirement.

By the time the summer season of 1896 had gotten underway, the *Eldorado* was ensconced on the run to Long Island, and the *Pilgrim* had begun regular service to Peaks Island, with frequent ''down the bay'' excursions. Greatly supplementing the *Emita* and *Forest Queen*, they aided in boosting the company to new heights of prestige.

The *Eldorado* was unlike any steamer the Casco Bay Line had ever operated, far excelling her predecessors in sheer passenger comfort and overall design. Smallest of the fleet, she was nevertheless a real favorite, with her spacious, extensively glassed and well-lighted main-deck cabin, as weather-tight as those of her running mates. A roomy second deck, despite the lack of a decked-over forecastle, was provided when her Buffalo builders carried it forward to a point just covering the main deck gangways. Like other newer steamers running among the islands, the *Eldorado* could make a handy 12 knots and was strongly built of white oak, with an interior finish, it is said, of quartered oak.

The years between 1889 and 1896 had seen the respective demise of the *Minnehaha, Express, Forest City* (ex-*Gazelle*), and *Cadet* in favor of newer vessels, and now the *Emita* enjoyed the dubious distinction of being the oldest steamboat in the Casco Bay Line fleet.

More than any other vessel in the line's history, the large three-decked steamer *Pilgrim* remains the brightest symbol of the second Casco Bay Steamboat Company's most prosperous days, spanning a busy decade prior to, and immediately following, the turn of the century. The *Pilgrim* could legally carry 1,100 passengers between Portland and Peaks Island, while being limited to some 900 on a more outside run, yet crowds were often so great that two or three trips might be necessary to accommodate everyone on certain runs each summer day. In order to handle these large numbers, two gangways, fore and aft, were commonly used on the *Pilgrim* at Custom House Wharf, smoothing considerably the flow of passenger traffic. An Assistant Ticket-taker, ranking just below Purser, was stationed at the second gangplank. Loading standards of all steamers were strictly obeyed, even if prompted more by the constant presence of U.S. Steamboat Inspection Service "counters" at Custom House Wharf than by the spirit of the regulations.

From these first years on Casco Bay, the *Pilgrim* became a tourist boat in the broadest sense of the term. Her routine was one of extensive summer operation, followed by long seasonal lay-up. Each spring, she would make her appearance among the islands as soon as the warmer weather would render profitable, or at least possible, the scenic sails for which the imposing three-decker became famous.

Beginning with the 1897 season, Manager Goding placed advertisements in local newspapers and other periodicals, extolling in capitals, in the ebullient journalistic style of the day, the wonders of "The Many-gemmed Casco Bay—Ideal Summer Resort of Maine." The *Forest Queen*, commanded by Captain Edward L. Parsons, together with the *Emita*, *Eldorado*, and the grand *Pilgrim*, often ran filled to capacity, making hourly trips in season to Peaks, Cushing, Little and Great Diamond, and Long Islands. On Peaks Island alone, they stopped at Forest City, Trefethen's and Evergreen Landings. A 60-ride ticket to any of the latter stops cost only three dollars, or a nickel a ride!

The line now owned the Gem Theater on Peaks, and during the show season a round-trip ticket, plus admission to the Gem, was priced at only 25 cents. Manager Goding had negotiated purchase of the one-time Forest City Skating Rink, then carefully supervised the transformation of the 16-year-old structure into a commodious summer-stock theater. The rebuilt edifice was placed under the direction of actor-manager Byron Douglas and opened its doors to theater lovers on June 6, 1898. First-night audiences were treated to a well-cast presentation of the play *Diplomacy* by Sardon. In the 1899 season, the regular daily service from Portland to the islands reached its all-time peak, when trips left Custom House Wharf every half-hour.

Able guardian of the old Casco Bay Line steamers and fleet operations since the late 1880s, General Manager Charles W.T. Goding went on to perform identical duties for the combined Casco Bay & Harpswell Lines.
Maine Historical Society

Opened as the Forest City Skating Rink in 1884, but renovated in 1898 by the Casco Bay Steamboat Company, the Gem Theater eventually became a ballroom, destroyed by fire on September 8, 1934. Fronting the flat-roofed Coronado Hotel at left are the Peaks Island House and smaller Innes House.
Walter T. Randall

The steamer Emita *is stripped down to the hull for her second major reconstruction at the South Portland repair yard and marine railways in 1901.*
Peter T. McLaughlin, from Warren N. Graffam

The Emita, *with a good crowd aboard, looks fit and ready following the extensive refitting project of 1901.* The Peabody Museum of Salem

These were the golden years, when the annual number of passengers reached and even exceeded 450,000, not including island commuters or inter-island travelers. During this period, the competing ''5-cent Line'' opposed almost all sailings with trips of its own, and many a race occurred over the shuttle route to Peaks between the four Casco Bay Line vessels and steamers such as the *Jeanette*, *M. & M.*, and *Island Belle*, with the *Belle*, especially, offering a rugged contest.

By 1901, the company's need for an additional vessel to meet the increasing trade became acute. However, even after carrying peak loads of freight and passengers, the cost of the three previous boats had been recovered too slowly. With a firm hand on the corporate pocketbook, line officials made a thrifty decision. Captain Wilbur Gates, with Mate Manley Littlefield, soon undocked the *Emita* for a short trip to the repair yard at South Portland. There she was stripped and dismantled until nothing remained above her guards except the tall stack mounted over her old-fashioned lake-type horizontal boiler.

Months later, a completely updated and improved *Emita* emerged from the yard. Her accommodations had been increased, and she could now carry as many as 500 passengers. She returned to service in time for the height of the 1901 season, and continued to perform handsomely under Captain James Foye through many active years. This same reliable Jim Foye thought himself quite psychic and often spent his off-hours over

a Ouija board. The captain's predictions always seemed to find a ready audience among his fellow workers at Custom House Wharf and many islanders.

Some five years after the *Eldorado* arrived, her ruggedness and durability proved instrumental in obtaining a government contract to carry workmen and supplies to Great Diamond Island during the construction of Fort McKinley as a Coast Artillery post. Though she was highly successful on her new home waters, the *Eldorado*'s greatest handicap was her small size, which limited her legal capacity to 250 passengers.

Always a favorite with her engineers, the *Forest Queen* was known as an ''easy steamer.'' One of her firemen of years ago, Ralph Bailey of Falmouth, said:

On the *Forest Queen*, you could go down, when you left the dock here, and put 10 or 12 good big shovelfuls of coal on either side of her firebox, and go up and hold the damper rope and you wouldn't much more than get it out of your hand before the old safety valve would go 'pop-pop-pop.' You'd have to eject a little steam to stop it. Then you wouldn't have to go down again until she got way down below Little Diamond. Then you went down, coaled her right over heavy again, and you never had to use a sluice bar or anything on those fires!

No longer identifiable by name, the crew of the old Forest Queen *pose beneath the jaunty gilded eagle of the* Queen's *early days. An open foredeck was a common feature in the fleet until shortly after the century's turn.*
Peter T. McLaughlin, from Warren N. Graffam

The Forest Queen *leaves Great Diamond Island Wharf. Her second deck has been extended to the forecastle head to increase her capacity and give more shelter to freight on the main deck.* R. Loren Graham

The *Forest Queen* was not always so popular with her captains or deck crew, though. Many recalled her as a hard boat to maneuver. She was a bit slow to turn, and being of deeper draft than her sister steamers on the line, she had a reputation as "long-legged." Indeed, it was said that she could only make Trefethen's Landing at Peaks on a half-tide or above. These faults notwithstanding, the *Forest Queen* was still generally recognized as one of the ablest boats to run locally.

The summer schedule kept the *Forest Queen* constantly busy, but the off-season found her hardly less active. She was often assigned the regular late-afternoon run into Portland, a busy trip, especially in the years following the completion of Fort McKinley. Artillerymen and other soldiers who rode the *Queen* to their favorite bars and brothels around the Fore Street district saw an irony in the spelling of the steamer's name and cleverly dubbed her the "Fore St. Queen," a nickname which stuck to her for decades.

During the day excursions and moonlight sails which immediately proved so popular, Manager Goding early realized the attraction of a good brass band, or string ensemble, to entertain the passengers during the inevitable duller moments of a cruise. Many a run was enhanced by the music of Portland's American Cadet Band, or Chandler's Band, long conducted by Charles M. Brooks of Portland, and still in existence today. Another daytime band of young children from Lewiston, ranging up to a maximum age of 12, was called the Boilermakers Band. This well-liked group packed the decks of the *Pilgrim* whenever it performed, and the phenomenon continued for several seasons. Florence Bailey of Falmouth remembered:

They'd run special excursions in the old days and have Chandler's Band or some other on the *Pilgrim*. As they left Custom House Wharf she would be flanked by two other boats, one on either side of her, and *all* crowded to capacity! They'd sail down the bay, with the *Pilgrim* keeping slightly in the lead with the brass band. Many times different groups of summer people along the route would set off Roman candles and other fireworks as a salute when the steamers passed by. The air would just ring with the answering three-blast salutes of the steamer whistles and the lively music of that band! Yes sir, steamboating in those days used to be quite a thing!

Seen during her earlier years on Casco Bay, the steamer Pilgrim, *carries no fewer than 800 excursionists for a day's outing among the islands. On the busy Peaks Island shuttle, the popular "grand lady" was permitted to carry up to 1,100 passengers.* The Peabody Museum of Salem

Not needed for the slack passenger trade of the long off-season months, the Casco Bay Steamboat Company's former lakers Eldorado *and* Pilgrim *are shown in a circa 1903 view in annual lay-up on the west side of Custom House Wharf.* James Stevens

The excursions of both major steamboat companies, not to mention the general quality of service, was never lost on the editors of the *Casco Bay Breeze*. This newspaper, published weekly between 1900 and 1917, was, if nothing else, noted for two characteristics: its consistent support of the steamboat companies, particularly the larger ones, and its inconsistent tone in reporting the news. It could be, by turns, saccharine or bittersweet, cosmopolitan or parochial, arrogant or humble, extravagant or factual, sometimes displaying several of its conflicting attributes within one issue.

It noted on July 7, 1904: "The excursion conducted every Tuesday evening to Peaks by the Casco Bay Line is proving a strong attraction and judging by the large numbers that went from [Long] Island, the Gem must have been crowded. The play this week is 'Charlie's Aunt' and is a great success."

Shortly after the close of the 1904 season, Curtis and Goding saw a golden opportunity arise with news that Bennett & Kerst of Bucksport had sacrificed their veteran steamboat *Merryconeag* to auction sale. Casco Bay Line's bid was successful and the *Merryconeag* arrived to take the *Eldorado*'s place on the island run, also relieving the chartered steamer *Verona*.

In light of the Casco Bay Line's energetic but faltering campaign for another steamer in 1904, the bargain purchase of the *Merry* was a tremendous cost savings coup. This maneuver made up for the company's failure to come to favorable terms with the Barbour interests at Brewer over acquisition of the chartered *Verona*. This beautiful vessel, last in the Barbour tradition of craftsmanship and so like Casco Bay's Dyer-built steamers in design, slipped away to New York waters only to be destroyed by fire three years later.

The Casco Bay Steamboat Company directors, in their zeal over the *Verona*, had allowed their ultimate goal of adding a smart new 120-foot steamer, modeled closely after the Harpswell Line's *Aucocisco*, but larger still, to become eclipsed. With the addition of the *Merryconeag*, the idea of another new steamboat died. Plan views of this impressive unnamed steamer, dated 1904, surfaced in the early 1980s in the Portland Company archives collection held by the Maine Historical Society Library on Congress Street, Portland.

A vessel as staunch and comfortable as the *Eldorado* did not have long to wait for a new owner. Within a short time she became flagship of the Popham Beach Steamboat Company, on the Kennebec River, operating daily between Bath's City Landing, Phippsburg Center, Hinckley's Landing at Georgetown, Cox's Head, Bay Point and Popham. Luck seemed to travel with the *Eldorado* as she rapidly gained popularity under Captain James E. Perkins, with Engineer Frank Oliver insuring that her boiler and engine received the best of care. She ran year round on this route without mishap until the early morning of December 16, 1908, when, for causes unknown to this day, she burned to the water's edge at Popham Wharf.

The biggest news of the year unfolded in the *Casco Bay Breeze* on June 8, 1905:

Casco Bay Line now owns *Merryconeag*—The well-known steamer *Merryconeag*, always a favorite boat, has been purchased by the Casco Bay Steamboat Company and added to the fleet. She is being handsomely repaired and altered to suit their needs, having electric lights and search light and will soon be ready for use. She will probably take the place of a leased boat [the steamboat *Verona*] which was pressed into service last season.

With her pilot house raised conspicuously high aloft to the boat deck, the *Merryconeag* eventually bore an uncanny resemblance to her Harpswell Line half-sister, the *Aucocisco*. The cost of overhaul for the new debut could be whistled to the tune of some $4,000.

Accolades from the *Breeze* were published perennially and the July 20, 1905, issue stated: "With Chandler's Band on the *Pilgrim* and the American Cadet Band on the *Aucocisco*, the rocks and woods of the bay resound with music on Sundays and the cottagers are appreciative of the concert as the handsome steamers glide by."

Much had happened to change the complexion of the company's affairs by 1906. Feeling the restrictions and setbacks caused largely by the overwhelming prosperity and success of the neighboring Harpswell Steamboat Company at Portland Pier, Casco Bay Line officials determined to strike for a share in the eastern island business. One step in the right direction was to "field" its steamers to the out islands. The *Forest Queen* now began to make special excursions into Harpswell Line territory, even venturing as far as Gurnet Bridge, with capacity crowds bent on shore dinners at local inns and summer hotels.

Even as the *Pilgrim* was hugely successful on Casco Bay's shortest run, between Portland and Peaks Island, she was also popular on the excursions to the bay's easternmost reaches. The *Casco Bay Breeze* of June 28, 1906, gave front-page coverage to "Another Popular Excursion: The steamer *Pilgrim* will make the beautiful Gurnet Bridge trip again next Sunday, sailing from Custom House Wharf in season to arrive at Gurnet for dinner."

In 1904 the Casco Bay Steamboat Company terminated the charter of the handsome Verona. *The last Barbour-built steamer to be launched at the famed Brewer yard, she was one of its best. Sadly missed by many islanders, the* Verona *soon met a fiery end on the Hudson.*
Warren N. Graffam Collection, from Hilda Cushing Dudley

Though the company had by now begun its run onto financial shoals, the *Breeze* of July 19, 1906, chose to honor one of the line's leading officials:

General Manager, Charles W.T. Goding of the Casco Bay S.B. Company is one of Portland's best known businessmen and merchants. He has made hosts of friends by his hearty, whole-souled manner of meeting people and has always worked for the success of the Casco Bay Line of Steamers, whose patrons numbering over 200,000 in a summer, always have a friendly greeting for him.

The number of special trips and excursions steadily increased and the company wasted no opportunity. As witness, an item from the *Breeze* of June 28, 1906, titled "Sunday Sails by Casco Bay Steamboat Company" read in part:

The *Merryconeag* took a party of excursionists down to Bath Sunday, arriving there at 12:30 p.m., while the *Forest Queen* carried a good crowd up to Gurnet Bridge for a shore dinner. The weather was not of the brightest, but was an appreciable improvement over the previous Sunday and a pleasant time was enjoyed by both parties.

Eastern Landing, Great Chebeague Island, was a Casco Bay Line route expansion landing built, and later enlarged, by Henry Bailey's work gangs. The overhead canopy, forming an archway between waiting room and baggage/freight shed was a Bailey trademark.
Barbara D. Munsey

Perhaps induced by the careful prodding of General Manager Goding, the *Breeze* was again enthusiastically blowing its Edwardian horn just three weeks later over "Another Fine Trip" and went on:

Steamer *Merryconeag* took a large party to Gurnet Bridge Sunday—The fast and able steamer *Merryconeag* of the Casco Bay Line had a large excursion party on board Sunday for the famous sail and dinner up to Gurnet Bridge. A band was in attendance and the trip up Merriconeag Sound gave complete enjoyment to all. The round trip was about 60 miles [and] a stop was made at Peaks Island, both going and returning.

The *Breeze* erred slightly in its account as the *Merryconeag*'s trip took her up the New Meadows River rather than Merriconeag Sound.

Through the cold winter months and on into the spring of 1907, the overall strategy of Goding and company became apparent. A number of parcels of shorefront land had been quietly acquired the previous year, most of these closely adjacent to the Harpswell Line wharves in many eastern bay locations. Now the wharf builders were set to work in force and by the peak of the 1907 season the *Breeze* could banner the story in its Fourth of July issue:

Now Plying Bay—Casco Bay Steamboat Co.'s Boats
Inaugurated Summer Schedule Monday
Touch at Chebeague Island, Hope Island, South Harpswell
and Gurnet Bridge in Lower Bay

The Casco Bay Steamboat Company is now running steamers to the Portland Harbor landings, including Hope Island, Chebeague Island, South Harpswell and Gurnet. The latter place is to be served by the steamer *Merryconeag* and one other boat, giving 4 round trips daily at Hope and Chebeague, 3 daily round trips to South Harpswell, the last boat leaving Portland at 6:20 p.m. One round trip to Gurnet Bridge daily will be given.

With the building of its own wharves eastward from Great Chebeague Island, the Casco Bay Line expanded its schedule considerably. The *Forest Queen*, under Captain Charles Howe, then operated the new route occasionally, but left most runs to the newly acquired *Merryconeag*, while the *Queen*, *Pilgrim*, and *Emita* routinely serviced islands nearer Portland.

This saga of Casco Bay steamboating is largely concerned with the island passenger steamboats, and not the regular Portland Harbor steam towboats or the less dignified and even lowlier steam lighters. But the story

An annual complimentary pass issued by the Casco Bay Steamboat Company. This 1907 card was among the last issued while the firm was still an independent line.
Steamship Historical Society of America

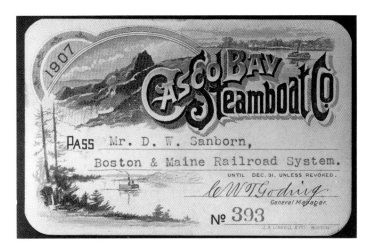

of one steam scow lighter, the *Venture*, uniquely does belong here. This homely old craft was peculiarly akin with the island steamers, among which she moored and worked for nearly all her years.

Back in 1902, the *Venture* had been launched by her builder and owner, the small Guy Lawrence shipyard, located well up the Kennebec River at Pittston. No more than a functional freight lighter and typically unattractive, the *Venture* had only simple houses located aft and was equipped with derrick and loading boom. She went to work between river ports, occasionally making a longer haul as far east as Rockland and sometimes westward to Portland. On one of these latter trips, the *Venture* was observed by Charles Goding, who had developed a considerable ship stores business through skillful use of his waterfront connections. In the *Venture*, he saw the perfect tender for Portland Harbor ship supply and purchased the steam lighter for his own account during the autumn of 1904.

By 1905, Goding's interest in the steamboat company had become keener and the sturdy *Venture* was transferred to the Casco Bay fleet in return for a greater share of stock ownership.

Since progressive improvement of regional wagon roads for the use of early automobiles and trucks caused the eventual abandonment of many steamboat routes, it is ironic that the Casco Bay Steamboat Company would play an important role in road construction. In 1904, a decision to drill and dynamite a wide cut through cliff and rock sought to insure a safer approach to the Orrs-Great Island bridge. The next year, when it came time to ship the heavy equipment needed for the work, the condition of the existing road demanded an easier and more direct water route. The *Venture* was ready and able, so Captain Ernest Hill took the heavily laden steam scow lighter far up Merriconeag and Harpswell Sounds to land her cargo of machinery on the Great Island shore, close by the old bridge approach.

Once the Great Island passway had been cut and a new roadway laid down, the *Venture* was called upon to reload the heavy steam drilling machinery. Captain Hill was again in command and all went according to plan until the *Venture*, at deepest draft, was well underway from the staging area. At this point, the overloaded lighter was caught unawares by the swift tide race of the narrow strait. Swept along by the strong current, the *Venture* struck and went hard on the foul ground off Dipper Cove Ledge. Frantic efforts of Captain Hill and her four-man crew were to no avail; the luckless vessel groaned and timbers crunched as her hull heeled over on the rock ledges. The weight of machinery caused her to hog and twist, and any less rugged craft would have broken up.

But it was not the *Venture*'s time, for destiny still had important roles for her to play. Later that week, the stranded lighter was hauled off and then jury-patched at the construction site. Under her own power, the *Venture* arrived at the South Portland marine railway for repairs. Although she was soon back at work, not all the hogging and twist were remedied and, from that time forward, local mariners considered her to be "crookeder than the Devil."

The Charles A. Warren *of the Harpswell Line is seen on her native upper Delaware River. After her brief local passenger service, the* Warren *returned to a berth at Central Wharf and the "tow and water" trade which first brought her to Portland.*
Steven Lang

The steam tugboat C. A. Warren, underway in Portland Harbor, circa 1904, looks no different here than she did in 1875, when she took the mantle of first steamer to run for the line that came to be the Harpswell Steamboat Company. In 1905, the elderly craft was renamed Casco.
Sullivan Photo Collection

CHAPTER 3

STEAMBOATS TO THE EASTERN ISLES
THE HARPSWELL BOATS

A Time of Passenger Towboats and A Pogie Steamer

Charles A. Warren and *Henrietta*

The story of steamboating among the islands of Casco Bay does not rest with the formative growth of the Casco Bay Steamboat Company alone. Other lines sprang up, one gaining particular notice.

Harking back a few decades to the year 1875, we find that the people of Great Chebeague Island followed a subscription plan similar to that of the Peaks Islanders before them. With this capital, they engaged the *Charles A. Warren* to provide transportation to and from the mainland.

The *Warren*, a steam screw towboat built in 1873 for the Delaware River trade, had led a fairly busy life in the "tow and water" business; as well as carrying out conventional towing duties, her built-in tanks supplied ships with their water requirements. Together with her running mate, the *Wm. H. Scott*, she plied Portland Harbor under Charles Sawyer's ownership until the Chebeague group chartered her.

The island service itself was scant, offering only once-weekly trips. This state of affairs soon dissatisfied many Chebeaguers, so on April 9, 1875, they subscribed additional funds to enlarge their cooperative enterprise, then purchased the towboat-like steamer *Henrietta*.

Fallen suddenly into disfavor, the *Charles A. Warren* returned to full-time towing duties, a pioneer vessel of the Central Wharf Towboat Company fleet. Originally, this boat was known on the Delaware as the *C. A. Warren*, then by her namesake's full name during mid-career and ferryage years, but the Central Wharf's owners later briefly resorted to the initialized identity again. The confusion was resolved when she was renamed *Casco* in 1905 and went about her harbor duties until her well-deserved retirement in 1917.

The *Henrietta*, though similar in appearance to the *Warren*, had more substantial passenger and freight space and the islanders accepted her readily. An urgent priority now was the construction of a sorely needed wharf landing on the island, since the *Warren* had tediously off-loaded passengers and freight into dories and other small boats, to be landed on the nearest beach or shallow-water "tide wharf." When finally completed, the wharf, located on the southeast shore and called Littlefield's Landing after the proprietor of the new general store there, had cost considerably more than the island residents expected.

The expenses encountered in operating the *Henrietta* came as a rude shock to members of the cooperative, headed now by Captain Stephen Ricker of Chebeague, who also served as agent and treasurer. But even though revenues fell far below expectations, the owners persisted in hope of recouping their investment. The continuing quest for funds soon brought into the enterprise many people from other islands, and the *Henrietta*'s route from Portland's Commercial Wharf was extended to include Long, Little Chebeague, and Cliff Islands, and South Harpswell. The last-named settlement, though part of the mainland, remained virtually isolated from its neighboring college community of Brunswick. The notoriously poor condition of the wagon roads, and the lengthy, tiring journey involved in trekking over dry ruts or through the mud, left Harpswell generally referred to as "the wild and rocky peninsula." Starting May 10, 1875, the *Henrietta*'s schedule provided two daily trips as far as South Harpswell all summer, with only semi-weekly service the remainder of the year.

Unable to construct wharves at other stopping points, the cooperative contented itself to continue with transfer by dories. Patience was rapidly running out, however, as well as the will and energy needed to keep the "soup strainer" operation afloat. Worried or disgusted according to individual temperament, the members now searched for a more business-oriented private enterprise to take over the helm.

The Portland, Little Chebeague & Harpswell Steamboat Company

Henrietta and Sea Flower (later Gordon)

They needn't have been so pessimistic. An avidly interested group, headed by E.L.O. Adams, John S. Morris, and Stephen C. Perry, was already watching from the sidelines and quickly purchased the *Henrietta* and other properties in 1876. Under the name of the Portland, Little Chebeague & Harpswell Steamboat Company, the Portland terminus was shifted to Custom House Wharf and with almost uncanny swiftness wharf landings similar to Littlefield's sprang up at all points served. The days of the dory transfer were ended, to the satisfaction of all but the boatmen, to be revived only when tide, wind, or freakish causes prevented normal wharf landings.

The *Henrietta* served well under Captains Thomas Matthews and Granville Lowell, often carrying her capacity crowd of 200 passengers, along with general merchandise, foodstuff stocks, baggage and mail. Many were the laden inbound trips to Portland, which also carried quantities of barreled fish, clams, lobsters, crates of apples and garden produce, poultry and livestock of the islands, all bound for the Portland market.

As Chebeague Islanders struggled to achieve adequate steamboat service on their section of Casco Bay, a remote and seemingly unrelated event took place during 1876 at Clark's Island, on the St. George River near Port Clyde. It was the launching of the "pogie," or menhaden fishery, steamer *Sea Flower*, and at a glance her purpose as a steam fisherman for local interests would appear totally unconnected with Casco Bay steamboating. But the *Sea Flower*'s fishing days were much less successful than anticipated. A cycle of mackerel runs had abruptly ended the reach of menhaden schools into Maine's coastal waters. By 1881, her owners had placed her on the block and former Portland mayor George P. Westcott was there to bid her in.

She received some minor conversion work after her arrival in Portland and soon shareholder Westcott had the *Sea Flower* in operation under the auspices of the Portland, Little Chebeague & Harpswell Steamboat Company. The firm found able leadership in two of Westcott's associates, president John S. Morris and manager George F. West, and quickly came to knock on prosperity's door. With offices at 22 Exchange Street and terminus at Custom House Wharf, in what amounted to a "sweetheart deal" with the Curtis interests and the Tourist Steamboat Line, the Harpswell Line now ran the *Sea Flower* daily to Long Island, Little and Great Chebeague, and South Harpswell, in company with the *Henrietta*.

The steamboat company, given new vigor by ambitious management and fresh capital, expanded its schedule to as many as six trips per week in summer and maintained two weekly trips the year round, despite buffeting winds and winter ice. Later, the company frequently chartered the *Minnehaha*, *Tourist*, or *Magnet* in summer and advertised them as "favorites" for excursions to the islands, while using the *Henrietta* and *Sea Flower* on regularly scheduled runs.

The early Harpswell Line steamboat *Gordon at the old Orrs Island Wharf in 1886. She was a pioneer on the extended route to Bailey and Orrs Islands.*
Steamship Historical Society of America

The Portland & Harpswell Steamboat Company

Henrietta and Sea Flower (later Gordon)

In 1881, the directors changed their corporate title to the more appropriate Portland & Harpswell Steamboat Company. At the behest of new investors, the firm undertook a reorganization which left the steamboat line a subsidiary of the larger Harpswell Island Company. This move led to a program of improvements which included the rebuilding of the *Sea Flower*. In the spring of 1883, the former "pogie" steamer emerged as the *Gordon*, with Captain Ricker relieving Captain Redman. Able to carry 250 passengers, the *Gordon* began a schedule which, when taken with the alternate steamer *Henrietta*'s, gave three trips a day to Harpswell and five to Long Island, Little and Great Chebeague, and Cliff Islands. In fact, peak-load summer traffic often made a six- to eight-trip schedule feasible. Service on Sundays was at first omitted, but hastily included once the weekend tourist potential became evident. A boon to weekend summer excursionists from the Lewiston and Auburn area was the 5:00 a.m. Monday departure from Harpswell, which made a good connection at Portland with the Grand Trunk Railway train to Lewiston.

Captain James Long began his steamboating career on the *Gordon*, starting as a deckhand in 1882 and becoming her master in 1884, when he was not yet 21 years old. This required a special permit from Steamboat Inspector George A. Pollister, duly granted upon high recommendation from owner Westcott. Another of the *Gordon*'s officers destined for a long and successful career was Engineer George H. Doughty, later of the *Aucocisco*, who served on many of the bay's major steamers.

The Waldo Steamboat Company

Alice

Another effort at local steamboat operations, quite apart from the Harpswell Line interests at first, began in 1884 with the formation of the Waldo Steamboat Company. Several prominent Portlanders, including members of the food-processing Burnham and Morrill families, Joseph B. Reed (an ex-Registrar of Probate) and Governor Cleaves, had begun a new venture in the large, palatial Hotel Waldo, nearing completion on Little Chebeague Island. Their intent was to provide a private steamboat service for patrons of this posh new summer hostelry.

An order placed with the well-known Barbour Works at Brewer for the company's sole steamer brought a small vessel of just over seven tons. Christened *Alice*, after Mrs. Alice Burnham, wife of one of the principals, she became one of the few vessels of the large fleet of Barbour-built steamboats ever to serve on Casco Bay waters.

The *Alice* entered service between the line's mainland terminus at Burnham's Wharf and the landing at Little Chebeague Island, and these were palmy days indeed for the island's tiny community. Its dozen or so houses were by now augmented by a bowling alley and a large indoor community clambake building, as well as the great hotel complex, with its typical wide verandas of that era.

The *Alice* was to perform her specialized service for only two seasons, always laying up during the winter in those first pampered years. Then events brought a sudden change in her career. A disastrous fire overtook

MAINE COAST STR. ALICE   2958

The Barbour-built steamer Alice, *while in Waldo Line service, backs from the landing at Little Chebeague Island.* Steamship Historical Society of America

the Hotel Waldo in the autumn of 1885, and the great summer establishment was totally destroyed. After assessing the ruins, the owners made no effort to rebuild, perhaps a clue to the limited success the project had enjoyed, despite the earnest endeavors of the many people involved in the hotel's development.

One of the best-known of the island's year-round families, that of wharf builder and marine contractor Henry Bailey, worked hard in the years afterward to raise Little Chebeague's social status from the ashes by catering to summer visitors. New arrivals always received a warm welcome, and the island clambakes were said to be memorable events. Mrs. Bert Stockbridge, one of the Bailey daughters, fondly remembered helping her mother to make her widely heralded and delicious clam chowder, using a common copper wash boiler. Many a Maine chef has found these large, old-fashioned oval kettles to be the only suitable ones for any sizable feed or benefit supper!

The Waldo Steamboat Company continued to exist, but never again did active business. Instead, it became passively managed by the owners, while the *Alice* was chartered to the Harpswell Line on a long-term basis. Captain John Berry continued in command. In company with the *Henrietta* and *Gordon* on the Harpswell route, the *Alice* performed yeoman service both summer and winter, all three becoming local hallmarks of reliability.

In 1885, a rebuilt *Gordon* made the first scheduled runs eastward to Orrs Island. The steamboat wharf here had been built near the niche in the rock ledges known as "The Grotto." It was the actual spot where Harriet Beecher Stowe had meditated while writing her novel *Pearl of Orr's Island*, coming often to this haven of solitude overlooking Merriconeag Sound. Mrs. Stowe was destined to bring literary fame to the region and, of course, to be immortalized for her *Uncle Tom's Cabin*, also written when she lived at Brunswick, but generations of local girls came to know, love and identify even more with Pearl, her Casco Bay island heroine.

The *Gordon's* time over the enlarged 22-mile system of courses was slow but adequate and she gained a loyal following along this route. Two years later, and fortified with $30,000 in fresh capital from Isaiah Daniels and members of his Harpswell-oriented mercantile family, the line took the official name of the Harpswell Steamboat Company. The Daniels family was already well known as owners or managers of many regional fishing schooners, not to mention its partnership in the large Orrs Island general store, ship chandlery and fishing supply, livery, coal and wood, building materials and supplies establishment known as Prince & Daniels Company.

The Harpswell Steamboat Company

Merryconeag and *Chebeague*

Old Captain Long, in later years, loved to tell of those cold and icy winters of the 1880s. He had many times seen ice so thick at South Harpswell that the mail from the *Alice* was landed in a dory on the back side, off Pinkham Island. Often, with severe icing conditions, the landing at Orrs Island became impossible, and the *Alice* used to be toggled to the offshore ice instead of the wharf. The gangplank would then be run out and passengers walked ashore.

During a severe winter's day in 1887, the *Alice* and *Gordon* lay at Custom House Wharf, frozen in by ice which covered much of Portland Harbor and the near bay. General Manager Isaiah Daniels, already keenly attentive to the islanders' needs after less than a year with the company, called in Captain Long for a hasty conference. Anyone about on that dark, overcast day would have been surprised to see Captain Jimmie galloping from the Portland Post Office an hour or so later on the manager's horse, mailbag across the saddle, and muffled against the numbing cold. The horse's brisk trot soon bringing the captain to the Yarmouth shore, he reined in, scanned the frozen expanse, then spurred his steed out across two miles of solid ice to Great Chebeague! That day, the mail, for Chebeaguers at least, certainly got through. With the *Henrietta* also iced in at Orrs Island, other stops weren't as fortunate.

Snow still lay deep on the ground during the late winter of 1887, as the Harpswell Steamboat Company began negotiations with the George Russell shipyard in East Deering for a new vessel. The contract with this well-known sailing-ship builder called for completion of the yard's second steamboat, the *Merryconeag*. True enough, she was also its last steamboat, but economic reasons lay at the root of that matter, not lack of quality. Many people have testified, before and since the *Merryconeag's* passing, that she was the best constructed and fastest of any of the Casco Bay or Harpswell boats. The Russell brothers insisted that the finest of the shipwrights' art went into her making. Built of sturdy hard pine, the new *Merryconeag* was completely copper-fastened, and her interiors finished thoroughly in varnished hardwoods.

The first of a number of Harpswell Line steamboats to be christened with native Abenaki place names of the Casco Bay region, the new steamer took that of Merriconeag Sound, once also applied to Harpswell as well. Honed by time and tradition, the original "Merrucoonegan" next became "Merryconeag", said to mean "golden eagle." Hence, the Russells fittingly perched a gilded wingspread eagle atop her pilot house.

The previous year ex-mayor Westcott had sold his interest in the Harpswell Steamboat Company to Isaiah Daniels, who became treasurer as well as general manager, with George F. West succeeding Westcott as president.

Westcott's departure did not spell the end of his local steamboating ventures, for by 1892 he had come to occupy the president's chair of the Old Orchard Steamboat Company, owner of the sidewheeler *S.E. Spring*, which previously shared offices with the old Portland, Little Chebeague & Harpswell Line on Exchange Street. What did vanish almost immediately was the rapport and influence the Harpswell Line formerly had with the moguls at Custom House Wharf. Bitter differences ensued, and with the handsome new *Merryconeag* about to enter service, West and company left Custom House Wharf to establish a new terminus at nearby Portland Pier. Good feeling between the managements of the two lines was never quite restored.

The launching of the *Merryconeag* in 1888 brought a new refinement to island steamer travel over the eastern bay, and her arrival at Portland Pier relegated the *Henrietta* to lay-up until she was sold in 1889. This left the old *Gordon* to run mostly in alternate status or on special excursions.

Many good years remained for the *Henrietta*, however, and she went on to prove her worth under ownership of the Eastern Dredging Company of Portland. Serving as a towboat, she steamed her way through the years until 1915, when she was retired and abandoned.

The new Harpswell Line flagship Merryconeag *departs York's Landing at Bailey Island, en route from Orrs Island in the summer of 1889. Seen inbound toward Portland, the* Merry *was the favored standard bearer for the Harpswell Steamboat Company until the advent of the larger Sebascodegan in 1895.* Lawrence and Ruth Piper

With the *Merryconeag* now plying the route, running time was cut considerably and service was extended to Bailey Island in 1888. Until 1885, all U.S. Mail for residents of Orrs and Bailey Islands had arrived or left the Orrs Island village post office via stagecoach from Brunswick. Thereafter, mail was routed from Portland by steamer, as had already been the case with South Harpswell. With no suitable wharf and no post office yet on Bailey, the mail, supplies and passengers not transported under sail came over by dory from Orrs. The efforts of Lendall M. York to establish a coal and wood business in conjunction with a large general store at Bailey central village provided impetus for several fruitful meetings with Harpswell Line officials in 1887. Bailey Island thus gained its first steamboat wharf, oddly combined in general usage as a community "coal pocket." Prior to this, only its resident farming and fishing families and a certain few vacationers had ever set foot on the island. Indeed, when Walter D. Crafts, who later became proprietor of the famed Ocean View Hotel on Bailey, first visited the spot in 1887, only five summer cottages graced the island, besides the few staid white houses of year-round fishermen and farmers. By 1903, over 60 cottages had been erected, with many more still in prospect.

The schedule remained inefficient, however, due to the slower steamer *Alice* and the only occasional operation of the *Gordon*, while the prestige of owning a three-steamboat fleet conflicted with the fact that two of the company's boats were outmoded. The attitude prevailed, from directors on down, that only first-class steamers would meet the line's requirements. Another boat was needed, but in spite of the bustling summer business with which the Harpswell Line fared so well, there was the long off-season to consider, when traffic dwindled. The directors had watched the profits of summer melt away in overall operational costs, and now planned for a new steamer to replace the *Gordon*, but a smaller, more economical one than the *Merryconeag*.

The Nathan Dyer yard, at Franklin Wharf, Portland, was keenly interested in what the now-defunct George Russell shipyard had accomplished in the *Merryconeag*'s construction. It took her design in the autumn of 1890 and built a similar but smaller craft of its own. Launched in April 1891, the tidy steamer *Chebeague*, named for the two adjacent islands situated well off the western bay, or foreside, shore (and meaning "land of many springs" in the Abenaki tongue), had graceful and well proportioned lines and sheer, a pilot house that spelled dignity, and that

Never destined for a long career in the island passenger trade, the perky little Chebeague *is shown at Jenks Landing, Great Chebeague Island, in 1892. Most of her days were spent as Portland's first modern fireboat.*
Steamship Historical Society of America

first hallmark of a Dyer-built steamboat, a well-rounded forefoot at the bow. Also conspicuous was her lack of a forecastle deck over the bow, more in the manner of the *Alice* and *Gordon* before her.

During the long 1890-91 off-season, the *Merryconeag* carried the brunt of the business. Advertisements in late fall and winter announced a daily departure from Orrs Island at 6:40 a.m., with the return trip leaving Portland Pier at 2:20 p.m. The *Chebeague*, under Captain Bert Daniels and Engineer Tom Gould, did a later afternoon trip down the bay. A frequent advertisement in the *Eastern Argus* read: "Harpswell Steamboat Company—On and after May 31, 1891, the steamer *Chebeague* will leave Portland Pier, Portland weekdays for Long, Little and Great Chebeague Islands, Harpswell, Bailey's and Orr's Islands at 3:15 p.m. Returning leave Orr's Island for Portland and intermediate landings at 6:40 a.m." On Sundays the *Chebeague* would terminate at Harpswell and run back to Portland, omitting stops at Bailey and Orrs Islands.

With the *Chebeague* on the schedules, it meant the ax for the little *Alice.* Her charter was terminated, but the Waldo owners wasted little time in finding work for their steamer. After a short lay-up, the *Alice* returned to service under lease to the new Falmouth Foreside Steamboat Company. We will take up her story later, with that of the Falmouth Foreside line.

As the 1891 summer season drew near, the *Gordon* refused to steam any longer. Her tired little low-powered steam plant had worn itself out and her hull was certainly in no better shape. The company turned its back on the weary vessel which had brought it so far in only ten years. Captain Long had graduated to command of the smart *Merryconeag* and was now delegated to tow the old *Gordon* to Jenks Beach on Great Chebeague. Here she was beached, stripped and burned. Some of her wreckage, including the keel and ribs, and even the pilot house, was still to be seen on the shore close by Jenks Landing in 1916.

A late spring advertisement in Portland's leading daily, the *Eastern Argus,* on Saturday, June 13, 1891, read in part: "Daily excursions down Casco Bay—Beginning today, steamer *Merryconeag,* Captain J.L. Long, will make daily excursions down the bay, leaving Portland Pier at 2 p.m. and return arrival at Portland 5 p.m. Fare for the round trip, 30 miles, only 25 cents!"

By June 29, long-time director and now president Henry P. Dewey gave approval for general manager Daniels to insert new advertisements in the Portland newspapers, bannering "The Elegant New Steamers *Chebeague* and *Merryconeag,*" leaving Portland daily for the islands. As the *Chebeague* ran steadily, with Captain Bert Daniels and occasionally Captain Jimmie Long at her helm, the Harpswell Steamboat Company earned the highest profits in its history. Revenue was boosted when the boom of the tourist season, starting in late June each year, signaled an increase to 50 cents for the entire run, with 35 cents round trip to Harpswell and 25 cents for other landings along the route. Business also soared through the early nineties, picking up at such a great seasonal rate that the two fine steamboats could not handle it adequately.

Immediately following the dockside fire of early Saturday morning, September 3, 1892 at Portland Pier, which claimed the South Portland ferryboat *Cornelia H.,* the Harpswell Line came to the rescue by loaning the *Chebeague* to the Peoples Ferry Company. Meanwhile, the *Merryconeag* easily handled the off-season business down the bay. Returned to the Harpswell Line, the *Chebeague* continued to render good service, but the company now desired a larger steamer. A chance to replace the *Chebeague* came in 1895, when funds were allocated for another boat. Nathan Dyer this time evolved the design toward a higher-capacity vessel.

The triumphant arrival of the steamer *Sebascodegan* marked a new day for the company and the lowest ebb of the *Chebeague*'s career. She was at once withdrawn, but not long afterward, following careful inspection at her slip by the Portland Fire Chief and officials of his department, the *Chebeague* was unanimously approved as suitable for conversion to harbor fireboat. The Harpswell Line received prompt payment from the city treasurer's office, and applied it directly to the cost of the *Sebascodegan*. The *Chebeague* next underwent a complete rebuilding of her deckhouses and machinery spaces. A new, larger boiler, powerful fire pumps and high-pressure water system were installed, the upper decks cut back, and the pilot house altered to provide officer accommodation at the rear. Finally, her smokestack was jacketed by a taller and heavier outer stack. In general appearance she now resembled a large but handsome white towboat and city dignitaries were well pleased with the results. In keeping with strict policy for classifying department firefighting equipment, the Indian name *Chebeague* was discarded and the more prosaic title of *Engine No. 7* was substituted.

On Bailey Island, an often dusty, coal- and wood-laden York's Landing offended the discerning and sophisticated summer visitors and led to the establishment of a second steamboat landing site. The year-round advantages of the sheltered and relatively ice-free Mackerel Cove were well known to the local residents. At any rate, David P. Sinnett, owner of a general store and flourishing fish wharf on the cove's eastern mid-shore, located between Bass Rock to the north and the fishing shanties of the "Nubble" to the south, answered the call. Sinnett was a shrewd businessman, having already worked diligently to enlarge the old Johnson general store and increase its clientele. The former owner, John M. Johnson, had relocated the store building itself to this spot back in 1855, using a clumsy barge-like scow to float it across Mackerel Cove on the tide, after jacking and shifting it off its original 1846-built foundation near the old wooden bridge at the head of the cove on Abner's Point.

David Sinnett became founder and principal shareholder of the family-held Bailey's Island Steamboat Wharf Company, and the Sinnetts soon contracted to have Mackerel Cove Landing built as a new section of the already sizable wharf on their property. Were it not for the mundane fisheries functions performed on one half of the length of the massive wharf, it might easily have berthed any two steamboats moored end to end. His confidence no doubt bolstered by the remarkable growth of the Harpswell Line, as well as the knowledge that its newest flyer, the *Sebascodegan*, was on the South Portland builders' ways, David Sinnett granted perpetual wharf rights to the Harpswell Steamboat Company on Monday, January 7, 1895.

*Approaching Cushing's Landing, Long Island, in 1895,
Harpswell Line's new* Sebascodegan *sports the addition of
an unskilled artist's "Old Glory" waving valiantly at the
stem, while real flags hang limp on a flat, calm day.*
The Peabody Museum of Salem

Steaming down Portland Harbor in her original rig, the
Aucocisco, *skippered by her first regular master, Captain
Ivan Bryan, carries a capacity crowd.*
The Peabody Museum of Salem

CHAPTER 4
DAYS OF GLORY AND FRUITS OF EXPANSION

Sebascodegan, *Aucocisco*, and *Maquoit*

The old Dyer yard had expanded to Ferry Village, on the South Portland waterfront, by 1894, when Harpswell Line directors first called at the new Portland Shipbuilding Company offices. Shortly, a new keel was laid, hackmatack frames were assembled and the sturdy hard pine hull of the *Sebascodegan* took shape. Hers was the old Abenaki name for both the largest island in Casco Bay and its smaller neighbor just southerly in the East Harpswell chain, more commonly known as Great Island and Orrs Island.

Launched in spring 1895 to the ringing cheers of a local throng, the new boat was engined and outfitted across the harbor at the Portland Company's factory pier. Instead of the all slide-valve arrangement of the *Merryconeag*, the *Sebasco*'s plant employed piston-valves on the high-pressure cylinder, with traditional slide-valves on the low-pressure cylinder. The new layout proved easier for the engine gang to steam and the *Sebascodegan*'s crew set out to knock down the *Merryconeag*'s speed title.

Somewhat longer and beamier, the *Sebascodegan* was a good eight tons heavier than the *Merryconeag*. Chance meetings on the bay became opportunities to race. Both were fast, but the old *Merryconeag* was not to be beaten by this newcomer. It was only the easier steaming qualities of the *Sebasco*, or a better head of steam, which allowed her to take the lead even occasionally.

Oldtimers recalled that the *Sebascodegan* always had a curious appearance when steaming at speed. Her stern and fantail rode extra low in the water as her screw dug in deeply, causing her pronounced Dyer forefoot to rise clear out of the water like an icebreaker. The *Sebasco* was a tremendous boat in the ice for just this reason, but, on the negative side, passengers had a hard climb to enjoy the view from the vessel's bow "eyes." Earliest runs took place under Captain Jimmie Long, but the 550-passenger flyer soon passed to Captain Bert Daniels, and Long returned to duties on the *Merryconeag*.

The end of a most successful 1896 season found the Harpswell Steamboat Company a profitable enterprise in every sense. In the *Merryconeag* and *Sebascodegan* it had the two finest and fastest steamboats on Casco Bay. The company's sphere of influence stretched over a wider area than that of the Casco Bay Line, although the latter's number of trips and volume of passengers were often many times greater. The Harpswell Line directors now determined to do even greater things. They would see how much better the Portland Shipbuilding Company could do in matching or exceeding their two steamers by ordering a third.

If it were possible to breach the barrier of time and travel back to the most rousing and successful days of the Harpswell Steamboat Company, we would find ourselves standing amidst a gathering crowd in the small shipyard at Ferry Village, South Portland. This would be Monday morning, May 3, 1897, just another in a series of overcast and showery days, except that everyone is assembled to witness the momentous launching of a glistening new steamboat. The vessel on the ways will soon become, and remain for all time, the most popular of the island steamers, a lucky craft destined to part Casco Bay's blue-green waters for more than 50 long and faithful years.

Months before, as the new vessel neared completion, Harpswell Line management had started pondering an appropriate name. *Norumba* had everyone's support until early April when another name surfaced, apparently considered a more musical one to the ears of owners and management. The queen of the fleet would bear Casco Bay's old Abenaki Indian name of Aucocisco, meaning "resting place."

Given the signal by yard officials at 11:40 a.m. on this launching day, workmen begin driving the wedges. Barely seven minutes later, the *Aucocisco* glides smoothly down the ways, her hull soon floating free on the waters of Portland Harbor for the first time. Cheers from those fortunate few aboard are more than matched by the din of the onshore gathering.

As the new vessel assumes her initial trim, the waiting tug *James Sampson* steams alongside, makes fast, and tows the *Aucocisco* to a nearby

Perhaps the only surviving photograph of two Harpswell Line sisters of yesteryear together, the newer Aucocisco *is on the east side of Portland Pier, behind the drifting smoke of a naval steam launch. Astern, the* Sebascodegan's *capped stack reveals her to be seasonally inactive.*
Jane Stevens, from Capt. James Perkins

The gambrel-roofed Merritt House, principal hotel at the south end of Orrs Island, fronted on what was then Steamboat Hill Road. Sharing the steamboat landing area with the S.J. Prince & Son general store, the Mascot House, and the Sebasco House Lodge, the Merritt House remained an important dining spot and transient hostelry for passengers through the late 1950s. Nowadays the renovated hotel is an apartment complex.
Robert and Grace Green

The former Chebeague, *rebuilt and wearing the black hull and red superstructure as originally used by the marine arm of the Portland Fire Department, carries the No. 7 badge on her stack.* David Crockett

The Harpswell Line's Merryconeag, *now sharing the "outside route" from Portland with the* Sebascodegan, *approaches the Orrs Island Landing in the spring of 1896. Although bow sheathing has been removed, and awnings added for warmer weather, that spring overhaul date on the railway has not yet arrived.* Robert and Grace Green

A Harpswell Steamboat Company advertisement of 1899 promotes the leading attractions of Casco Bay.
Willis H. Ballard, from Allie Ryan

The Portland Company 15"x32"/22" marine compound steam engine differs only in minor details from those installed aboard Harpswell Line's Merryconeag, Sebascodegan, *and* Aucocisco. *The main difference was in the size of the large low-pressure cylinder, which varied between 26" and 30" on these three steamboats, and all had a slightly shorter stroke of 18".* William B. Jordan, Jr.

outfitting dock. Here the finishing touches need to be applied before the short cross-harbor tow to the factory pier of the Portland Company to receive her compound engine and Scotch boiler.

The *Auco's* steam plant differed from the *Sebascodegan's* in that both engine cylinders were equipped with easier-steaming piston valves rather than the *Sebasco's* slide-and-piston valve combination or the hard-steaming slide-valves of the *Merryconeag*. As sturdy as any steamboat yet built by Dyer's Portland Shipbuilding Company, the *Aucocisco* had an oak frame, with hackmatack "knees," each four feet long, and hard pine planking. While many other vessels on the bay were not double-planked, or, like the *Emita*, only partially double-planked, the *Auco* was strongly planked inside and out and "kneed off," for better support of her hull shelf, from bow to stern.

Placed under the honorary command of ever-popular senior master, Captain James L. Long, the *Aucocisco* was ready for her maiden voyage on Monday, June 21, 1897. An account appeared in the *Portland Express*:

Every whistle on the boats in the harbor shrieked a salute to the *Aucocisco* this morning, as she backed out of Portland Pier, and steamed away down the bay. The handsome new steamer was gaily decorated with flags and streamers, her sides glistened with fresh paint, and her shining brass-work was spotless. It was the occasion of the [Elks'] Annual Field Day, and more than 100 members of the Order were on board. The *Auco* took the merry party to Hope Island, where a shore dinner was served. The American Cadet Band accompanied the excursionists, and furnished delightful music.

At day's end, Captain Long passed the temporary command over to the selected regular skipper, Captain Ivan W. Bryan, and returned to his assignment on the *Merryconeag*.

One singular hallmark of this gracefully built steamer was the pleasant tone of her whistle, a melodious sound, said to have been pitched F in the musical scale. To many who remembered, that sound was part of the romance. Former deckhand Lovell B. Sawyer was to call the *Auco's* whistle "softly hoarse, like a husky-voiced girl's and just as fascinating." Others thought of the sound as portentous and special. It had a low resonance which could blend with the listener's mood to seem either comforting or melancholy. Through the depths of an ominous fog it could be sharp and frightening. The customary salute of three blasts even had a joyful ring!

The Sunday forenoon arrival of the steamer Sebascodegan *in early summer 1900, as seen from Jockey Hill on Bailey Island. York's Landing appears behind the trees at the far right.* George A. Hill, from Lawrence Piper

The *Aucocisco* proved to be more comfortable than her predecessor *Merryconeag* and boasted more freight space up forward. The owners and Portland Shipbuilding Company's founder Nathan E. Dyer, who had supervised construction, were justifiably proud of her. The *Aucocisco's* picture henceforth graced the company's advertisements, represented on most literature by artists' sketches, to herald "Harpswell SB.Co.—The 365 Island Route—Swift and commodious steamers *Aucocisco* and *Sebascodegan* for the principal islands and landings on Casco Bay." Their only chagrin was in finding that even the *Auco* could not match the speed of the old *Merryconeag*. Frequently she raced both her sister ships, whether or not the company benefited. The winner was often the boat which could mount the most steam pressure, and the rapid roaring "choo-choo" of efforts to raise pressure by forcing draft and clearing coal smoke was always exciting to passengers.

For the 1897 season, the two newer boats held down the route and the *Merryconeag* was laid up for sale, since the company had no need of more than two steamers. Captain Isaac Edson ("Ed") Archibald, brother-in-law of local steamboat purser Judson Webber of Orrs Island, and a resourceful Yankee from Port Clyde, purchased the *Merry* to found his Portland & Rockland Steamboat Company. To render the *Merryconeag*

suitable for the outside run to Rockland and waylandings required some remodeling, and initial costs were steep. At first the freight business did so poorly that making some scheduled trips seemed ridiculous, but Captain Ed soon had a business boom on his hands. A reboilering job by the Portland Company in 1899 for better performance gained the *Merryconeag* no friends among her engineers, as will be seen later.

Under Captain Archibald, occasional mishaps marred the record. Early in October 1900, *Merry* suffered her first casualty by grounding on Morse Island, southwest of Friendship. Luckily, her keel found only the sandy bar, and she was pulled off by tug on the next high tide. A few months later, the *Merryconeag* struck on Johns Rocks, south of Cliff Island, en route from Boothbay on her usual winter route into Portland Harbor, which entered the channel past Great and Little Chebeague and Long Islands. This time she was gotten off with some damage to her bottom timbers.

By 1901, the former Harpswell steamer was no longer able to carry all the freight alone on the amazingly successful Portland-Rockland line. That year the new and larger *Mineola* came on and the older *Merryconeag* became spare boat. A "dungeon" fog overtook her in spring 1902, when she piled onto Green Island Reef, between Inner and Outer Green Islands.

This time the *Mineola* was present to carry on the service without interruption. But, as Captain Cliff Randall expressed it, "The *Merryconeag* sat there on that reef for a week. Nobody ever thought they would get her off. She sat right up between two big boulders. But she wasn't too badly damaged. They went down and plugged a hole in her, pumped her out, and took her right out of there."

All the while registered at Rockland, the *Merryconeag* turned up on the Portsmouth-Isles of Shoals line, under short-term charter, during the summer seasons of 1901 and 1902. When Captain Archibald offered her for sale in 1903, the *Merryconeag* passed into the eager hands of Captain W.D. Bennett and Daniel W. Kerst of Bucksport. They immediately set her to work on their opposition service to Captain Oscar Crockett's popular Blue Hill Line, which kindled another fierce Penobscot Bay steamboat rate war.

The time-honored Crockett line and its two neat little steamers *Catherine* and *Juliette* caused Bennett & Kerst to struggle bitterly just to pay operating costs. The *Merryconeag* went for two years without maintenance, though often running the year round to points as remote as Stonington. Soundly beaten by 1905, Bennett & Kerst's properties and steamer were seized for debts and offered at U.S. Marshal's auction sale, though the tenacious Captain Bennett would eventually start yet another Penobscot Bay and River line. What happened next is a most telling irony in Casco Bay steamboat history, for when the resounding echo of the auctioneer's hammer had faded, the dilapidated *Merryconeag*'s new owner was none other than the Casco Bay Steamboat Company of Portland.

Regardless of doubly threatening circumstances, the 1898 season was to be another banner year for the Harpswell Line, with a reported passenger count for the season exceeding 100,000 travelers, most of them enjoying a leisurely sail over the 22-mile route. The Spanish-American War brought both a shock and a thrill as Mainers read first of the tragic sinking of their namesake battleship in Havana Harbor and then of the naval engagements with inferior Spanish fleets, both in the Caribbean and at Manila Bay. In Portland Harbor, visiting battleships and other men-of-war boosted business for excursion steamers, taking crowds out to the naval anchorages.

An indirect competitor had also arrived on the scene in the unlikely person of Portland fish dealer, James MacDonald. He and his associates had failed to gather up their organizational skirts in time to snap up the cast-off *Merryconeag* before the wily Captain Archibald made a successful offer, but they came up with the light Kennebec River steamer *Percy V.* to start the Portland & Small Point Steamboat Company. The company title sounded innocuous, but by using the inside route, the *Percy V.* actually covered many of the same islands as the Harpswell boats on her way across

An early view of a serene Mackerel Cove, looking down old Steamboat Hill Road, at Bailey Island. The steamer approaching in the distance is the Harpswell Line's Sebascodegan. Author's Collection

the bay toward Cape Small. This "Johnnie-come-lately" even had the nerve to rent space on the opposite side of Portland Pier from the Harpswell Line, under its competitor's watchful eyes.

Before long, the MacDonald interests made a stunning decision to purchase an additional steamboat. The newly acquired *Pejepscot* of New York was considerably more powerful than locally built boats, a real racer, having twin screws and a pair of triple-expansion engines, even one of which might outperform the compounds of any Casco Bay steamboats. It was a regretful time for Harpswell Line directors. To rapidly cover the costs of the *Aucocisco*, they had chosen an early disposal of the *Merryconeag* and now, when she could have brought even more profit their way, she was plying Captain Archibald's coastwise route. Added excursion business thus fell to the vessels of the Casco Bay Line and the rival MacDonald Line's powerful, large-capacity *Pejepscot*.

The Harpswell Line management endured the unpleasantness of having the MacDonald Line as next-door neighbor for only a few years. If James MacDonald's cross-bay line had not turned from a juicy plum to a sour lemon, the Harpswell Line's prospects might have been considerably dimmer. The new line died, though, and its princely steamer disappeared from local waters. Once again, the *Sebascodegan* and *Aucocisco* were Casco Bay's finest. The watchword was still prosperity, on an ever-increasing scale.

The versatile Captain Wm. Henry Sinnett of Bailey Island, skipper of steam lobster smacks, turned farmer after retirement and also provided stage and carriage service in the early 1900s. Augustus P. Johnson

Maine historian and author Harold B. Clifford, while setting down many dialogues in the long-undiscovered and unpublished manuscript which became *Charlie York: Maine Coast Fisherman* in 1974, stayed close to the old man's vernacular as he told of his boyhood on Bailey Island:

When I was a kid, everything and everybody come to Bailey's by water. Before the bridge was built, my Grandfather Burnham used to set people across the narrow channel to Orr's in his dory, ten cents a person, three or four for a quarter, or bring 'em on when he heard 'em shoutin' for the ferry.

The Harpswell Steambo't Company run year-round service to Portland. The steamer would leave Orr's Island at 7:00, put into York's Landin' on Bailey's, then across to South Harpswell and on to Cliff Island, Chebeague, Long. . .and dock [at Portland Pier] about 10:30. She left on the return trip with passengers, mail, express, and freight at 2:00. We young ones knowed the name of every bo't and we could tell which was which as fur as we could see 'em, or hear the whistle: *Merryconeag, Sebascodegan, Aucocisco, Machigonne.* Indian names, probly.

The most excitin' time of day was when we'd hear the steambo't blow about 4:00 P.M. All the local people that could spare the time went to the wharf and, as it was summertime, the rusticators flocked down. The steamer's side would be lined with men,

women, and children as she come near, and the cap'n would bring her in at a smart clip. Then he'd give the engineer two bells and the jingler and fetch her right up on a dime. I can see the mate now, standin' with the forrard spring line, and how easy he'd flip that hawser over the pilin' just right as the bow come by the dock. He'd hold a strain and she'd come against the wharf with hardly a jar; then he'd snub her tight.

The gangplank would drop for the passengers to go ashore. Everett Sinnett, he was postmaster for fifty years, would be there for his bags of mail. Deckhands would roll out barrels of sugar and flour, crates of groceries, maybe a bunch of bananas, and other fresh fruits. Then the skipper would give the whistle a toot, they'd haul in the gangplank, and she'd git underway for Orr's Island.

Cap'n Henry Sinnett had wagons for the passengers. Lish Leeman had a pair of horses and a cart to take the freight, trunks, and heavy baggage. Come the end of August, he dreaded to handle them trunks again; they was usually half full of smooth, round rocks from Pebbly Beach. A lot of us follered the mail to the store and waited for it to be sorted. In them days all first class mail had to be backstamped. We could hear Mr. Sinnett go kerthump, kerthump; sometimes he'd stop and we figgered he was readin' a postcard. Friends would be talkin' with friends. Kids would be skylarkin' around. If they was a girl you wanted to see, she was sure to be there. When the mail was out, everyone went home.

Whenever they was something special goin' on in Portland, the steambo't company would run an excursion, with reduced rates. The one I remember best was in the late spring of 1899, when the first automobile come to Portland. They put the fare for grownups from fifty cents down to forty cents and kids up to twelve could go for twenty cents. A lot of people went from Bailey's and more from South Harpswell and the islands. We landed at [Portland Pier] and I had to foller mother around while she shopped, and then we had dinner in a restaurant.

That same Captain Wm. Henry Sinnett that Charlie York had spoken of was an honored and respected retired skipper of steam lobster smacks which ranged the coast from Boston to Eastport. Turned gentleman farmer after coming ashore, he owned a large Bailey Island cattle and produce farm. Throughout the early 1900s, "Cap'n Henry" also provided stage and carriage service between the two steamboat wharves and homes, inns, and points of interest on the island, carrying mostly passengers. Heavy freight and baggage were left to the wagons of Elisha Leeman or Perley Sinnett.

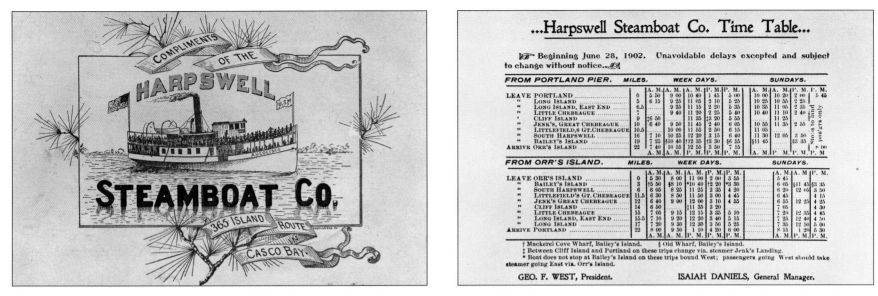

The Harpswell Line timetable for summer 1902 as it appeared in the company's tour booklet. The artist-engraver may be forgiven for not presenting the Aucocisco *with the true eye of a draftsman!* David Crockett

The "steamboat society" of the day flourished in the war's aftermath. At wharf landings all across the bay it had become fashionable to walk down to meet the boat each summer evening after dinner, the men dressed in white flannel suits and, perhaps, carrying a favorite ivory-headed cane, more for appearance than support. The ladies were typically attired in bustle and stylish long, sweeping skirts. The up and down revenue trends and operating headaches of officials in the steamboat offices were not always apparent to the public, and so the social mores of the elite summertime "rusticators," and some of the islanders as well, remained aloof and unruffled as tourism gained momentum in the region and the bountiful turn of the century grew nearer.

A characteristic advertisement appeared in the 1902-03 *Casco Bay Directory*:

Harpswell Steamboat Company—The 365 Island Route— Swift and commodious steamers *Aucocisco* and *Sebascodegan* for the principal islands and landings on Casco Bay including Chebeague, Long Island, South Harpswell, Bailey's Island, Orr's Island, Hope Island, Little Chebeague, Cliff Island, etc. Extra service and special excursions during the summer season. Steamers leave Portland Pier.
(signed) Isaiah Daniels, Gen'l Manager

The *Sebascodegan* steamed through the turn of the century under newly appointed Captain Charles B. Morrill, unscathed until Friday, July 31, 1903. Then, while backing out of her slip at Portland Pier for the 5:45 a.m. trip, the piston within her high-pressure cylinder let go. Only a short distance from the wharf, the *Sebasco* drifted helplessly until shouts from the crew reached the shore before she was carried by the tidal current to a point off the Grand Trunk wharves. The steam tug *Naos* soon puffed onto the scene, however, made up alongside and returned the disabled *Sebasco* to her berth. That day the line's service was crippled, depending as it did on both boats. The *Aucocisco* carried the ball, though, and made three speedy trips from the city, leaving at 9 a.m., 2 p.m., and 7 p.m. Back aboard the *Sebasco*, three machinists from the Portland Machine Company worked feverishly throughout the night. They had her ready, with steam up, only 20 minutes late for Saturday's scheduled 10:40 a.m. trip.

The situation rapidly returned to normal, but the casualty coming at such a heavily traveled time profoundly upset an already ailing Manager Daniels. The strain on the old gentleman over the previous worrisome hours was apparently much more severe than anyone realized. The news broke shortly after nine o'clock Monday morning. Isaiah Daniels was dead. The greater Portland waterfront community was stunned, and plunged into mourning. The flags of the *Sebascodegan* and *Aucocisco* were dipped

A.E. Pinkham's 44-room Merriconeag House was advertised as the finest hotel at South Harpswell as early as 1881, when daily communication was either with Portland by steamer or with Brunswick by stage. Barbara D. Munsey

to half-mast by crews dedicated to their capable manager. At Custom House Wharf, flags of the rival Casco Bay Steamboat Company followed those of the Harpswell Line down the halyards in tribute to a great steamboat man now passed on.

The funeral notice appearing in the August 6, 1903, issue of the *Casco Bay Breeze* included these excerpts:

Isaiah Daniels, the well-known and genial Treasurer and General Manager of the Harpswell Steamboat Company, died at his [Portland] residence at 8:15 o'clock on Monday morning. While Mr. Daniels was confined to his house for only a brief period, he has not been a well man for at least two years. . . . Mr. Daniels has long been one of Portland's best known citizens and his connection with the Harpswell Line has given him an acquaintance which extends all over the country. He was born September 23, 1836 at Hopewell Cape, New Brunswick, but at the age of nine years left that town and came to Portland. . . . Sixteen years ago he bought an interest in the Harpswell Steamboat Company and at the same time was made General Manager of that line. The route was then but a small affair, with but one steamer [owned], the old *Gordon*, which has long since gone to pieces on the shore at Great

Chebeague Island. Mr. Daniels must therefore be given the credit for the wonderful growth of the line and for the splendid condition in which it is at the present time. . . . The funeral service took place Wednesday at 2 o'clock from his late residence. The floral tributes were extremely beautiful. Among the most prominent [was] an immense anchor from the Harpswell Steamboat Company, a large wreath from the crew of the *Aucocisco*, and a handsome pillow from the crew of the *Sebascodegan*. These each had the steamers' name across the front. There were other floral tributes from George F. West, President of the Harpswell SB. Co., Edgar L. Jordan and from different organizations to which he belonged. George F. West, President of the company; Frank B. Morse of the Board of Directors; Captain James L. Long of the steamer *Aucocisco*; Captain Charles B. Morrill of the steamer *Sebascodegan*; Captain Andrew J. York were pall bearers.

The line recovered from its emotional setback and it was once again business as usual. The heyday of the steamboat on Casco Bay was truly at hand. Islands and scattered mainland stops dotting the bay were united as never before into a close-knit waterborne community, linked by the steamboat's course and further stitched together with bustling inter-island business and a social life long since gone and perhaps impossible to repeat.

An important major social factor of the era, and not to be overlooked due to its unusual partisanship toward local steamboating, was the seasonal publishing empire of Crowley & Lunt of Harpswell and later of Portland. With their reputable Beverly, Massachusetts firm literally moving with them to summer quarters on the bay each year, they published many regional directories in New England, not the least of which was the *Casco Bay Directory* of people, places and services. These volumes were at once as interesting as a travelogue and nearly as informative as today's Yellow Pages. The glittering star of their publishing empire was the idiosyncratic weekly newspaper, the *Casco Bay Breeze*, which used its mixed bag of journalistic attributes to attract its eager readers in the fishing, farming and tourist society of the region.

The steamboats were a lifeline, as desperately important to the newspaper's circulation as to the people, and the *Breeze*'s publishers and staffers knew this well. Its pages always contained complete schedules of the major steamboat lines, and any information released by their managments was regarded as news of the first magnitude. If a steamboat captain or crew member became open to criticism following a mishap, the *Breeze* was right by his side, fighting like a dedicated soldier, solidly in his favor. If, by chance, circumstances rendered a steamboat man at fault in any incident, then the *Breeze* fell as silent as death, allowing no editorial barb against even one thread of the people's lifeline. In fact, for the *Breeze*, silence became the common weapon against social negatives of almost any kind.

Not only did its pages cover major steamboat happenings, but they included every trifling item and nuance as well. An example appearing on the front page of the *Breeze* on September 3, 1903, read: "Lost His Panama Hat—A passenger on the 10:40 Saturday lost his new $15 Panama Hat while off Cliff Island. Engineer McShane, of the *Sebascodegan*, loaned his derby to the unfortunate gentleman, who has undoubtedly seen the last of his 'Panama' unless it floats to safe harbor, in which case the finder may find the owner by communicating with Mr. McShane."

With their two "white flyers," *Aucocisco* and *Sebascodegan*, producing excellent revenues in 1903 on the outside route, the Harpswell Steamboat Company considered extending its influence. It set its sights on the much-neglected inner route, through inside channels and tranquil, tree-lined backwaters of Casco Bay. With landings seldom serviced since the last days of the old steamboats *Phantom* and *Haidee*, the route, which became the South Freeport Division, fairly cried out for attention.

The Harpswell Line placed an order for its first new vessel in over six years with the Portland Shipbuilding Company. Adapting a model similar to the early *Phantom* and the old Harpswell steamer *Gordon*, the builders launched the sparkling white *Maquoit* in the late spring of 1904. Though some 20 feet shorter than either the *Auco* or *Sebasco*, she was every bit as trim in appearance. Solidly constructed of hard pine, and equipped with a Portland Company Scotch boiler and compound engine, her pilot house squatted on the second deck. Stepped on her open foredeck was a samson post with a swinging derrick boom. Unlike her fleetmates, the *Maquoit*'s main deck housing did not extend flush to the guard rails, so there was less cabin space. The Portland Company's selection of a whistle for the new boat seems to have been the only flaw. A widespread opinion was that the *Maquoit*'s shrill, high-pitched whistle would have done more justice at the business end of a freight train.

At Bailey Island, meanwhile, the spring of 1904 had brought an operational tragedy for residents, as well as the Harpswell Steamboat Company. The great wharf formed by Mackerel Cove Landing and the abutting fish wharf, all property of the Sinnett-owned Bailey's Island Steamboat Wharf Company, caught fire and succumbed to a raging and wind-whipped inferno which completely destroyed the premises, though island bucket brigades saved the E.E. Sinnett Company general store and post office. Steamer schedules were immediately altered to make all stops at York's Landing until such time as the ruins were cleared and a new wharf built on the site.

A photograph taken about 1904 aboard the Aucocisco *shows, standing, left to right, Purser Judson Webber, Mate James Foye, and Captain James Long. Seated, from left, are an unidentified deckhand, Engineer George Doughty, and Quartermaster Bert Stockbridge. Note the old-fashioned kerosene lamps and the U.S. Mail storage locker.* Mrs. Amy Stockbridge

The Portland Company steam compound engine is of the exact size and appearance as that installed aboard the Harpswell Line's Maquoit *in 1904. The photograph may indeed be a factory view of this same engine as completed and awaiting the steamer's launching.*
William B. Jordan, Jr.

Under command of Captain Eugene A. Barker, with Mate Manley Littlefield and Engineer Alonzo Small, the *Maquoit* commenced the new Inner Bay service on May 23, 1904. The temporary end of the line, and the steamer's overnight stop, was Bustins Island, but only until completion of the Mere Point wharf allowed extension of the route. On May 27, the newspaper *Six Town Times* offered that "the *Maquoit* of the Harpswell Steamship [sic] Co. made her first trip on the new route Monday. She will leave South Freeport on weekdays at 6:30 and 11:45 a.m. and Sunday at 7 a.m. and 2 p.m. . . .one of the best steamers, carrying 350 passengers as the limit."

The *Casco Bay Breeze* provided its usual fanfare in the issue of June 16, 1904:

The Harpswell Steamboat Company has for years been operating successfully what has been known as the 'outside route'. . .which makes a pretty sail. . .but there is an inside route, equally beautiful though less developed, which is now being covered by the new steamer *Maquoit* of the Harpswell Line. This steamer will make regular stops at Long Island, Sunset Landing, Hamilton's Landing, Cousin's, Littlejohn's, Bustin's, and at South Freeport. These islands are masterpieces of nature's art, but have been seriously handicapped on account of not having had proper boat service until this season.

In the same issue, the Long Island columnist added a few more enthusiastic notes:

The 2:15 p.m. trip from Portland, given by the *Maquoit* of the Harpswell Line, is proving quite popular, judging from the large number who come down on it daily. As the season advances, we expect it will be the popular trip. A large number of excursionists from Portland and vicinity came down Sunday several of which were entertained at the cottages here. The day was perfect and it was the first real Sunday crowd of the season.

Henry Bailey has been busy the past week making improvements on the two wharves of the Harpswell Line. The freight shed and waiting room at the East End [Cleaves Landing] has been overhauled and is now in keeping with the others along the route. Several improvements were made at the West End pier [Cushing's Landing], so now the patrons on this island have not reason to complain of the wharf property here.

For its part, the June 17, 1904, issue of the *Six Town Times* chimed in:

Mrs. Alonzo Small [wife of the *Maquoit*'s engineer] and son have gone to Bustin's Island to remain there until the boat change over to Mere Point. Capt. Barker's wife has also gone to Bustin's where they will occupy "Sunset" [cottage]. The steamer *Maquoit* will remain overnight at Bustin's for the present instead of this [South Freeport] wharf, coming from there before going to Portland, leaving here at 6:30 a.m. as before.

Once again the Inner Bay had been tamed to the wash of a swirling propeller, the rhythmic timing of a reciprocating engine, and the echoing steamboat whistle, but weeks passed before anything like clockwork regularity arrived. Difficult low-water landings at Cousins Island, and after July 11 at Mere Point, found use of the derrick boom essential in lifting baggage, freight, and mail up onto the high level of the wharves. If the tide was dead low, passengers were landed at Cousins Island by lowering a lifeboat and rowing them in to the wharf. Another thorn was the impossibility of making Hamilton's Landing, Great Chebeague, at low tide, although service was provided by off-loading into small craft or a lifeboat. On July 7, however, the *Breeze* reported:

Walter W. and Alfred H. Hamilton are dredging the channel at Hamilton's Landing to prepare the way for the steamer *Maquoit*. Work was started last Friday and will be completed this week, after which the boat will touch regularly 4 times daily at low tides. Walter W. Hamilton is captain of the dredger, which is the same one formerly owned by Hamilton & Sawyer.

The same issue contained another entry: "Misters Levi and Abie Bernstein are the hustling news dealers and shoe polishers on the *Aucocisco* and *Sebascodegan* respectively. They carry the *Casco Bay Breeze* and sell them. Get the local paper and all the local social news of the bay from them on your way down."

Following her 1903 piston failure, the *Sebascodegan* had continued without mishap until Monday afternoon, July 18. Thick fog had settled in as the *Sebasco* made the usual course for the channel markers on her afternoon trip down the bay. Dreary weather had cut sharply the number of travelers that day; only 40 passengers were aboard. They included popular Bailey Island storekeeper Lendall M. York, returning home following a run of errands and escorting his young daughter Mertie, who had come along to enjoy the sights. Also aboard was the noted author

After her 1904 collision with the U.S. Revenue cutter Woodbury *in Diamond Island Roads near House Island, the awesome wreckage of the* Sebascodegan *is clearly evident.* Steamship Historical Society of America

Found at fault in the collision which severely damaged the Sebascodegan, *the well-known U.S. Revenue cutter* Woodbury *enjoyed a lengthy career that was otherwise beyond reproach.* Captain Howard L. Wentworth, Sr.

Clara Louise Burnham, a member of the aristocratic Root clan of Bailey Island, who summered and wrote many of her 30 published novels at the Moorings cottage, an annex built for her by the Roots adjacent to their large, rambling gambrel-roofed cottage "Tekitesi" on Jockey Hill.

Captain Morrill and Mate Herbert Webber both occupied the pilot house, with fog lookout Fred W. Doughty stationed at the bow. Fog signals sounded continuously on the *Sebasco*'s whistle and she was running at under half speed, facts verified later by all on board. Meanwhile, unknown to anyone on the Harpswell boat, the U.S. Revenue cutter *Woodbury*, a much larger ocean vessel equipped to run with either steam or full-rigged sail, approached from the opposite direction, off House Island. Under steam, she too was sounding fog signals and operating with caution. But signals of the two vessels went off almost simultaneously, making it impossible for either one to determine the presence of the other.

The large black hull of the *Woodbury* loomed out of the fog, headed directly for the steamer's starboard bow, with scarcely enough time for startled passengers up forward to scatter toward the stern on the run, while shouting warnings to others aboard. Captain Morrill quickly rang the stop bell to the engine room, followed by the reverse signal. Mate Webber now left the pilot house by the starboard door and got clear only seconds before the heavy jib boom of the *Woodbury* smashed right through it. It was

1:45 p.m. The cutter's raking bowsprit connected with the second deck rail and main deck house, and sheared aft so quickly that poor Mate Webber had to run down the deck as the broken bowsprit followed closely behind him, wrecking everything in its path clear to the midship gangway.

Moments after the impact, Captain Morrill himself dashed from the port door of the pilot house with destruction already ensuing, not realizing just how close he had come to death or serious injury. The story has been handed down, though, of how he stepped dazedly aft toward a group of passengers, still clutching a broken wheel spoke in his right hand!

When the cutter bowsprit finally lost its raking momentum and ground to a shrieking halt, the *Woodbury*'s lower bow had not quite found a mark in the *Sebasco*'s hull, a fortunate circumstance indeed. But the steamer's upperworks lay demolished almost beyond belief, with almost exactly half of her pilot house carried away completely and the major part of her main deck cabin also carried away or smashed in. Scattered everywhere lay bent and twisted rail, crushed and splintered deck, broken glass and debris. Numerous pieces from the area of the *Sebasco*'s bow could even be found close by her undamaged smokestack. The thunderous crash had been heard as far away as Willard Beach, at South Portland.

Amazingly enough, a cursory inspection around the decks showed no serious injuries aboard either craft. In fact, the only casualty, other

Shown as it appeared around 1903, the Ocean View Hotel at South Harpswell began as the Lawson House, but enjoyed greater prominence after its owners gave it the more definitive seaside identity. Barbara D. Munsey

A tranquil scene at Portland Pier, circa 1905, finds the new Maquoit *as she was designed for the Harpswell Line's Freeport Division. The Perkins steam tug* John C. Morrison *is barely visible at left, while the* Aucocisco's *fantail appears at right.* Orville R. Cummings, from Charles Heseltine

than a good shaking up for most on the *Sebascodegan*, was a Philadelphia visitor summering at the Ocean View Hotel, Bailey Island, who escaped with a cut hand. Aided by crew members, passengers were transferred to the *Woodbury*, which limped off to land them at Central Wharf. Meanwhile, at the South Harpswell Landing a large crowd gathered to meet the boat, this being a mail trip, and anxiety resulted when she failed to appear. When news came of the collision, a curious populace lingered, then slowly dispersed from the landing, rumors and opinions flying thick and fast among them. The islanders assembled at other landings were equally incredulous.

The *Degan*, as she was also popularly labeled by many Harpswellians, was towed from the scene and tied up at Portland Pier while a frenzied management made hasty arrangements for survey at the Portland Shipbuilding Company's South Portland yard and marine railways. The severely damaged steamer was then hauled out immediately; it was decided that topside rebuilding was feasible, and the yard even ventured to estimate repair time at just over a week. Nightmarish visions of a total loss in prime season dissolved and the Harpswell Line set about to jury-rig the schedule for one boat. The *Aucocisco*, on her next Portland landing, commenced an extended schedule of three round trips daily.

Those three round trips meant steaming over 140 miles a day, and dense fog daily rolled in and out over the bay for much of the time, making working conditions even more trying. A crew member who had to tumble out of his bunk before 5 a.m. often found himself still on duty as late as 9:30 p.m. But, although Captain Long, Engineer Doughty and the crew were overworked, they withstood it with little complaint.

The *Sebascodegan-Woodbury* collision left the *Casco Bay Breeze* editorially flat-footed; close to the front page news of the wreck was an article, written before the accident, extolling the safety of the bay's "white flyers" and the virtuous competence of their handlers. It had been drafted as a local buffer against the account of the tragic burning of the New York Harbor excursion steamer *General Slocum*, with a loss of 1,021 lives on June 15, only weeks previous. In view of the *Sebascodegan's* mishap, the article now seemed inept. Still another lame-duck piece dealt with the question of Harpswell Steamboat Company deckhands agitating for higher pay, despite the line's pronouncement that it could not afford it. At any rate, the accident ended all talk of higher pay in 1904.

On July 27, the rebuilt *Sebascodegan* left the repair yard after less than nine days off her run. A monumental effort by yard workers to get her shipshape again had kept a gang of 25 men laboring steadily at the insistence and pleas of President West and General Manager Jordan. Public opinion over the collision favored Captain Morrill's actions as above

This view of Birch Island Landing reveals the outline of the stubbier original Brunswick & Portland Line wharf, from which it was extended and reconstructed for Harpswell Line use. Stewart P. Schneider

reproach and the best possible under the circumstances. Letters expressing satisfaction with his splendid discipline, conduct, and courtesy effectively found their way into the columns of the *Breeze*, further vindicating him.

Clara Louise Burnham never forgot Captain Morrill's bravery, and in gratitude had provided strong witness to authorities along with several other highly respected individuals. Well along on her successful literary career now, "Aunt Clara" had begun with the 1893-published *Dr. Latimer*. A Christmas 1906 gift to her hero, Captain Charlie Morrill, and so inscribed, was her latest novel *Open Shutters*, set at Basin Cove, South Harpswell. Such remembrances became her habit.

The official hearings were convened in early August of 1904 by the marine Board of Examiners. Captain O.E. Willey of the *Woodbury*, and his Chief Engineer, Lt. Charles Sederly, testified, as well as Captain Morrill, Mate Webber and fog lookout Doughty, and several less prominent witnesses. Neither vessel had the right of way due to the fog, but as the inquiry progressed the burden of guilt fell toward the cutter, and the board finally ruled the *Sebascodegan* to have been run down.

The summer season of 1904 ended as a moderate success for the new South Freeport Division, despite the somewhat rocky start. The autumn schedule saw fewer trips, just as on the outer route, but the service would continue, for the *Maquoit* was never intended as merely a tourist steamer, but as a rugged, reliable link to the city for the off-shore people she served. During the prime season, command of the new steamer had passed to Captain Manley Littlefield. Captain Barker eventually became longtime skipper of the Portland-Peaks Island sidewheel ferryboat *Swampscott*.

With only one boat necessary to meet fall and winter schedules, the able *Sebasco* was leased to the Rockland and Vinalhaven Steamboat Company on Penobscot Bay. She had cut her teeth on runs out of Rockland a few seasons earlier and had continued to run on Penobscot Bay during each subsequent winter. Occasionally Captain Ed Archibald had her briefly take the Portland-Rockland run in place of one of his own steamers. This charter work was obviously good business and the Harpswell Steamboat Company was always well rewarded for its prudent tactics. Though repairs to the *Sebascodegan*, plus costs in placing the new *Maquoit* in service, had crimped the summer profits of 1904, the treasury made a handsome comeback and the season of 1905 dawned bright for the Harpswell Line.

Harpswell Line's Aucocisco *is at Cushing's Landing, Long Island. The Casco Bay Steamboat Company's Ponce Landing and the Granite Spring Casino and Hotel can be seen just astern.* The Peabody Museum of Salem

The Sebascodegan's *officers and crew look deadly earnest in this 1906 photograph. Top center, Captain Charlie Morrill; far right, Engineer Bill Cook; second from right, Purser Cliff Hamilton; seated right, Mate Jimmy Nichols; seated left, deckhand Frank Merriman; standing in companionway, shoeshine and newsboy Abie Bernstein. The cook at left is believed to be Angus MacDonald.* Mrs. Amy Stockbridge

CHAPTER 5

BOLD TRIUMPHS AND MORE MISADVENTURES
THE SEEDS OF DECLINE

Sebascodegan, Aucocisco, Maquoit, and *Machigonne*

By the following May, business for the new line had increased, and the *Maquoit* had proved herself a highly versatile boat. In mid-June, two round trips per day were once again being made as the Harpswell Steamboat Company launched its summer schedule for 1905. Enhancing business to Hamilton's Landing this season was the new nearby summer hostelry on Great Chebeague known as the Hamilton.

Captain Littlefield had built a popular following in a very short time, and many *Casco Bay Breeze* readers were pleasantly surprised to find on June 22:

Married—Captain of Casco Bay steamers Wedded to a Chebeague girl Wednesday—The marriage of Miss Bessie A. Hill and Captain Manley Littlefield took place at the home of Mr. & Mrs. L.A. Hamilton at Woodford's yesterday at 11 o'clock, a local Methodist minister performing the ceremony. Captain Littlefield is a son of Mr. George W. Littlefield of Chebeague Island and Miss Hill has also been a resident of the island, stopping with her uncle and aunt, Mr. & Mrs. Eben E. Bates. Both are very popular young people and are well known in Casco Bay.

Breeze subscribers might not have thought it such pleasurable reading had they known that married life would shortly call Captain Littlefield from the *Maquoit*'s wheelhouse for a life's work as a shoreside Inspector of Hulls. Succeeding him was Captain Joseph T. Upton, who came over from his old position on the South Portland steam ferry *Elizabeth City*.

Ready by June 22, the *Aucocisco* took up her role in the Orr's Island Division double service, each of the two larger steamers making two daily round trips. After winter and a spring interlude of charter work and spotty local service, added to considerable lay-up time, Captain Long had

superintended three weeks of work on "the queen of the fleet." The captain took great pride in the always smart appearance of the *Aucocisco* and admired her adaptability over any other vessel he had commanded.

The *Sebascodegan* was brilliant in fresh paint and polish, with a new forward companionway installed for greater convenience. She was still commanded by Captain Morrill, with Mate Cliff Hamilton serving under him; William H. Cook succeeded Engineer McShane.

Perhaps the highlight of this season for the *Aucocisco* came with her charter, during the Merchants' Exposition of 1905, to carry 500 participating members of the 53rd and 65th Regiments of His Majesty's Royal Canadian Infantry on a sail to Long Island. The capacity load of soldiers enjoyed a shore dinner at Ponce's Hotel Casino during their stopover. In addition to as much charter excursion business as its three-vessel operations would permit, the Harpswell Line's four round-trip Orr's Island Division service reflected a higher patronage than in 1904 and the regional island community took on an even greater air of wellbeing.

At this juncture, the *Breeze* launched its first annual contest, centered, of course, on steamboat operations. It had been noted from pursers' records that the Harpswell Line, during June, July, and August of 1904, had carried 89,265 passengers to and from Portland on its three steamers, not counting inter-island travelers or daily commuters. The object of the contest was to guess the number of passengers to be carried in 1905. No one connected with the newspaper or steamboat company was eligible to enter and the Grand Prize was a coastal trip to New York, via a steamer of the Maine Steamship Company, plus one day's board in New York City at a first-class hotel. Really quite an incentive, especially to some poor island fishing or farming people who might otherwise have lived unexciting and meager lives. As it turned out, the islander who won guessed 90,000 people.

The fascination of his old sidewheel ferryboat would not leave Captain Upton and he departed the *Maquoit* to return to the *Elizabeth City*'s broad decks at the end of July, 1905. Next in succession was the familiar face of Captain Safford Macomber, who handled the *Maquoit* only briefly before his retirement from steamboating. Following him as skipper came Captain Prescott Taylor, the first of the *Maquoit*'s commanders to linger awhile.

On July 15, the *Maquoit*'s first publicized breakdown occurred at Portland Pier when a broken flange on her main steam feed pipe blew out just before her last trip of the day. Four hours later she was able to leave and could be heard far into the star-studded evening, as her whistle announced each island landing.

The *Sebascodegan*'s 1905 season went along routinely until the evening of August 24, when a heavy summer squall struck just as she was making the West End (Cushing's) Landing at Long Island. Driving rain, fog, and intense winds had reached their height when Mate Herb Thompson spotted Jake Bailey's motorboat struggling toward the wharf. Overloaded and rolling badly, the launch had been returning a good-sized party of South Harpswell theatergoers home after a performance at the Gem on Peaks Island. With Bailey vainly trying to head her up for the leeward side of the wharf, the force of the wind blew his boat up against the piles on the windward side, where the suddenly heavy chop of the seas might capsize or batter her severely. A treacherous few minutes followed, but the drenched passengers were landed on the wharf safely with assistance from Mate Thompson and deckhand J.W. Gilliam of the *Sebasco*, who were acclaimed as heroes by the wet and bedraggled group after all had embarked on the steamer.

Though deckmen on the island steamers labored daily in the limelight of passengers' attention, crew members down in the darkened fire rooms and engine pits gained only occasional distinction. Again this year, the *Sebascodegan* boasted fireman John Lamy, who had sailed into Manila Bay behind Admiral Dewey's flagship during the Spanish-American War. Then a navy fireman aboard the first-class cruiser *Baltimore*, he had gone on to make a Far East cruise of almost 9,000 miles after transfer to the cruiser *Brooklyn*. Upon leaving the Navy, he had obviously settled down to a quieter way of life, content to steam never more than 40 miles out of his way.

In an era long before the pattern of modern practice called for placement of a powerful and readily directed searchlight atop coastal steamer wheelhouses, the *Sebascodegan* nearly came to grief one Sunday evening in early September 1905. At South Harpswell, on the way back to Orrs Island, the last glimmer of twilight had passed as Captain Morrill rang a slow bell to ease her ahead, and most lines were let go. The stern had swung away from the pier as the spring line took tension, and the usual groaning and creaking of guard against wooden pilings halted with

a stop bell and slackdown on the spring and now the order to "take her in." Next the backing bells, and the *Sebasco* was off and into the stream once again.

Now to Captain Charlie's dismay on this moonless evening, the rising heavy vapors in the night air prevented him from making out the locations of the unlighted buoys marking the tortuous channel off Potts Harbor and Thrumcap Islet. Evidently thinking that his night vision would improve as the *Sebasco* slowly proceeded, the skipper decided the run through could still be safely made despite extremely low tides lately.

The *Sebasco*, like most bay steamers, was not yet equipped with a searchlight, and after making the elbow bend, the steamer moved ahead slowly. Suddenly, a jolting thud shook the hull timbers, followed by a dull grinding which ceased as quickly as it had begun. She had struck a rock; three bells for full astern immediately clanged after the stop bell as the steamer sheered off. Another stop bell now and Captain Morrill knew well that to advance under such doubtful circumstances would be foolhardy. Judging his boat to have drifted to the right, after a few minutes he could look back to locate only the lights of South Harpswell village and the steamer wharf with any certainty. Drawing an obvious conclusion, Captain Charlie backed and turned the *Sebasco* slowly to regain the safety of the berth she had vacated only minutes before. She lay at the wharf until dawn, with passengers able to find overnight lodging in the village, and happy to do so, rather than risk calamity on the darkened waters. No significant damage could be found after a hull inspection at South Portland the next day.

With the new four daily round-trip schedule inaugurated in 1906, the *Sebascodegan* commenced her morning run from the Orrs Island wharf at 5:40 a.m., making all stops Portland-bound and arriving there at 8 a.m. In the meantime, the *Aucocisco* would start her day by leaving Portland Pier at 7 a.m., again making all stops and arriving at the Orrs Island end of the line about 9:15 a.m. Evidence that the *Auco* was not always limited to the Orr's Island Division outside route is found in the *Breeze* of June 28, 1906:

Steamer *Aucocisco* Takes Out Party—Shining with bright brass and new paint on first Sunday Sail—A sail Sunday afternoon by the steamer *Aucocisco*, Captain James L. Long, was an inner bay trip among the beautiful isles of this section. The boat carried a fine company out and the trip was much enjoyed. On Monday the *Aucocisco* was put on the regular line again and is running with the *Sebascodegan* on the double trip service for the season.

Photographed about 1905, the Hotel Rockmere, overlooking the wharf, was Littlejohn Island's principal inn during the steamboat era. Both the hotel and a sizable cottage colony had been built in 1893 by the Atlantic Improvement Company of Massachusetts, on property purchased from the Hamilton family. Barbara D. Munsey

The summer schedule found the *Maquoit* under command of Captain Prescott Taylor, with Cliff Hamilton as Mate. Leaving from her nightly layover at Mere Point at 6 a.m., she made all landings and arrived in Portland at 8:30 a.m. Her first trip outbound was at 9:30 a.m. The principal complaint on the South Freeport Division this year had been the dismally rickety condition of the old, hurriedly patched-up wharf at Cousins Island. Only hours before the impending Fourth of July rush, Henry Bailey and his work gang completed its reconditioning. Cousins Islanders were once more content now that service had improved. Reassured by such attention, inner island residents accepted both boat and crew with renewed enthusiasm.

Not the least of the steamer's new admirers was Pete, the pet hound dog of Postmaster Glover on Littlejohn Island. Even though the wharf lay a good mile from his home at the Post Office, Pete would bound down the wagon road at the first sound of the *Maquoit*'s shrill whistle and arrive on the dock, panting and with tail wagging happily, as the first line looped over the bollards. The boatmen took a great liking to the gentle mutt and the cook's tin pan of table scraps, often placed for him on the wharf planks, was a bribery which made the feeling mutual. Pete became a constant attendant, trotting back and forth between the steamboat wharf and Post Office no less than four times each day.

In July 1906, the *Casco Bay Breeze* came out with a new weekly feature titled "Steamboat Men You Know." Each week a photograph of one of the better-known steamboat personalities on the bay appeared, with a brief sketch of his career. The first was honored on July 5:

Captain James L. Long of the steamer *Aucocisco,* though a comparatively young man, has a record of 22 years in the steamboat business and has been with the Harpswell Steamboat Company for a considerable part of this time. He is considered one of the best informed masters in this section and is familiar with courses and harbors from New Hampshire to Bar Harbor.

Soon commemorated in similar fashion was the *Sebasco*'s master:

Captain Charles B. Morrill of the steamer *Sebascodegan* is a well known steamboat man who has had years of experience. He navigates Casco Bay in a manner which has often earned him the confidence and deserved praise of his many passengers. His career as a steamboat man includes some years of towboating with the Eastern Dredging Company and also Morris Cummings & Company of New York. He recently spent some time about the Pacific Coast and Alaska.

"Steamboat Men You Know" on July 26, 1906, stated:

Captain Prescott Taylor of the steamer *Maquoit* enjoys the enviable position of master of one of the finest small steamers on the coast of Maine. He has had a captain's license for 12 years and has been in the steamboat business for 17 years. During this time holding positions with the Maine S.S. Co., The Freeport & Portland Steamboat Company, and on the *Island Belle* one season to Peaks Island. He has been captain of the *Maquoit* two seasons and is very popular on the Inner Bay route. He has never had an accident.

Engineer William H. Cook of the Sebascodegan, *shown in a 1906
photo, became an expert on towing vessels and opposition line
craft. Once he came over to the Harpswell Line he remained with it
and successors throughout the rest of his steamboating career.*
Maine Historical Society

Ironically, only weeks later, a rowboat being towed from Mere Point to Portland by the *Maquoit* was drawn down by the steamer's propeller suction, as Captain Taylor backed away from Hamilton's Landing on his 1:40 p.m. departure. The rowboat, consigned to Samuel Hodgdon at Merrill's Wharf, suffered a badly crushed stern.

In August, for the first time, the *Sebascodegan* made moonlight sails instead of merely lying idle at the Orrs wharf each pleasant summer evening. These cruises proved very popular and were long remembered among the older generations. If weather permitted, just before 8 p.m., with full steam up again following the supper hour, the *Sebasco* would wait in readiness as happy throngs of island residents trooped over the wharf planking to board her for the leisurely run. Under way on the hour, she would soon stop at Old Wharf (York's Landing), Bailey Island, where many more pleasure seekers waited to board. South Harpswell followed, with the final stop made at Littlefield's Landing on Great Chebeague, before the *Sebasco* turned back over the route toward Orrs Island. These runs greatly aided in popularizing inter-island baseball games, played in the early evening, by offering both the teams and spectators a later trip homeward.

On August 2, the *Breeze* leaned toward anecdote:

George H. Doughty, Chief Engineer for the Harpswell Line of steamers, is considered one of the best informed marine engineers in the business. At present Engineer on the steamer *Aucocisco*, a position he has held since she was built, he counts his period of service with this line back to 25 years ago when he ran the steamer *Gordon*. Following this boat, he took, in order, the *Alice*, *Merryconeag*, *Sebascodegan*, and *Aucocisco*. Previously he was on the Portland-Boston line for nine years. He was quite widely noted a few years ago for diving, having on one occasion taken a look at the bottom of Portland Harbor to see if the *Auco's* screw was digging it away too fast. It was said to have been an accident but George denies this firmly.

The following week "Steamboat Men You Know" was more business-like, stating in its August 9 issue:

Judson A. Webber, Purser of the *Aucocisco* holds one of the responsible positions of the Harpswell Line. A purser for the company is in his capacity a traveling Treasurer, handling large sums of money and keeping numerous freight and passenger accounts. The position is one requiring strict application and can be filled only by very competent men. Mr. Webber has for four years filled this occupation on the *Aucocisco*, to the complete satisfaction of the Harpswell Steamboat Company and has gained also the warm friendship of the summer tourists who know him well.

Then came Bill Cook's moment of glory as the *Breeze* said of him:

William H. Cook, popular Engineer of steamer *Sebascodegan* is widely and favorably known to all patrons of the Harpswell Line. Mr. Cook served his apprenticeship with the Knickerbocker Steam Towage Company [of Bath]. After receiving his papers, his first assignment was with the steamer [tug] *Frederick N. Wilson*, since which he has served on the following boats: *C.A. Warren*, *Madeleine*, *Percy V.*, *Pejepscot*, *Mineola* . . . .He is an expert machinist and a valuable man for this line.

There's evidence here that Cook served some time on the opposition MacDonald Line but was now a loyal convert!

The *Sebascodegan*'s crew held the limelight as the *Breeze* came on strong the very next week. "Steamboat Men You Know" declared:

William L. Purington, one of the best known steamboat men about Portland, holds the position of Purser aboard the steamer *Sebascodegan*. In this capacity, he has during the past four years, endeared himself to every passenger by his cheerful good nature, under conditions often strenuous enough to disturb the most positive equanimity. He transacts the large cash and charge business of the boat in his office on board, besides following the loading and unloading of every piece of freight and attending to the passenger's service. He is certainly entitled to the words 'well done' in these columns. Hats off to Will!

Many in Casco Bay steamboat circles would later wish they had fathomed more accurately the importance of hushed inner-office planning sessions among Harpswell Line directors and management throughout the year 1906. Toward the end of another successful season for the Harpswell Line, an account in the *Casco Bay Breeze* of August 23 foreshadowed the future:

At present the company has under the most serious consideration several plans for making next season's accommodations such as will make the beautiful trip down Casco Bay, the favorite sail out of Portland, even more pleasurable for patrons. We hope to be able to announce before the close of the present season just what the company contemplates doing. Those who have been taken into the company's confidence say that, both for passengers and freight, next season's accommodations on the Harpswell Line will be unsurpassed by any other steamboat company of its class. This year has been the most prosperous one that the management has yet known. The pursers report that they never before have carried anything like the same number of passengers and this is the most convincing proof of the growing popularity of Casco Bay.

Late in August, "Steamboat Men You Know" proudly announced:

Engineer Harry Hill . . .of the steamer *Maquoit*, is the youngest licensed marine engineer in the state, if not in New England. When this boat was built . . .Mr. Hill had just received his papers and was 21 years of age. His experience had been gained on several boats, the *Aucocisco*, where he finished his days as fireman under Engineer Doughty; the *Percy V.*; and Eastern Dredging Company's boats. He is a resident of Chebeague Island and is a popular young man ashore and afloat.

During the winter of 1906-07, the lonely bay route was taken by the *Sebasco*, while the *Aucocisco* took her turn substituting first on the Portland-Rockland route, Captain Archibald at her helm, and then augmenting the light and less enclosed winter boat on the Rockland-Vinalhaven line.

That winter on Casco Bay was a memorable one for its bitter cold and the great expanse of thick ice that formed over most of the inlets and sounds all the way from Portland to the New Meadows River. The alternating Captains, Long and Morrill, had their crews up as early as 3 a.m. some mornings to clear the decks of ice and snow, then break ice close

The Ocean View Hotel at Bailey Island, owned by Walter D. Crafts, an astute and efficient hotelier, overlooked picturesque Mackerel Cove. Author's Collection

Following a 1907 reconstruction, intended to leave her better suited as running mate to the bold new Machigonne, *the* Aucocisco *had reached her zenith of overall usefulness and trim appearance.* The Peabody Museum of Salem

around the hull with shovels, pickaxes, and stout timbers, just to improve the chances of getting away from the Orrs Island wharf in the first place. Under such severely ice-locked conditions, the alternate route ran into Mackerel Cove, Bailey Island, then outside Little Mark Island, through Green Island Passage, around Ram Island Light and into the main ship channel entering Portland Harbor. Getting back to Orrs in late afternoon was often a demanding exercise as well, and Captain Long recalled vividly the time the *Sebasco* was forced to wait well off Prince's Point until townspeople had cut a channel through the heavy ice with handsaws and axes so that she could make it to the steamboat wharf.

On the approach of spring in 1907, the web of the company's expansion plans was fast being spun. At a far-off shipyard on the Delaware River, a bold new luxury flagship was taking shape on the ways. On the home front, builders were not only enlarging wharves for the new Harpswell Line steamship, but also constructing new landings for the expansion of the Casco Bay Steamboat Company. Other important changes came too, and soon the *Aucocisco* was on the South Portland marine railway for alterations. She was to leave the railway cradle many weeks later with the striking new appearance and profile which would see her through the years, dignified and handsome, and part of the lives of generations who came to know her well.

Following leads supplied by the Maine Central Railroad, Harpswell

Line officials had journeyed to the Neafie & Levy Ship & Engine Building Company at Philadelphia, negotiated a deal and watched over plans for an updated version of Maine Central's much-admired *Norumbega*. Ordered at a cost of $75,000, the new flagship was christened *Machigonne*, after an early Abenaki Indian settlement where the city of Portland now lies. Reflecting the geographic shape of the promontory crowned by Munjoy Hill, the name translates as "great knee."

In May, Henry Bailey's wharf-building gangs, aided by a tug and a steam pile driver, built a 12-foot addition to the South Harpswell Landing, others of 20 feet at Cushing's Landing, Long Island and at Little Chebeague, a 30-foot extension of Littlefield's Landing at Great Chebeague, and 20 feet to the pier at Cliff Island. Lesser repairs were made at Beals Ledges (Sebasco) Landing before work gangs concluded with new wharves for the company's expansion at Gurnet, Cundy's Harbor, and finally Harpswell Center.

Senior Captain James L. Long and Chief Engineer George H. Doughty were selected to bring the *Machigonne* home from the Delaware River builders' yard. After a long maiden voyage, the *Machigonne* entered Portland Harbor on Friday, June 21, amid a clamorous welcome from local harbor and small craft. At Portland Pier, the queen of the steamboat fleet became focal point as curious crowds came down to Commercial Street to pass judgment.

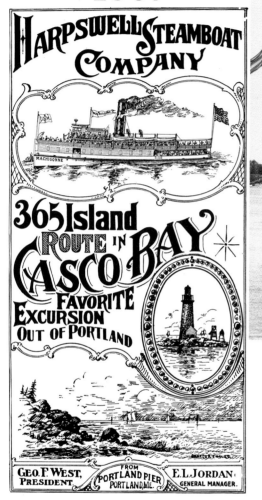

1907

HARPSWELL STEAMBOAT COMPANY

365 Island ROUTE IN CASCO BAY

FAVORITE EXCURSION OUT OF PORTLAND

GEO. F. WEST, PRESIDENT

FROM PORTLAND PIER PORTLAND, ME.

E. L. JORDAN, GENERAL MANAGER.

The Harpswell Steamboat Company's 1907 timetable opened up to reveal a detailed map of the company's routes. Author's Collection

Backing from Portland Pier during the summer of 1907 is the stately Harpswell Line steamer Machigonne *with a near-capacity crowd.*
The Peabody Museum of Salem

By island steamer standards, the *Machigonne* was an incredible advance, with durable hull of steel, five watertight bulkheads and wood-sheathed superstructure. The almost lavish decor of her interiors included a main saloon handsomely upholstered and finished throughout in white-and-gold trim, while the sedate men's smoking room had been finished in quartered oak and its seating padded in expensive Spanish leather. Seating in the attractive ladies' cabin aft was upholstered in blue plush. All interior spaces were laid in rich wine-colored carpeting and the glitter of polished brass rails and brightwork shone everywhere. Compared with the limited open area aboard many of the older wooden-hulled boats, the *Machigonne*'s promenades were spacious and airy. On the second (or observation) deck, the large extensively glassed cabin offered passengers a practically unbroken view. Ample freight space below was sufficient for any demand and the new flagship was certified to carry 1,000 passengers.

The *Machigonne* was equally well fitted in her engine spaces. First island steamboat to employ a triple-expansion engine since the defeated MacDonald Line flyer *Pejepscot*, and now alone in this class, still she seldom logged better than 12 knots on Casco Bay.

The *Machigonne*'s first regularly assigned crew numbered 14, with the deck gang under the practiced eye of Mate Len Hamilton, and a sizable Stewards' Department, which included the Steward and Stewardess, a Mr. and Mrs. Noblett, and, for a time, two southern blacks who served as Porter and Messenger.

Since the close of the 1906 summer season, Harpswell Steamboat Company directors and management had outdone themselves. The firm now had four well-defined divisions, more and larger landings, expanded schedules and greatly increased tonnage. There seemed no end to its progress. Its principals truly believed in Casco Bay, the myriad Calendar Islands, and the city of Portland, now known as the "Sunrise Gateway."

While the *Aucocisco*, under Captain Clifford Hamilton, would run opposite the larger *Machigonne* on the Orr's Island Division, the *Sebascodegan* was promptly placed on the lately formed New Meadows line. Henry Bailey had completed a 75-foot landing on the Great Island side of Gurnet Strait, as well as a 150-foot wharf at Cundy's Harbor, and the use of an existing wharf was arranged at the resort town of Sebasco on the eastern New Meadows shore. The *Sebascodegan* would now leave Portland daily at 9 a.m., cover all the stops to Bailey Island except Orrs, then, following the Mackerel Cove stop, continue around southward of Jaquish Island, to head northeast for Sebasco. Next came the stop at Cundy's Harbor and finally a six-mile trip around the tree-lined eastern shore of Great Island, with occasional waylanding flag stops made at the Winnegance and Foster's Point Landings on the New Meadows east shore, before turning westward into Gurnet Strait and the Gurnet Bridge Landing. Here a one-hour stop was made for the shore dinner customers before the steamer departed at 2 p.m., to make all the stops on the 40-mile return trip to Portland. The *Sebasco* would arrive back at Portland Pier at 6 p.m., which still allowed her passengers time for supper or connection with evening trains or coastwise steamship departures.

The indomitable *Casco Bay Breeze* fairly glowed over the new run, its July 11, 1907, issue stating that "travel is getting heavier every day on this route." It continued:

Completely refurbished by the Casco Bay Line, the Merryconeag *appears at Gurnet Landing in the summer of 1907. The rival Harpswell Line's* Sebascodegan *is also evident at Gurnet Bridge Landing.*
The Peabody Museum of Salem

The elegance of the Machigonne's *interior accommodation is evident in her upper deck cabin showing the detail of upper clerestory lighting and staircase to the main deck. Seated are Casco Bay & Harpswell Lines Superintendent Walter Locke and fleet ''commodore'' Captain James L. Long.*
Warren N. Graffam Collection, from Hilda Cushing Dudley

The Gurnet trip on the Harpswell Line. . .is one of the most popular trips on the bay this summer. Beginning this week there will be another restaurant running at Gurnet Bridge and accommodations will be ample for the large number who are taking the sail of 80 miles among the islands. Twenty-four miles of this trip is up the New Meadows River and, at Cundy's Harbor and Gurnet, connection is made with a subsidiary motor line which runs to the electric car connection at New Meadows. . . .The magnificent scenery and the fragrance of the balsam-laden air up in the secluded section of the bay is enough to tempt the most timid across the gangplank of the staunch steamer *Sebascodegan* on a pleasant morning. . . .Dinners at the terminus are not a disappointment either, for they are liberal, with well-cooked seafood and reasonable in price. . . .The crew of the steamer are always ready to point out the places of interest on the way and are courteous and accommodating to all.

Since this easternmost bay area had no regular or connecting steamer service to and from Portland following the demise of the MacDonald Line, except for the New Meadows Steamboat Company, the Cundy's Harbor correspondent for the *Breeze* summed up the general feeling on July 18 by writing "The *Sebascodegan* had a large number of people on board Sunday and we are so glad to see the liberal patronage."

The crew of the *Sebasco*, under Captain Morrill, remained about the same as when on the Orrs Island route, with the notable exception of Will Purington, who had taken the important position of Purser on the *Machigonne*. He was succeeded on the *Sebasco* by W.E. Leighton, of Portland, who was to continue with the steamboat company for several summer vacations while attending Wesleyan University.

The *Machigonne*'s first run brought enthusiasm mirrored by the *Breeze* in its issue of June 27, 1907. Under the lead line "Popular Sunday Excursion," its account read:

The first public trip of the new Harpswell Line steamer *Machigonne* was held on Sunday afternoon last at 2:30 p.m. With a crowd of 850 passengers on board, the boat left Portland Pier and sailed down the harbor. Captain James L. Long took the steamer on a most delightful trip, going down the inner bay route and returning passing the islands of the outer bay. The passengers enjoyed a very pretty afternoon sail. The American Cadet Band was aboard and rendered a delightful concert during the trip.

The regular schedule had the *Machigonne* leaving Portland Pier daily at 9:45 a.m. and making stops at Long, Cliff and Chebeague Islands, South Harpswell, Bailey and Orrs Islands. Back in Portland, she would depart again at 2:15 p.m. for an identical round trip, popularly called the matinee sail. This arrangement offered an all-day trip for excursionists or a four-hour, 50-mile sail among the islands.

Those first days were not all as glorious as the Harpswell Line could have hoped for. The *Machigonne* had cost some $20,000 over the original estimate, and wharf alterations alone amounted to a small fortune. Already, management was hard put to admit that its pride and joy seemed possessed of demons when it came to maneuverability, was cranky down below and so continually hungry that coal bills were monumental.

Leading a series of problems which kept line officials reaching for the aspirin bottle, the idea of making a stop at Mackerel Cove Landing, Bailey Island, surfaced as impractical. While it took courage to bring the balky *Machigonne* around Abner's Point in a breeze to begin with, Captain Long's troubles at this point were still elementary. Undocking and turning the big steamer in the restricted wharf area caused frequent damage to pilings and she often touched bottom whenever the tide was low. Captain Jimmie was soon forced to complete his bow-in calls there by backing over half a mile out, past the entrance buoy, before he could safely turn out around Abner's Point. Classing this matter stoically as an acceptable peril, the company changed its attitude after Captain Long and the magnificent *Machigonne* went hard aground while leaving Mackerel Cove with a falling tide. Passengers removed by small craft remained stranded on the island until the mid-afternoon run by the *Aucocisco* returned them to Portland. Freed on the next high tide, the *Machigonne* steamed back to Portland, never again to round "the Point" into Mackerel Cove.

With wharf builders at work to enlarge York's Landing, the *Machigonne*'s two daily stops at Bailey Island were shifted there. This wharf, once known as Mineral Spring (due to its proximity to a cupola-capped spring house just south of it along the shoreline of Lowell Cove), but lately referred to simply as Old Wharf, was the first steamboat landing on Bailey, built in 1888 for the steamers *Gordon* and *Alice*. Centrally located at the seaward end of tiny Lowell Cove, it was just down the hill from Lendall York's large general store and livery stable, which shared the knoll with the island school house, the prosaic and unsteepled Community Church and a small village cluster which included a boarding house or two. The old wharf had served the company well, despite being a difficult place to land in a southwest wind and frequently ice-jammed in winter. It now returned to prominence with the *Machigonne*.

The Robin Hood Inn at the northeasterly end of Bailey Island was a favored destination of a brisk carriage trade from York's Landing, especially in the palmy days when the Machigonne *or* Pilgrim *landed their matinee sail passengers in great numbers.* Barbara D. Munsey

By early July it became clear that the *Machigonne* was very hard on all the island landings. Captain George "Cliff" Randall expressed it this way:

Those old wharves, the way they were built then, they just couldn't take her. She'd come alongside and when she touched she'd come up too hard against them. The Mate used to keep men busy with slush buckets, greasing around her guards to reduce the damage there might be if she ever 'dry-ironed' into a piling and fetched up on it. Many's the time those wooden pilings were broken up or torn away from the wharf!

Added to a snarling string of troubles, the *Machigonne* could reach Potts Harbor, South Harpswell, only on a high tide and the channel, from this wharf toward Merriconeag Sound, was so difficult and risky that Captain Long began taking the *Machigonne* out around Haskell Island on foggy or windy days.

When the South Freeport Division was first expanded beyond Mere Point Landing, it was to serve the old Brunswick & Portland Steamboat Company wharf, built in 1899 at Johnson's Point on the west shore of Birch Island. Disused since the abandonment of the line, and the legal seizure of the firm's steamer *Corinna* in 1903, the landing had been the product of a mid-1890s euphoria in the face of any number of mostly deceptive speculative real-estate ventures, all supposed to culminate in refined inner bay resort colonies of summer cottages. Some of these had elaborate plans, duly filed with the Cumberland County Registry of Deeds, and on Birch Island the visionary Birchmont was just such a project. Founded by the Birch Island Land Company owner and trustee, George P. Dewey, this overblown proposal was laid out in 242 cottage lots, occupying 68 acres of the former Merryman farm, purchased on July 6, 1895. Since successful promotion of this scheme, together with others on Frenchman's Island and both Upper and Lower Goose Islands, needed a reliable system of steamer transportation to proceed properly, not one but several companies were spawned or expanded from Portland, all heavily dependent on the paper potentials of these wondrous new cottage colonies. But when no dramatic progress, or even general acceptance by the public, was seen to be forthcoming, the smaller steamer lines intending to service the Portland to Brunswick inner bay route went broke one after another, as later chapters will testify.

Although a less grandiose Birchmont plan pared down the number of house lots to a more spacious and exclusive 80 on the same acreage in August 1903, and gave particular attention to reserving some fields and

The Maquoit *waits at the Harpswell Steamboat Company's Cushing's Landing at Long Island. This wharf lay close to the old Casco Bay Line's Ponce Hotel Landing and the Granite Spring Hotel.*
R. Loren Graham, from Myron R. Currier

pasture lands or woodlands to natural usage along the six acres of a central avenue right of way, with seven planned streets to have crossed it, nothing much more happened. A thoroughly disillusioned Dewey resorted to selling much of the subdivided land in piecemeal fashion until shortly before his death in December 1925. The last nine unsold lots were left to his widow.

Frederick C. Johnson, another Birch Island dreamer and developer, but more down to earth in his dealings, had purchased the old childhood farmstead home of Pulitzer Prize-winning poet Robert P. Tristram Coffin in 1883. A hard-working farmer and sometime fisherman in the hard-scrabble island tradition at first, Fred Johnson gradually shifted focus and turned the old Coffin farm into a seasonal boarding establishment in 1901. It became the first of his two Johnson House hotels. Later subdividing his land holdings on Johnson's Point into the house lots of the Crawford Plan cottage colony, and acreage on The Ridge to Arlington Heights, he garnered more outside interest than George Dewey had.

Intrigued with Johnson's latest activities, George F. West, President of the Harpswell Steamboat Company, brought a party of his friends from Portland to Birch Island in his private steam yacht *Philomena* on July 1, 1904. Fred Johnson parlayed the occasion into a series of meetings to negotiate a lease of the existing Birch Island wharf to the Harpswell Line.

He found the Portland Pier solon to be a hard sell at first. The disastrous record of predecessor steamer lines was not lost on the shrewd Harpswell Line official. Since one of his close business associates and shareholders was a relative of George P. Dewey, this was not the first time his Harpswell Line board had been courted. The upshot was that West and company wanted to see more actual progress in island development and F.C. Johnson set out in earnest to provide it.

The new service was finally instituted once the old wharf had been extended another 20 feet seaward and widened to ''down bay'' standards. Continuing improvements brought a new Johnson House, with its screened piazza and Tea Room restaurant, which often served upward of 30 steamer passengers each day. A well-stocked store and a post office were provided, as well as a 50,000-gallon cistern water system, tennis courts, a baseball field and, some years later, a new casino and bowling alley. Hotelier, storekeeper and fuel merchant, Fred Johnson also served as Birch Island's summer postmaster for a quarter century.

The Harpswell Line summer schedule for 1907 revealed changes for the former South Freeport Division. The morning departure from Portland was a quarter-hour earlier, but the biggest news was the newly rebuilt wharf at Harpswell Center, where townspeople had known no regular service since the retreat of Captain Ed Baker's steamer *Corinna* several years before. By midsummer the line reached beyond Mere Point and Birch Island landings to begin serving Center Harpswell's Lookout, and this run was labeled the Harpswell Division. The *Maquoit* was spruced up in grand style for the lengthened run, with her old samson post and boom removed to allow for a decked-over forecastle. To most of her passengers and crew, the dapper little *Maquoit* was "as smart as they come" and Joe Feeney of Stroudwater thought well of her years before he ever stepped aboard as her Purser. The genial retired Portland schoolteacher revealed: "I rode as a passenger on the *Maquoit* one time in 1907, from Peaks Island to Portland and it was the fastest trip I ever knew her to make. She was all overhauled and better than brand new—and she fairly flew!"

At the height of the 1907 season, the *Aucocisco* suffered her first and only setback on Tuesday, July 30. Leaving Orrs Island wharf on her 1:30 p.m. trip to Portland, and starting her customary wide swing around Cox Ledge off Garrison Point, Bailey Island, she suddenly refused to answer the helm for her bewildered quartermaster. Captain Hamilton felt her take a "rotten sheer" to starboard instead, toward the distant West Harpswell shore across Merriconeag Sound. The clanging of engine bells stopped her dead in the water and inspection found an unshipped rudder. The *Auco* was forced to drift and await assistance, but the Orrs landing was within hailing distance and her whistle brought out a well-manned dory from Prince & Daniels' wharf nearby. Captain Hamilton was able to dispatch a message, to be telephoned to Manager Jordan from the general store. More than two hours later, Central Wharf Towboat Company's steam tug *Portland* hove into view, coming around past Pinkham Island. To the relief of passengers, the *Auco* was soon under way again, plodding along under tow. Returning from her regular trip to Gurnet, the *Sebascodegan* was recruited to take the belated last trip down the bay that evening. At the marine railway, the *Auco*'s rudder was easily repaired and she returned to service on Wednesday morning.

Deep down in the fabric of difficulties lately experienced with the grand new *Machigonne* ran a few golden threads. Two such strands were the Nobletts, Steward and Stewardess, a kindly couple who became an institution of a novel sort. Though the Harpswell Line had ambitiously envisioned a fleet of up to five vessels of the *Machigonne*'s class, no more were ever built, and the Nobletts were thus the first and only personnel to hold their title and position. Popular with bay travelers from far and near, they both busily saw to every want and need of passengers, while carefully maintaining the interior finery and cleanliness of cabins, as well as manning the galley to cook for the entire complement.

The first season for the *Machigonne* was disappointing, though, with almost never a scheduled trip at capacity load. Repairs to damaged wharf structures from one end of the line to the other were a hefty expense not anticipated. The Harpswell Steamboat Company, riding the surging crest only four months before, had been cruelly set back by fate, and not only in this arena, but also with a failing Gurnet line and marginal Harpswell Division revenues.

Meanwhile, the neighboring Casco Bay Steamboat Company had ambitiously expanded on a paper foundation and its business affairs were entangled almost beyond hope of recovery. What a year to remember and regret among the Casco Bay steamboat fraternity!

The end of the 1907 season was also the end of an era. For over three decades there had been two major independently strong steamboat companies on Casco Bay. In desperation the directors of the Casco Bay Line met with those of the Harpswell Steamboat Company. Hoping to offset declining revenues through expansion, the older firm had instead slipped hopelessly into debt. The despair of honorable men blurred the vision of the Harpswell directors and management now, making their own financial problems seem less acute. When the Indian summer of 1907 came to the region, the two companies had voted to unite, merging to form the Casco Bay & Harpswell Lines, with combined operations from Custom House Wharf.

This may well have been the final September trip departure of the Merryconeag *from Gurnet Landing in 1907. If so, she would never again run farther east than Orrs Island.*
William E. Hitchcock

Opposite the Great Island side of the old Gurnet Bridge, the Merryconeag *awaits her flock of shore dinner excursionists. Casco Bay Line's 1906 route expansion to Gurnet used the wharf originally built for the old MacDonald Steamboat Company.*
Maine Maritime Museum

CHAPTER 6

CASCO BAY & HARPSWELL LINES
BRIGHTEST MOMENTS AND FLEETING FORTUNES

The Consolidation of 1907

By autumn the amalgamated Casco Bay & Harpswell Lines had become a reality. Portland Pier ceased to be a terminus and Custom House Wharf became the sole bustling activity center for all arrivals and departures. The old Casco Bay Line steamers *Emita*, *Merryconeag*, *Forest Queen*, and *Pilgrim*, with their silver-and-black top-banded stacks, now shared berths with the black-stacked Harpswell Line steamers *Maquoit*, *Sebascodegan*, *Aucocisco*, and *Machigonne*, as well as the South Portland ferry steamer *Mary W. Libby*, and the steam lighter *Venture*. The *Venture* continued a fairly busy life doing island freight transport, dock repairs, and the like. For many years she was regularly skippered by either Captain Ernest Hill or Captain Jim Foye of Portland.

The year 1908, with newly organized Casco Bay & Harpswell Lines now providing services throughout the bay, was laced with bitter medicine for many islanders and and summer residents. Profit potential had increased, but the consolidation of 1907 actually brought a decline in services, created one excessively large fleet, and combined the debt of the founding companies. Wharves were discontinued at an alarming rate as the new joint management sought the most efficient system of stops. Tempers and anxiety ran high as C.B. & H. Lines' planning errors found the under-populated Jenks Landing amply provided for, while the *Maquoit*'s stop at Hamilton's Landing on Great Chebeague's east shore was eliminated, depriving one thousand or more natives and summer cottagers of adequate service. Freight for that section was now landed at Eastern Landing where, because of distance, it failed to reach its destination in reasonable time. Butter, meats and other perishables often melted or deteriorated in the summer sun. Harried officials worked to meet demands and attempted to stem further complaint from irate patrons all across the bay. Most often the solution was only a compromise and the people's dissatisfied murmurings would never quite be stilled again.

The company spared no pains, however, in overhauling its eight passenger steamers and sprucing them up in impressive style. The *Machigonne* was, of course, still its brightest star and she had lost nothing of her stateliness and handsome appointments. Since the fleet had an obvious excess of steamers, a partial solution was reached by leasing the *Forest Queen* to a line running from Portsmouth to the Isles of Shoals. On June 30, the *Queen* proceeded down the coast with Captain Charles Howe at the helm. He, in fact, remained with her during her entire stay in the New Hampshire seacoast region. Operation of the large steamboat on the run to the microscopic isles and tiny settlement of Gosport on Star Island was evidently not yet the highly successful enterprise it would later become. At any rate, the lease on the *Forest Queen* was not renewed and she returned to Portland in the autumn, to be laid up at Custom House Wharf.

The *Merryconeag* was back in the pink, ever admired by passengers, officers and crews alike. Only her engine department tended to run hot and cold over her performance. Retired fireman Ralph Bailey revealed:

The *Merryconeag*, *Sebascodegan*, and *Aucocisco* all had Portland Company compound engines, each with variations. The *Merryconeag*, now, had slide-valves on both high- and low-pressure cylinders. She was the fastest boat of the three, but the hardest one to steam! Oh boy, when those slide-valves opened, they opened wide—while a piston-valve cracks open only partially—and the *Merryconeag* could really put her foot down when you opened her up, if you had any pressure at all. But you had to be a real honest-to-God fireman to fire her! Oh, yeah! There weren't any greenhorns around!

Other boats, like the *Forest Queen*, were easy steamers and their fireboxes were a pleasure to tend . . . but the old *Merryconeag*, brother, you had to have either the sluice bar or the devil's claw in your hand all the time to break up the clinkers.

The Merryconeag *was always put to consistently hard use. In this late spring view, her bow sheathing has been removed, but the* Merry *has not yet had her turn on the marine railway for prime season refurbishing.*
Peter T. McLaughlin, from Warren N. Graffam

It is July 1908 and, in the midst of her second summer season on Casco Bay, the Machigonne *shows off her sparkling white livery and the International Code flags of "Captain Jimmie Long's wash." She approaches Doughty's Landing, Long Island, on return of the matinee sail from eastern bay points. The 1907 consolidation has retained the former Casco Bay Line wharf at Doughty's, while abandoning the Harpswell Line Marriner's Landing seen in the distance.* Philip H. Lee

Then the generators in most of the other old boats were powered by a small steam engine and belt-drive. You take a boat like the *Merryconeag*; she had an inside generator. But her boiler used steam so hard that when you used the generator, boy, you had very little steam pressure to run with. At night you might have lights with her, but you didn't steam much. You could row about as fast as you'd go! If you had 50 pounds of steam with that generator running, you were doing pretty well!

Through the chaos of reorganization and thereafter, the *Aucocisco* retained her place on the Orr's Island Division. This line, together with the inner route and the Gurnet line, continued as they had before the merger. The *Machigonne*'s pre-eminence on the outside route was never in doubt. Again in 1908, her crew remained much as it had been that first season with only one new, but familiar, face aboard. The *Casco Bay Breeze* offered a salute in the July 2, 1908, issue:

Ralph Sprague, the popular purser of the Casco Bay & Harpswell Line is now purser on the steamer *Machigonne* for the season. Mr. Sprague is a student at the Bowdoin Medical College at Brunswick. Last season Mr. Sprague was purser of the *Aucocisco* and pays courteous attention to the wants of the patrons of this line. He has made many friends, all of whom are glad to see him with us again this season.

The operations of the large C.B. & H. Lines fleet made old, historic Custom House Wharf busier than ever before. Always the primary seat of steamboating on the bay, the wharf was the focal point of island travel. At this bustling terminus even the proud *Machigonne* was never beneath her dignity as she departed daily to cover far-flung island stops, and, like other steamers, apparently shrinking at times in importance alongside the gangways, stacked and piled freight, a maze of waiting rooms, ticket booths, offices, sheds, shops and business establishments of varied sorts, and eateries. In those times, the entire length of the great wharf was steamboat domain and the vessels lining its slips in the late evening presented an arresting spectacle as they lay idle after countless daylight trips. Perhaps one of the South Portland shuttle steamers might be active at the float landing within the lead dock space, but the larger bay queens began a nightly slumber, unbroken until the small hours of the next morning. The old buildings on Custom House Wharf had high peaked roofs, only much later reduced to flat roofs.

From its earliest days, the wharf had been the property of the influential Barker family, and even now venerable Peleg Barker made himself memorable by standing on the wharf at practically all hours, merely to collect a quarter from any boatman who might tie up there. Old Barker had no need of more money, but collecting that twenty-five cents from unwitting users became a real pastime. On the frugal owner's death, the wharf property passed to his estate, which eventually sold out to the Custom House Wharf Corporation, also known as "The Proprietors of Custom House Wharf."

There was also a modest touch of grandeur, if one had a mind to notice, in the many staunch and weathered island landings scattered across the bay. Most of the wharves had been built or improved by the tireless work gangs of carpenter and wharf builder Henry Bailey, of Little Chebeague Island. Some of his finest efforts resulted in the picturesque canopied wharves constructed for the old Casco Bay Steamboat Company at Doughty's Landing on Long Island, at Little Diamond, both Western and Eastern Landings on Great Chebeague, at Cliff Island, and at South Harpswell.

The consolidation affected operation of the *Pilgrim* very little at first. She continued to be used primarily on the Peaks and Diamond Islands run, excursion charters and moonlight sails. Soon, though, she customarily made one daily trip as far east as Bailey and Orrs Islands, and sometimes more often on weekends. The former Harpswell Line practice of a scheduled layover at Orrs Island, continued by C.B. & H. Lines, was never delegated to the *Pilgrim* or *Machigonne*, but fell to either the *Aucocisco* or the *Merryconeag*.

The *Pilgrim*'s memorable moonlight sails continued just as they had under the old regime. A trio of musicians often graced the *Pilgrim* on summer evenings as she steamed serenely through moonlit waters, the popular dance music of the era echoing over her decks and surroundings. Alice Flynn Davis thought highly of these trips:

> Why, when I was invited out on those moonlight sails by older fellows—I was 16 or 17—it was beautiful! We used to have a string ensemble called the St. Angelus Trio, playing a piano accordion, a violin and a cello. They would collect money while performing, I think, and pay C.B. & H. Lines on a seasonal basis for the privilege of riding. But, oh, they could certainly play lovely music!

Following the annual September exodus of summer people back to their permanent homes in Eastern and Middle Atlantic locations, the *Pilgrim* would take a turn on the South Portland marine railway for a

The landing at Harpswell Lookout eventually became overnight terminus for the steamer Maquoit *as the Harpswell Steamboat Company's South Freeport Division expanded eastward.* Barbara D. Munsey

few timely repairs and then ease into her Custom House Wharf berth for the long winter's hibernation.

As the *Sebascodegan* entered the second year of her new Gurnet assignment, a traditional thick summer fog came along to dog her on Thursday, July 2, 1908. At her helm, Captain Charlie Morrill left Abner's Point and Mackerel Cove astern and began his long arcing turn around the western point of Bailey Island, supposedly leaving tiny Turnip and Jaquish Islands well on the port hand. Perhaps no more than an erratic magnetic compass or a stopwatch timing error, coupled with unreliable currents off the point, left the *Sebasco* turning far too soon and well to the left of her track. Near the narrow Jaquish Gut at Land's End, she struck bow-on to the shelving ledge, startling everyone, none more than Captain Morrill. Riding high onto solid rock almost at an even keel, her good fortune ran deeper than that. Some rock ledges in the vicinity would have seriously damaged the hull, but she had found a smooth, sloping, seaweed-covered ledge on which to fetch up. While acute embarrassment marked the episode, the *Sebasco* lay on her unaccustomed perch only until the next tide, which easily floated her off. Furthermore, she went on to complete the run, and showed no signs of damage other than scarred bottom paintwork when hauled out at South Portland. Gurnet line operations proceeded the next day without hindrance.

The Aucocisco *approaches Central Landing at Great Chebeague Island on a calm summer's day in 1908. In the days of the old Harpswell Line, the wharf had been known as Littlefield's Landing.*
Captain Carleton R. Morrill

Officers and crew look forward from the boat deck of the Aucocisco *in 1908. Front row, left to right, are Purser Ralph Sprague, Captain Charles Morrill, Mate Bert Stockbridge, Engineer William Cook, and Quartermaster Peter Schyler. Among those standing to the rear are deckhand Fred Wilson at left; fireman Frank Pinkham, top center; deckhand Frank Merriman, rear right.*
Mrs. Amy Stockbridge

On the *Maquoit*, Captain Taylor had left local employment for broader horizons with Eastern Steamship Company, being relieved by an equally sea-minded Chebeague Islander. Captain Clifford S. Hamilton had come up from deckhand to serve as quartermaster, then purser and finally mate under Captain Morrill, performing capably on the *Sebascodegan* and *Aucocisco*, sometimes as relief skipper, before stepping up to command of the *Maquoit*. The engineer was Spanish-American War naval veteran John Lamy, fresh off the Gurnet steamer *Sebascodegan* and doling out greetings and wry good humor to everyone within earshot. When one New York socialite lady, riding on the *Aucocisco*, sniffed, "I think it is an outrage that tea is not served to passengers on the steamers!" Jack suggested that perhaps the stokers could brew tea down in the boiler room and the deck hands could pass cups around on little silver trays. In fact, he insisted, he would be very glad to serve it up himself!

The toast of the socially prominent "rusticators" all across the bay area in 1908 was novelist William Jasper Nicolls, who had given the *Aucocisco* a starring role in his latest book, *Brunhilda of Orr's Island*. A readable and nostalgic work, the book featured an illustration in color

Not a single telltale trace of the 1904 collision damage remains to be seen in a summer 1908 view of the Sebascodegan *at Gurnet Bridge Landing. The added main deck cabin space and a forward companionway between main and forecastle deck are evident.* Steamship Historical Society of America

of the heroine, Brunhilda, as a frontispiece. Many people thought the picture bore a striking resemblance to socialite summer resident Esther Sayles Root of Bailey Island and New York, and the whisperings were distinctly audible. Nicolls and Root shared a love for things romantic and an abiding affection for the *Aucocisco*, if nothing else more scandalous.

The 1908 season ended, and as the first summer of the consolidated Casco Bay & Harspwell Lines, it proved decisive. The amalgamated management, with the former Harpswell Line's Edgar L. Jordan as superintendent and the old Casco Bay Steamboat Company's Charles W.T. Goding as general manager, had taken a long, hard look at prospects and reached some sober conclusions. The company owned too many wharves and too many steamboats. Only those landings in the best locations were retained, while many others, some not yet two years old, had fallen into disuse and disappeared from the new C.B. & H. Lines schedule. Unhappily, the cherished dual services had narrowed to one. Most islanders of the eastern bay had greeted the new arrangement with anger; their resentment over the consolidation would take years to subside.

At the insistence of President West and Treasurer George W. Beyer, Jordan and Goding faced hard reality in considering the next move. The Gurnet line, so recently operated in keen competition by the rival companies, running their steamers *Merryconeag* and *Sebascodegan* in opposition, had slipped badly in patronage. It would not be operated again. Since only the *Sebasco* handled the run under C.B. & H. Lines, she was now chosen for disposal.

Though it would later cause misgivings and remorse, the able *Degan* was tied up in the spare slip at Custom House Wharf for sale. Officials of a Hudson River excursion firm soon showed up in Portland to inspect her, and within days the *Sebascodegan* steamed past the islands for the last time, bound for a new career, both in New York waters and beyond. Many local admirers were left in her wake and Harpswell's Frank Linwood Bailey even penned a poem titled "The Sebascodegan," part of which survives in local memory:

Pull in the gangplank, we're on our way
For an old-time sail down Casco Bay. . .
We're on our Harpswell way at last
With bright flags flying from the mast,
Blue sky above, blue sea beneath . . .
New scenes before closed eyes unfold,
The years have flown and we are old;
The *Degan* ne'er again will make
That Harpswell trip we loved to take;
Denied that bygone priceless joy
To see her round Old Thumbcap's buoy;
No longer does her wheel and spoke
Yield to the hand that once did stroke
Each part, not unlike a caress
With loving pride and tenderness;
And may her crew, where'er they be
On this or on another sea,
Sail bravely on that final run
When day is gone and night has come.

The *Sebascodegan*'s 22-year career away from Casco Bay may be traced in the appendix titled Wayward Steamboats, but one final encounter seems to belong here. The wreck of this old Casco Bay steamboat was destined to lie undisturbed for many years on the shore of the Savannah River in Georgia. There amid quiet whisperings of a high overgrowth of trees and bushes encircling a mud-filled old basin, lapping tidal waters

Gathered on the boat deck of the Sebascodegan *in 1908 are Purser Ray Varney at far left; Engineer Bill Cook, lower center; Captain Charlie Morrill, front, second from right. Deckhand "Red" Herring stands at upper right; fireman Ralph Bailey is at lower right.*
Mrs. Alice Davis

washed around the *Sebasco*'s ancient timbers. This writer rediscovered those last active years and her 1930 demise there, thanks to several calls at the city of Savannah, Georgia's leading seaport, while he was serving on merchant vessels.

In June 1966, the author contacted Earl Gallovitch, youngest son of the river salvage man who had dismantled the *Sebascodegan* 36 years before. A workboat trip to the derelict at the next low water brought us near the site and we anchored and put into the basin by rowing a "bateau" to the plainly visible old hull. It was a long sentimental look at a tangible piece of Maine steamboating history. The Gallovitch brothers had a more practical interest. The eldest knew his father's final illness had come before the *Sebasco*'s bronze shaft and propeller could be removed. They still lay deep in the steamer's hull, buried under decades of accumulated mud. The aim that day was to investigate the possibility of inexpensively dredging up this valuable scrap metal. Although no word of progress in the endeavor has ever filtered back, candid opinions that day indicated that the

essential heavy equipment would have been financially prohibitive.

The pleasantly toned old Portland Company whistle of the *Commander* (ex-*Sebascodegan*) still survived in 1967, used as a time signal for employees of the nearby Savannah Machine & Foundry Company shipyard.

The days of stage plays at the steamboat company's Gem Theater on Peaks Island faded and the large showplace was converted to a motion picture house to reap greater profits from this new industry. Where George M. Cohan had produced some of his first stage hits, on the heels of Bartley McCullum and the top-billed stars of New York and San Francisco, C.B. & H. Lines employees Alice Flynn Davis and Phil Sherry remembered with fondness the many long extra hours put in at the Gem, selling tickets and attending the theater doors. Features such as Mae Erwin's *Kiss* and the Western *Bronco-busters* were the first silent movies to be shown anywhere in the region, and Portland native John Ford, later ranked as one of America's great film directors, started his meteoric career as an usher at the Gem.

This view is a good character study not only of the rebuilt Aucocisco *as she steams out of Chandler Cove, but of the Long Island landscape between Cleaves and Doughty's Landings in the summer of 1908. The unknown photographer has set up his camera on the southeastern point of Little Chebeague Island.* Philip H. Lee

In September 1908, the crew of the *Aucocisco* set a record over the *Machigonne* in fire and boat drills. It was claimed that they had four hoses rigged and streaming just 15 seconds after the sounding of the firebell atop the wheelhouse. The steamboat inspectors also proclaimed a record boat drill time over the other vessels. Pride in the *Auco* helped her crew to consistently walk away with such honors.

Within a month after the discontinuance of the Gurnet line, and sale of the steamer *Sebascodegan*, Captain Charles B. Morrill, second in Harpswell seniority to Captain Long, was transferred to the *Aucocisco*, succeeding Captain Hamilton. Except for periods of winter service in command of the rugged *Merryconeag*, Captain Morrill would remain with the *Auco* until his retirement.

The idle *Forest Queen* was not long inactive, because the larger *Pilgrim* and *Machigonne* were both laid up in September 1908, remaining out of service until late spring. Now, with the *Sebascodegan* gone, the company again needed the *Forest Queen* for year-round service. With Captain Herb Thompson in command, he was joined by Purser Sam Rogers of Long Island.

As with all New York-built steamers to serve with the Casco Bay fleet, the *Forest Queen* had a hull of live white oak construction and a lake-type horizontal boiler, rather than the hackmatack and hard pine hull and Scotch boiler common to most Maine-built boats. Annual spring overhaul in 1909 found the *Queen*'s hull as strong as ever, but her boiler and engine had both seen better days and it was decided to recondition her old plant. Then, too, the addition of an open deck over the forecastle some years before caused a visibility problem from the pilot house when passengers stood up forward during landings and thoughtlessly blocked the view of the captain and quartermaster. The wheelhouse was raised to the boat deck and weeks later, when the *Forest Queen* returned to service, she performed like a new boat, with Portland Company efforts at updating her steam plant and a retubed boiler increasing her speed markedly. Under Captain Herbert Thompson, her youthful mate was Earl Stockbridge, who had just earned his license in a steady climb from roustabout and deckhand.

Due mostly to extensive rebuilding over a five-year period, the *Emita* had survived the faster and more comfortable *Eldorado* when expansion dictated a larger replacement. The *Emita* became a mainstay of the year-round business, for the cold months cut the island populations down to a skeleton of their summertime numbers. Her size and dependability again caused the management to keep her in service after the 1908 season when the *Sebascodegan* was put up for sale.

In 1908, the Aucocisco *approaches the slips at Custom House Wharf on her first inbound trip of the day from Orrs Island. In the forward slip are the* Maquoit, *with* Forest Queen *and* Pilgrim *astern, all idle until later in the morning.* The Peabody Museum of Salem

It is summer 1909, and the Auco *has just left Central Landing at Great Chebeague Island. She is doubling back to the southward over her outbound track, an essential retracing maneuver to clear easterly shoal waters and then make good the course out toward Cliff Island.* The Peabody Museum of Salem

The Sebascodegan *was still a handsome steamer in a 1908 view just prior to her sale. Once she had left Casco Bay, her owners regretted their folly in selling this rugged and trouble-free steamer.*
Peter T. McLaughlin, from Warren N. Graffam

Built by the Sunset Land Company of Great Chebeague, Sunset Landing was intended for the exclusive use of the wealthy cottagers of the select colony.
Barbara D. Munsey

In 1908 the crew of the Emita *posed on the boat deck as she lay at Portland. At left is Captain James Foye; third from left is Purser Ed Richardson. Deckhand Golden is second from right, the mate stands at the far right, while the fireman is at center with folded arms.* Mrs. Alice Davis

The steamer Maquoit *eases into the slip at Doughty's Landing on Long Island in 1908.* Peter T. McLaughlin, from Warren N. Graffam

The winter cold of 1909 still locked the Maine coast in its firm grip, as C.B. & H. Lines officials mulled over the prospects for the coming season. The profit picture still lay obscured by indebtedness. But again optimism outweighed the sense of risk and the *Aucocisco* was berthed alongside the Portland Company factory pier. Her old steam plant was removed and replaced with a more powerful compound engine, the boiler modified and a new outer jacket for her stack lowered into place over the original. Across the harbor, the *Aucocisco* went onto the railway at South Portland to receive a new propeller and another flush-to-rail addition to her main deck cabin aft. Once she was off the ways, no time was lost in pitting the revitalized *Auco* against the Orr's Island Division winter boat, *Merryconeag*, for a race. Never fairly beaten by the *Auco* before this, the old *Merryconeag* could still "take a bone in her teeth" when occasion demanded. In a stout effort to retain her laurels, the older steamer lost nothing of her agility, but still succumbed to the *Aucocisco's* greater power. It had taken a dozen years to achieve, but the *Auco* was finally speed queen of all the wooden steamers. Her faster performance in service prompted a light-hearted item in the *Casco Bay Breeze* of June 24, 1909: "Who said the water was cold Sunday? Not the bathers at Bailey Island. They said

'twas fine! Perhaps it was the speed of the *Aucocisco's* new screw which warmed up Mackerel Cove by friction."

Early in the 1909 season, it was Captain Hamilton's turn to take a bride and though his friends rejoiced, they were perhaps recalling the loss a few years earlier of Captain Littlefield to a shorebound position following matrimony. But sporting and cheerful they were, and his crew no less so, for the *Breeze* of June 10 tells how "Friday evening last the steamer *Maquoit's* pilot house was gaily decked with the American colors, the same being in honor of Captain and Mrs. Clifford S. Hamilton, who were aboard after their short honeymoon. The boys serenaded their popular chief."

Various personalities seemed no less enduring than the steamers they served on. Witness an item from the *Breeze* on June 10, 1909: "Ralph B. Sprague, one of the popular pursers that serve during the summer season, is back again with us and his genial countenance is daily seen on the *Merryconeag*. During the past winter, Mr. Sprague has been traveling representative for William Lenox, importers of high-class novelties and silk and dress materials, with headquarters at 133 Fifth Avenue, New York City."

The Machigonne *makes a call at Great Diamond Island in the summer of 1909.*
Casco Bay Lines

In describing her earliest years at Custom House Wharf, C.B. & H. Lines' attractive "girl Friday," Alice Flynn Davis said:

One day I was in the freight office and there was a drunken soldier there who said something fresh to me. Captain Herb Thompson was there and heard him. Herb was about six feet two inches tall, a big man, and was the skipper on the *Forest Queen*. Anyway, this soldier thought he'd get wise with me and before long Herb came over, picked this fellow up bodily and carried him right out of the shed! The tide was pretty low at the time and the boats sat low in their slips, but still Herb dragged that man and threw him the length of the gangplank, down onto the deck of the *Forest Queen*! Why, it really jolted the guy. He certainly didn't come back to bother me again!

Captain Herb could be really docile, or a terror, according to his degree of spirit and he was really something of a legend on the boats in those days. But then, at Custom House Wharf, if it wasn't one thing I had to contend with, it was another! Mr. C.W.T. Goding, General Manager, was my boss. Charles Widgery Thomas Goding was his full name, but when I got mad, I used to call him "Old Hundredweight." He had been a rascal in his youth and I heard tell he had gotten kicked out of private schools in Newton, Massachusetts, and different places, before settling down to business. But he had the knack in him and besides the position at C.B. & H. Lines, he also ran a grocery store over on St. Lawrence Street. It was more than just a store, too, since he had a commission to supply every ship of the British White Star-Dominion Lines that came into Portland.

Though the *Machigonne*'s detractors could scarcely be ignored, both company and regional populace continued to back her valiantly against opposing views concerning the large steamer's practical worth on the island route. A prime example of this loyalty came in the *Breeze* of July 22, 1909:

Is it not a pleasure to step aboard the *Machigonne* and speed down the bay on a sunny afternoon? The luxurious boat, with its comforts and its two commodious decks with plenty of promenade space seems a great relief from the cramped room on such steamers as were formerly thought the thing for this service. When to the *Machigonne*'s comforts are added an orchestra which is on board every afternoon, a smooth sea and a balmy breeze there's nothing further to be desired than to sail on in quiet and rest, inhaling peace from every breath . . . and absorbing it from every vista of green woods that is passed.

An echo of the same tone, in the *Breeze* of August 26, appeared under the lead line "Heavy Travel":

The pride of the bay, the magnificent steamer *Machigonne* is carrying at least one-third more passengers than last year. Drawn by her size, comforts and luxurious furnishings, the crowds board her in preference to any other steamer of the C.B. & H. Lines fleet. She draws for all boats indirectly, as people take other steamers to junction points and leave them then for the *Machigonne* where otherwise they would refrain, perhaps, from making an excursion at all on the boats serving their own landings. The new steamer has been receiving her share of knocks, claims of expense and running her often being heard, but she is the pride of the line and comments in her favor are heard everyday by one who listens to the talk of passengers. There is no doubt that the company made a wise move when they built this boat and the future business will show this even more than at present.

For the editors of the *Breeze*, 1909 was the banner year of that newspaper's major campaign in defense of the big *Machigonne*. An impatient editorial of September 2 proved instrumental in stirring the government to blast away some of the ledge extending from South Harpswell Point, to ease the sharp Potts Channel s-turn so difficult for the *Machigonne* to negotiate. As it stood, she always stopped, then backed and filled around in order to get through. That following spring the channel to South Harpswell Wharf was dredged at last and initial blasting was done on the rocky turn. But this did not render any vastly improved channel into Merriconeag Sound and Captain Long still frequently needed to steam around, outside Haskell Island.

Perhaps the most impressive summer resort on Great Chebeague Island in the early 1900s was the handsomely appointed Hamilton Hotel, easily accessible from Eastern Landing. Its broad verandas offered a grand panorama of the Casco Bay islands. Barbara D. Munsey

A major hostelry on Great Chebeague Island in the salad days of steamboating was Charles W. Hamilton's Hill Crest Hotel, just up the slope from the old Stone Wharf. A disastrous fire destroyed the hotel in August 1924, but by the following season a new Hill Crest had arisen on the site. Barbara D. Munsey

Hard times for the Casco Bay & Harpswell Lines had come to stay as 1909 revenue diminished toward the refurbishing needed for the 1910 season. Though patronage had slipped only slightly, profit potential seemed to wash away in a relentless ebb tide.

For the 1911 season, C.B. & H. Lines undertook the usual general overhauling of the fleet's engines and hulls. But the *Maquoit* received extra attention. Her pilot house was lifted and placed on the boat deck to improve visibility, a change which lent her a new kind of dignity, appreciated by crew and passengers alike. But then, Lines' "Commodore," Captain Jimmie Long, and Chief Engineer George Doughty, had brought the entire fleet up to top-notch condition, with "clockwork" machinery, gleaming paintwork, polished brass and many minor improvements.

Everything went along hearteningly well in 1911 until Long Island spokesmen met with C.B. & H. Lines officials to protest the mere 4 round trips made to Long Island. Weighed against 19 round trips daily to Forest City Landing on Peaks and 13 trips to that same island's Evergreen Landing, and, even worse, 6 trips to islands farther across the bay, the Long Island petitions forced the company to reconsider its schedule.

The root cause of the Long Island problem was shoaling off Ponce's Landing, which prevented the deeper-draft *Machigonne* from stopping on her two daily round trips. Cushing's Landing, close southeastward in deeper water, fronting the grounds of the Cushing House hostelry, had been discontinued following the 1907 consolidation, since Ponce's was nearer the post office, stores and shops, and the Granite Spring Hotel & Casino, a larger inn and a landmark for tourists. C.B. & H. Lines seized on the quicker solution of repairing Cushing's, still a company property anyway, over the probable long delays prior to dredging. By mid-August a large crew were busy with repairs and replacement of bad wharf timbers to accommodate service by the *Machigonne*. With Ponce's remaining on the schedule as before and the reconditioned Cushing's Landing now seeing four daily stops, Long Islanders once more enjoyed their rightful share of service to Portland.

An additional benefit to the Inner Bay service this year, the stop at Eastern Landing, Great Chebeague, was restored after long removal from the *Maquoit*'s schedule, the fruit of labors by residents who had circulated and signed petitions to C.B. & H. Lines the year before.

A newcomer to the company at about this time, Joe Feeney, remembered:

Before being assigned to the *Maquoit*, I was broken in for the job of purser by Win Hodgdon on the *Pilgrim*. That first day that I was ever aboard a boat to learn the position, we went to Western

During the heyday of the Harpswell Steamboat Company, Engineer Harry Hill enjoyed the distinction of being the youngest licensed marine engineer in the State of Maine. He was assigned to the Maquoit *after her launching in 1904.* Maine Historical Society

Landing, Great Chebeague, and came back up through on that noon trip. It was the 1st of July and at Great Diamond we had loaded up with soldiers. When we left Little Diamond, Win emptied his pockets and gave the cash and ticket stack to me, saying, 'Go get 'em.' Well, when we whistled for the dock, I hadn't gotten around the engine room yet, to say nothing of the upper decks! Hodgdon came looking for me as we got in and he and I stood on either side of the gangplank and took whatever people would give us for the price of tickets—and with Walter Locke, C.B. & H. Lines' Superintendent, up at the head of the slip, watching us all the while! That's the way Hodgdon broke me in as a purser! Gee whiz, that was a day!

Upon Captain Hamilton's transfer to the *Merryconeag* in 1912, he was succeeded on the *Maquoit* by Captain Adelbert Stockbridge, a native of Swan's Island in the Penobscot region, who became equally well liked in his friendly yet reserved manner. Joe Feeney was soon to learn that his own new assignment was something more than the ordinary run-of-the-mill steamboat route:

The old Inner Bay run over the years came to be like a family institution. After a time, everybody used to get together on special occasions and take a ride with us to Harpswell Center and back, or to Portland, just for the lark of it. One such occasion was Captain Bert Stockbridge's birthday each August 30. When I first went on that line, though, Walter Locke took me aside in the waiting room and talked to me, with his hand on my shoulder for what seemed like an hour, explaining I was going on a run where 'people don't know us from Adam. They don't want us, they don't care about us, they're just our passengers. You can't go down there and have the same attitude toward them that you do with Peaks Islanders and Long Islanders, or even Chebeaguers. They're a different people and you've got to go along that way.' Mr. Locke then sent me to buy a blue serge uniform, as was customarily worn by all the officers then. I bought a three-piece outfit, including vest, for only eight dollars and gave it to my aunt, who sewed on the brass buttons and added canvas pocket linings to hold the heavy supply of coins necessary to make change and hold tickets, etc.

I can also remember how the *Maquoit* had, in the rear of the pilot house, a spare room for the private use of the mate and purser. It had only one door, centered in the after bulkhead and opening close to the smokestack and whistle. Anyone who left this door hooked open and settled down to relax while under way soon learned his lesson! The *Maquoit* always retained the same high-pitched whistle and, if it chanced to go off, the sound was well nigh enough to blow out a person's eardrums!

In 1912, Captain Clifford Hamilton, a well-liked and respected native Chebeaguer, came over from the smaller *Maquoit* to the *Merryconeag* and thereafter was her master during each summer season. No stranger to the outside route, he had previously worked his way up to mate on the steamer *Aucocisco*, serving there with Quartermaster Bert Stockbridge.

Ever since the consolidation in late 1907, the *Merryconeag* had been the accustomed winter boat on the long Orrs Island route. Captain Charles Morrill handled her in the off-season, the regular skipper on that run, no matter what steamer was assigned to it. Whenever it was necessary to haul off the *Merryconeag* for any reason, the *Aucocisco* would run temporarily in her place.

Prior to the introduction of the 1912 summer timetable, additional steps toward modernizing the old Union and Star Line *Emita* took place, and her New York builders would scarcely have recognized their vessel.

It's "boat time" at Mackerel Cove Landing, Bailey Island, with the usual crowd come to meet the Aucocisco *on a bright July day in 1911.* Lawrence and Ruth Piper

The Emita *pays a scheduled call at Cousins Island Landing on a summer day about 1910. The shoreline opposite is the Division Point area of Great Chebeague Island.* Peter T. McLaughlin, from Warren N. Graffam

The *Emita*'s pilot house was raised aloft to the boat deck, and her tall, ancient smokestack, once red with a wide yellow center band in Forest City Line days, had been jacketed by an outer stack, painted in silver with wide black top band. These stack markings carried over from Casco Bay Line pre-consolidation practice, but were adopted by Casco Bay & Harpswell Lines for general fleet use, including the ex-Harpswell steamers, for only a short period between 1914 and 1917.

One of the most notable events of the steam scow *Venture*'s career on Casco Bay was the day in August 1912 when she transported the first seaplane ever seen in the region. That morning, she steamed out to Little Chebeague Island with this strange flying machine loaded precariously on the foredeck. Later, on September 12, under the lead line of "Good Steamer Service" the *Casco Bay Breeze* stated: "One of the biggest things for which C.B. & H. Lines was responsible was bringing Harry Atwood to Little Chebeague for his hydro-aeroplane flights, and Manager Goding surely has the heartfelt thanks of people all over the bay who witnessed those flights. We are speaking for the residents of Casco Bay in wishing Mr. Goding a year of unparalleled success in 1913."

Without a doubt, Harry Atwood's aviation feats were the chief tourist attraction both among the islands and for hundreds of miles around that summer. Alice Flynn Davis recalled: "I can still clearly remember seeing the *Venture* at dockside and the men at work with her derrick, lifting that airplane onto the lighter. Once they got her out there to Chebeague they began to take up anyone who wanted to fly at a price of 50 cents each. I had a chance to go up for free, but no thanks! Sitting back of the pilot on bamboo chairs, with not even a floor to prevent looking down, just wasn't for me!''

The *Machigonne* finished the 1912 season as a contributor to a corporate sea of red ink. By this time the last dreams of a larger and better system of fine steel-hulled steamers had died away for C.B. & H. Lines and the romance with its ''white elephant'' steamer was over. At the first conference of directors following the *Machigonne*'s lay-up in the autumn, it was voted to place the big steamboat up for sale.

The year 1913 was a time of many woes for the Casco Bay & Harpswell Lines. While serving as secretary to the General Manager, Alice Davis viewed these days from an inside perspective:

The *Machigonne* was a lovely boat, but oh, they lost a batch of money on her! She was just too much steamboat for the income she would bring in here. I remember writing up the deficits on her, so I know. They lost a lot then, and kept right on losing until 1913. Take Charles W.T. Goding's wife, for instance; I wouldn't dare say how much she'd invested in that company, but since her father had been very wealthy and a shipowner with many three- and four-masted sailing ships, she had no doubt inherited a great deal of money. Well, she lost a barrelful, I'll tell you! I used to make out the office trial balance every month and there came to be such a terrific amount of loss that just doing that job was heartbreaking to me. They were the finest group to work for. I had been acquainted with most of the steamboating people for years, since my father's auto-painting shop was on Custom House Wharf, right next to the steamboats.

I loved the waterfront and when I was 15, and just graduated from Gray's Business College, I was offered a position in the steamboat offices and was thrilled to accept it! Mr. Goding was General Manager and the Superintendent, Mr. Walter Locke, was in charge of the office then. I really think I was in love with that guy! He was about 18 years older than me, but he was a wonderful, a brilliant, fine-looking man and always a gentleman! He knew his bookkeeping too, and whenever I'd have to work nights or on occasional Sundays from 9 a.m. to 2 p.m. he'd stay and help me.

On lunch hours I used to roam the waterfront for the pure enjoyment of it. One time I took a path running back of the buildings on Commercial Street, which led to a small candy store over on Portland Pier. 'Old Hundredweight' Goding had told me not to go over there, but I went anyway. He met me coming back and fired me! A little later he came to our house in a Franklin touring car to get me to go back. I returned with him that day, but [eventually] managed to get fired three more times. Each time, Mr. Goding took me back and once even gave me a raise. Years after, when I left them for good, they hired a girl replacement who wouldn't do all the office work and they were forced to hire both an office assistant and an office boy to do the filing on the passengers, which I had done all by myself!

Those years were the happiest times of my life, even though I was so naive then that I couldn't understand why so many girls took the boats down to Diamond Island on military paydays!

Since no acceptable purchase bids had surfaced with the arrival of spring in 1913, the *Machigonne* had a limited overhaul, bitterly reminding residents and steamboat people of what had been, for bay travelers, a better way. Then, in mid-May, prospective buyers appeared at Custom House Wharf from the Boston, Nahant & Pines Steamboat Company, a long-established Massachusetts Bay ferry and excursion line. Greatly enthusiastic, they were anxious to close a deal in time for the upcoming tourist season on Boston Harbor and North Shore waters. The shrewd Bostonians were successful, and records tell that they paid only $60,057.42.

During the first week of June, the *Machigonne*'s crew raised steam in the long-dormant boiler for the trip to Boston. Local crew members and some Nahant Line personnel manned her, commanded by Captain James Long, who first brought the ''queen of the fleet'' from Philadelphia and remained her captain throughout. When finally she cast off from her old berth and backed into the channel, it was to a mournful serenade of boat whistles from sister steamboats, harbor tugs, ferryboats, steam fishermen, with which she had crossed wakes so often on her daily runs. Many escorted her to the harbor entrance, their whistles sounding out long farewell wails. The *Machigonne* answered them all with her own deep, mellow-toned whistle, as was Captain Long's style. Such tribute few vessels are ever accorded. Eight hours later the big *Machigonne* passed through Boston Harbor toward the Atlantic Avenue wharf of her new owners. There Captain Long warped her into a berth close aboard her soon-to-be running mate, the older sidewheel steamer *Gen'l. Lincoln*, turned her over to waiting officials and quietly took his leave.

As she commenced the Bay State run, the *Machigonne* was hailed by Boston newspapers as a worthy addition to that city's fleet of harbor

The proud and luxurious Machigonne, *seen in June 1907, was without a doubt the all-time glamour queen of Casco Bay island steamboats. High operating costs and inadequate patronage led to her sale in 1913.* R. Loren Graham

excursion vessels, noting with satisfaction that her equipment resembled a private yacht's in many respects. The *Machigonne*'s run originated at the city's famed T-Wharf, crossed the harbor and then branched off the main ship channel to pass between Winthrop's Point Shirley and Deer Island. Interestingly, this passage was the one in which the old Casco Bay steamer *Cadet* had been wrecked almost 13 years before. Rounding off toward Nahant, the boat would steam well offshore of Winthrop and Revere Beach, then make for Bass Point and Point of Pines at the mouth of the Saugus River. With a call completed there, the *Machigonne* would proceed to the northern end of the line at the island of Nahant, which at this time had no connecting causeway to the Lynn mainland and thus lay pleasantly isolated.

Only two weeks after her arrival in Massachusetts waters, the *Machigonne* had her first bout with ill fortune. On Tuesday, June 24, 1913, the crowded steamer collided with the fishing schooner *Priscilla* off South Boston's Commonwealth Pier, while outbound on an afternoon trip to Nahant. The badly holed *Priscilla*, just in from a swordfishing trip, quickly filled as her crew escaped by jumping into dories lowered from her deck.

Within minutes the unlucky schooner had sunk to the bottom of the channel, only her topmasts visible above water, while the *Machigonne* had hove to in order to pick up fishermen in the drifting dories. Fortunately, no lives were lost and the schooner was later raised. The *Machigonne* sustained no apparent damage, but before June had passed the steamer was in the shipyard for repairs and a new shaft. After this ill-starred episode, the *Machigonne* settled down to a less eventful though busy career at Boston.

Unlike so many of her sisters, the rugged *Machigonne* is still with us as the dieselized *Yankee*. She has had several names and worked many services from Maine to Delaware, but until 1984 had been a regular Providence-Newport-Block Island line boat for decades with the Interstate Navigation companies, doing her daily duties faithfully after almost nine decades of operation. Today, taken together with the little steamboat *Sabino* at Mystic, Connecticut, she provides one more tangible reminder of bygone days, when the steamboat was a watchword among the isles of Casco Bay and all along the rockbound coast of Maine. Details of the rest of her story away from Casco Bay may be found in the Wayward Steamboats appendix.

Despite the seven years she was overshadowed by the Machigonne, *the* Pilgrim *high-stepped her way to great popularity as the principal special charters vessel in the Casco Bay & Harpswell Lines fleet. Her flags and festooned bunting signal a gala occasion.* Warren N. Graffam Collection, from Captain Harold H. Cushing, Jr.

The Emita, *with a good crowd aboard, backs out past the old Randall & McAllister coal pocket. Rebuilt as shown from a more primitive original styling, the long-lived vessel retained this appearance for more than a decade into the 20th century.* Orville R. Cummings, from Charles H. Heseltine

CHAPTER 7

CASCO BAY & HARPSWELL LINES
DARKEST HOURS—THE ROUTE TO OBLIVION

Overshadowed for a time by the magnificent *Machigonne*, the *Pilgrim* once again took the limelight when "the pride of Casco Bay" proved a dismal financial failure and steamed clear of local waters in 1913. Captains Wilbur Gates and James L. Long now began to alternate in command of the *Pilgrim* because of the heavy charter business plus her regularly scheduled trips.

With his affable manner, Captain Long was the more memorable of the two men. As the volume of charters diminished in the years of foment leading toward World War I, it was he who became exclusive master of the *Pilgrim* in 1917. A 1969 interview with Captain Earl Stockbridge at his Portland home revealed:

I've been on the *Pilgrim*, as Mate, when she carried 800 or more people. Captain Jimmie Long had her after the *Machigonne* was sold, and he was the finest man to sail with! All down the bay, people would shout greetings to him and he'd answer with three blasts on the whistle. We had an old-timer, Harry Ricker, on as Engineer. Well, all that whistling would cause his steam gauge to keep dancing up and down. Boy, it used to make him awful mad! It was probably his engine gang that came away calling the captain 'Tootie' Long.

Engineer Bill Ricker, aboard the dieselized *Emita* in her latter days, lent more insight into the ways of his father's cousin:

Harry Ricker was a bit cranky, a cantankerous old cuss. He always kept a clean, bright and polished engine room on the *Pilgrim*. He was likely to snap at anyone who entered the engine room if they even chanced to step on his polished brass threshold! He always lived with his sister, by the way, in a large frame house on the Portland side of Martin's Point Bridge.

To further please its often wealthy summer clientele, a unique service was initiated by C.B. & H. Lines in 1913, in which the *Merryconeag* figured prominently. Set up in connection with the Portland Post Office, each steamer was to have a mail sorting room and hired clerk aboard. The first so earmarked was the dependable old *Merryconeag*, and her postal clerk, young Portland High School graduate James Feeney, daily sorted all Portland and non-regional mail into one sack and all local island mail, canceled aboard, into sacks marked for each stop. This system allowed direct mailing within the bay and some islands were to receive four mails per day. Here was a vast improvement over an older custom, in which a letter might be mailed by someone at Bailey Island to a friend on Great Chebeague. That letter would ordinarily travel in a sack marked for Portland, right past its destination, be re-sorted and then journey back over the same route on a later boat for delivery at Great Chebeague! Unfortunately, even before the *Aucocisco* was similarly equipped, the mail volume proved insufficient to support a full-time mail clerk. Long before the end of the 1913 summer schedule, the new system was summarily scrapped.

Captain Charles Morrill and his *Aucocisco* became legend on Casco Bay, and their popularity thrived among all who traveled the steamers to their island homes and vacation spots. Always, Captain Charlie would stand by the door or at a window of his pilot house as the *Auco* waited in readiness to sail from Custom House Wharf, greeting everyone he noticed coming over the gangplank. He knew most passengers by name, whether summer vacationer or native islander. There were times, though, when Casco Bay's "old reliables," as captain and steamer were often called, would become separated. When Captain Morrill suffered a broken leg in the middle of May 1913, he was confined to his Orrs Island home until well into July. During this time, Captain Clifford Hamilton replaced him, remaining aboard throughout August to physically handle the steamer after Captain Charlie came back, until strength returned to the injured skipper's leg.

York's Landing, Bailey Island, in the days of the Machigonne. *Often called simply "Old Wharf" on steamboat schedules, it fell into disuse after the sale of the* Machigonne *and had largely succumbed to the elements by the mid-1920s.* Author's Collection

Wearing the aluminum paint and wide black top-banded stack of the fleet's pre-World War I days, the Pilgrim *runs a special charter excursion on the Saco River.* McArthur Library, Biddeford

The *Casco Bay Breeze* published a piece on August 24: "Captain Charlie Morrill is back at his post in the wheelhouse of the *Aucocisco* and his friends now feel that Casco Bay will pull through the season alright. It hardly seemed natural...to go through the summer without the knowledge that Captain Morrill was on the upper deck....All the regular summer visitors as well as the islanders are expressing their satisfaction over the latter's recovery and extend him a warm welcome back to his accustomed position."

To better sense the mood and rhythm of the days when the two "old reliables" served together on Casco Bay, we look to the pen of Mrs. Esther Adams, long-time summer resident of Bailey Island and wife of the famed poet and journalist Franklin P. Adams (F.P.A.). In her article "S.S. *Aucocisco*, A Saltwater Sound," appearing in the June 1956 issue of *Yankee Magazine*, she wrote:

The *Auco* started to serve us in her youth....She brought us food and freight and friends and mail and news, kerosene for our lamps, fuel for our stoves...and she was our touch with the world....As children we did not realize that she was fundamental to us. She was as much a part of Maine as the wind that blew black smoke out behind her or that took aloft the white steam when her whistle blew. At sunset time we would look west and see her, miles away, steadily coming toward us on the bright water. As she rounded the point at the head of the harbor she was majestic, she was beloved...

Mrs. Adams continued her account, tracing childhood memories of the *Aucocisco*, towering awesomely over island youngsters who dared to scull rowboats close enough to be tossed like shells by her bow wave; of teenage years and a young lady's ardent search for the romantic stranger who seemed certain to come to Bailey Island someday as a passenger on the steamer's crowded decks; of the scores of neighbors carrying armloads of packages from the city; of pipe-smoking fishermen and summer people meeting on the wharf at boat time; and of Captain Morrill, kindly to all, but especially to children. She remembered that "perhaps you'd catch Captain Morrill's eye and he might smile and say, 'Crate of watermelon coming off tonight!'"

Once the *Auco*'s call at the landing was completed, lines were cast off and the steamboat backed away from the dock before coming ahead for the arcing turn past the wharf and then slowly around, to head once again for Abner's Point and the open sound beyond. Now the ever-curious among women might cast carefully guarded glances from the wharf to the steamer's secluded settees around the fantail half-circle, a favorite spot for lovers.

To those who rode the Casco Bay steamers during the first half of the century, no less legendary than the steamer *Aucocisco* herself was the reputation of Captain Charlie Morrill. Passengers never ceased to marvel at his competent handling of the vessel in any weather. With a great sense of respect and admiration, Mrs. Adams recalled the concern island people often felt while listening for the distant whistle signals of the *Auco* on days of typical Maine coast ''dungeon'' fog. Usually just as those on the wharf might be imagining the worst, the steamer would suddenly sound a blast on her whistle and loom abruptly out of the heavy gray shroud, on a straight and true course for the landing. She noted that ''one of the fishermen on the wharf, perhaps out of relief or praise, would look up toward the pilot house and observe: 'Thick out there this evening,' and Captain Morrill would respond, 'Yes, 'tis!' as genial as though he had been steering through the glories of an orange sunset.''

By mid-July 1913, public embitterment culminated over the *Maquoit*'s service to Peaks, Long and the Diamonds, which really did more to deprive the original landings of their formerly fast service. Instead of the old running time of one hour and twenty minutes from Eastern Landing to Portland, the inner route steamer now took nearly two full hours. Railroad and coastal steamship schedules from Portland certainly could not be integrated to please a relatively small group of passengers trying to make connections. The certainty of bigger revenues from added service to the nearer islands precluded making any change and Inner Bay people were left, for the time being, to their stormy discontent.

The *Machigonne*'s seasonal place opposite the *Aucocisco*, on the Orr's Island Division, was taken by the three-decked *Pilgrim*. With this move, the outlook improved somewhat, but Casco Bay & Harpswell Lines continued its operations in a tense, uneasy manner. The going was disheartening, and downhill all the way. C.B. & H. Lines secretary Alice Flynn Davis recalled: ''The Lines' steamers were in the 'Ocean Class' under the U.S. Steamboat Inspection Service, so Superintendent Walter Locke and I used to compose letters to try to get the vessels into the 'River Class,' so that lifeboat and liferaft requirements would be reduced.'' By 1914, for instance, the *Forest Queen* could not have carried enough lifeboats on her deck to meet these strict lifeboat requirements, all brought about by the tragic sinking of the White Star liner *Titanic* after her collision with an iceberg in the North Atlantic in 1912. The alert and animated Alice Davis went on: ''The fleet continued to operate on temporary waivers until we did finally get reclassed and mostly through the efforts of Arthur O'Brien, who worked in the ticket office with Eddie Roundie and was the son of the chief Steamboat Inspector in Portland at the time.''

Photographed about 1914, the Merryconeag *leaves Portland Harbor for the eastern bay islands.* The Peabody Museum of Salem

Still under the Casco Bay & Harpswell Lines houseflag, the Pilgrim *has passed through the tortuous Potts Harbor channel and is making her way along the shore toward the South Harpswell Landing, June 1918.*
Robert and Grace Green

Posing on the boat deck with a lady passenger, around 1914, are the Forest Queen's *Purser Sam Rogers (left) and Captain Herbert Thompson.*
Mrs. Geneva Rogers

Purser Sam Rogers stands atop the guard rail as the Forest Queen *departs Forest City Landing at Peaks Island, circa 1910. An old Casco Bay Steamboat Company leaden mooring cap crowns the dock piling. These were all cast with the imprinted legend "C.B.S.B. Co."*
Mrs. Geneva Rogers

Life had become harder now for the *Maquoit* and her crew, since the steamer's plant had suffered the benign neglect of a financially strapped C.B. & H. Lines. Corners had been cut on precious operating funds. Another annoyance was Captain Oscar Randall's snappy little steamer *Tourist*, newly entered into the nearer bay island trade to skim off a share of the bustling residential and tourist business. Purser Feeney described the predicaments of the moment by stating:

During the summer of 1915, we used to come up the Inner Bay from Harpswell Center with the *Maquoit*, leaving at 5:15 a.m. to arrive for the 7:30 a.m. trip from the 'Roads.' We were in competition with the *Tourist* now, which came up from Long Island. We were having a horrible summer. The *Maquoit* was constantly under repair and 'half on the dock' most of the time. Bill Cook, the engineer, used to spend half the night down there at Harpswell Center, night after night, just 'hooking her together' so we could run her another day! She was in terrible shape and we were slow, so the *Tourist* would be in there and take the whole 'Roads' crowd away from us, day after day!

It was a discouraging season all right, but I forgot to mention July 4th. For Independence Day, there was a historical pageant of some kind on Great Chebeague Island. They ran the *Maquoit* special to Peaks Island at ten o'clock that morning to pick up spectators for the event. Well, they came aboard in droves and we were so loaded, we had to shut them off. We were allowed 350, I think it was, in those days. As we got near the Chebeague landing, they all went over to the side where we'd be shoving out the gangplank. That made her list suddenly. Boy, did we lay over! We were scared to death she'd go on her beam ends, but still we had to beg those people to move back!

Opinion was mixed among old-timers as to the *Maquoit*'s stability. Alice Davis thought, "That boat was top-heavy as anything," but later purser, advertising manager, and informal historian Warren Graffam, while admitting many people thought her beam was too narrow, felt that the steamer always behaved well in heavy seas. The *Maquoit* steamed throughout her years without serious mishap of any kind, which testifies to her seagoing qualities.

Captain Bert Stockbridge was, no doubt, one of the finest, most restrained gentlemen that could be found on Casco Bay steamers, choosing to serve his company both quietly and efficiently. Probably the greatest vocal pleasure he allowed himself was to call out an amiable "Goodbye, darlin'!'' from his pilot house window whenever he chanced to see the company's pert secretary, Alice Flynn, leaving the wharf at the end of the day. It was no secret that a few people around the waterfront mistook reserve for slow-wittedness and thought him a prime target for ribbing. It was only in jest, of course.

There were many times, naturally, when Captain Bert was not the butt of humorous incidents but still managed somehow to get involved. Retired fireman and machinist Ralph Bailey, son of the old-time Casco Bay wharf builder and carpenter, recalled:

There was an old guy around the waterfront years ago by the name of Murphy, who used to have a junk boat he'd row around the docks, collecting whatever people would give him, or whatever he could steal. They used to make fun of him a lot and it would plague him. One day, in the winter, he came around to Custom House Wharf, making his rounds, I guess, and I was sitting out there on a bench with Herb Thompson and Bert Stockbridge and one or two others. Well, he happened to be turned around back to us, so Herb picked up a snowball and tossed it. It hit old Murphy in the back and he went strutting off, madder than a hornet! We just sat there and laughed. Well then, down came Murphy with a policeman! The cop says to Murphy, 'Now, who threw the snowball at you?' Well, he pointed right at Bert, because Bert was the smallest of the bunch, and said, 'That's him!' The cop looks at poor Bert, winking at him, you know, and gave him the devil for Murphy's benefit. Then he turned to old Murphy and said, 'There, that'll teach him a lesson!' and he left. Well, Murphy was wearing a big grin on his face now and started walking away. But soon as he got turned back to us, Herb lobbed another snowball and hit him square in the back of the head! We all just roared, I'll tell you, and old Murphy got away as fast as he could.

Long before the drama of World War I had passed, subtle and irrevocable change had come over Casco Bay. Once a mecca for the vacationing elite from all over New England, the Middle Atlantic states and Canada, the region had suffered a marked decline. Partly a result of the campaign to forego travel during the war, there were other factors to explain the lack of recovery, even after the struggle ended. Nationally, those who could best afford it began to range farther afield over better roads in their own improved automobiles, or were now casting far across the oceans in search of vacation pleasures. The once-stentorian voice of the *Casco Bay Breeze* was stilled in 1917. The publishers sensed that those

Casco Bay & Harpswell Lines' Merryconeag *was a good boat in the ice, and had ample opportunity to prove it. In this World War I-era view, however, she loads and discharges her passengers well off an island wharf, unable to maneuver closer.* Warren N. Graffam Collection, from Captain Harold H. Cushing, Jr.

who had listened most attentively to its news, editorial and gossip content had widened their own horizons and were scattering to the four winds. People who summered on the islands constantly demanded to know more about events in the outside world, which they could learn by reading the more substantial newspapers of Portland, Boston, and New York. With the loss of the faithful old *Breeze*, the structure of the water-borne community weakened and diminished.

Many an epic winter challenged the steamboat fleet to a fierce and continuing duel with the ice, which frequently formed thickly over the bay reaches by early December. The *Merryconeag* was always prepared for the worst. At the South Portland marine railway each autumn, her hull was sheathed over with hard-grained yellow birch and soon afterward, in bucking the ice, it would begin to serve her well. Annually, many of the wharves along the route were left damaged or almost destroyed by a menacing crush of ice. Wharf locations often became inaccessible, except for those like Mackerel Cove Landing at Bailey Island, built within a naturally sheltered area. Captain Morrill was often forced to make his

Gus Johnson of Bailey Island met Bertha Lena King of Pembroke at a dance in Eastport. After their marriage, he brought his bride home to Bailey Island in January 1918 on the Merryconeag. *That first year on Casco Bay for the author's Grandma Johnson was to be the last for the sturdy* Merry. *Months later, the steamer was destroyed by fire.*
Author's Collection and The Peabody Museum of Salem

steamer fast to the ice far out from shore. Wagon teams sometimes had to drive out over 13-inch ice as far as Haskell Island to take off loads of supplies when the *Merryconeag* could get no closer to the South Harpswell and Orrs Island wharves. The years rested lightly on the aging *Merryconeag* as she maintained her schedule over the 36 different courses she took each way on trips across Casco Bay.

By the last week of November 1918, old *Merry*, as her crew often dubbed her, had been back for two months on her familiar off-season runs to Orrs Island. On Friday evening, November 29, she made the final landing of the day at Orrs Island wharf. As the steamer lay in on a spring line, screw turning over slowly, her passengers trekked over the gangplank, exchanging perhaps a last ''Good night'' with Captain Morrill or the two deckhands tending the gangway. With everyone off, the crew tied her up securely for the night. Engineer Bill McMullen answered the stop bell and then climbed below to shut down his plant while his fireman banked the fires.

Before long, Captain Charlie and his engineer walked up Steamboat Hill Road to their homes on the long knoll overlooking Merriconeag Sound. Most of the crew went their own ways to spend the evening at various haunts, not the least of which was the local pool parlor over at the village, or the traditional poker game in the backroom of the Prince & Daniels General Store. Two deckhands were left aboard as a sleep-in watch and, with only the prospect of a long dull night ahead, both turned in early.

The acrid smell of smoke brought them rudely out of their slumber at about 10 p.m. Hurrying topside, they were greeted by flames already roaring and well advanced over the varnished woodwork of the main cabin and engine spaces. Realizing quickly that the situation was far beyond what they could handle alone, a swift exchange of words sent one bounding onto the dock and dashing off to seek help. The other, hoping that a head of steam might have built up with all that tremendous heat around the boiler, raced up the ladders to the pilot house and hauled frantically on the whistle cord. He was immediately relieved to hear the strong blast of steam hit the chime and pierce the still air with a sharp wail.

The urgent whistle coming through the air at such an ungodly hour jolted islanders on both sides of Will's Strait! Poker hands had been tossed down and chairs thrown aside, while mackinaws and caps disappeared from wall hooks at Prince & Daniels'. A small army of men rushed headlong toward the first deckhand almost before he had set foot on the dirt road leading from the wharf.

At the top of the hill, Captain Morrill, with Mrs. Morrill close by his side, stared momentarily in disbelief from their porch as the whistle blasts continued and the flames glowed through the evergreens sloping down toward the shore. His heart in his throat, and his wife left standing on the broad veranda, the skipper made for the roadway just as a motorcar chugged toward him, bound from the village with more of his crew. When it abruptly halted, he climbed on the running board and yelled for the driver to hurry along. By now, most islanders were rushing down toward the wharf. Over on Bailey Island people had bundled up against the cold and were standing on the beach, their anxious faces illuminated by kerosene lanterns. Even now, several lamp-lit dories were pulling away out of Garrison Cove toward Orrs, loaded to the gunwales with hardy farmers and fishermen, all bent on doing their best to save a faithful old friend—the steamboat *Merryconeag*.

Bucket brigades were forming as Captain Morrill arrived and quickly surveyed the scene. He judged the fire to be out of control now, and Engineer McMullen concurred. Fighting the fire proved futile, but fortunately a small U.S. government war patrol vessel had anchored nearby that afternoon, and although it possessed little firefighting equipment, it was soon underway and standing off the wharf. Once the patrol craft positioned itself close off the *Merryconeag*'s bow, its crew let fly a heavy line and grappling hook. When the hook had landed and bitten its way solidly into the wooden guard rail just aft of the burning steamer's stem post, all lines on the wharf were axed away and the patrol boat went ahead on her engine, hauling the blazing *Merryconeag* slowly away. After a great effort, the steamboat was clear and the fire brigade began quenching fires on the wharf. Everyone at the scene stopped short in a moment of suspended animation as a massive boiler explosion shook the doomed *Merryconeag* in a deafening report, but most could not see the port side of her main cabin as it was blown seaward by the pressure of the blast.

One of the *Aucocisco*'s firemen in those days, Ralph Bailey, had still-vivid memories of that disastrous night in 1918:

Just that night we came off the railway and I'd cleaned the boilers and everything. They got hold of us some time after midnight to tell us we'd have to go to Orr's Island in a hurry. They told us right off that the *Merryconeag* was afire! Not knowing much more about when the fire had got going, I guess we all thought we could get down there and help out. George Doughty was engineer on our boat, but they didn't know where he was or how to get in touch with him so they got Bill Cook to make the trip. I used to run the engines, though, about as much as they did. So when Bill came down, I had her all warmed up and turnin' over.

We backed out of the dock and I went below to close the firebox door and dampers so as to give her some steam. Bill Cook asked me, 'How far does Doughty open her throttle?' and I said, 'Wide open!' Well, he did; opened her up all the way, and you can ask Carl Morrill if you don't believe me, 'cause his father was captain on the *Auco* for years. That was the record fastest trip ever made by any steamboat across the bay to Orr's Island. We made it in one hour and seventeen minutes between bells!

It was low tide at Pott's Harbor, where the channel bends around sharp, and they called down from the pilot house to have her slowed down to make the turn. Bill had me call back up and I told them 'Won't be no slowin' down now! You'll just have to put enough men on her wheel to twist her through!' It would take three or four men to hold her over under those conditions. The safety valve blew nine times between here and Orr's Island. We called it 'puttin' her to the blow.' The engine was wide open. The last time she blew, it was right off that side of Pinkham Island, you know, over by Harpswell.

Bill Cook come up and looked out the window where you could see Orr's Island, then he walked through the companionway and looked out the other windows. He said to me, 'My son (he always called me his 'son'), you go down and pull the dampers out and then open them doors wide, because otherwise when I shut down this throttle it's likely to blow both ends out of that boiler!'

At Orrs Island the incoming tide prevailed and the fiercely burning pyre, once a proud steamer, grounded on the flat-ledge bottom just offshore from the Sebasco House Lodge. The *Merryconeag* continued to burn, but the island wharf was clearly in no further danger and many exhausted islanders began to drift home for a few hours' rest, though most in their excitement would not get any sleep. Now a bewildering sight greeted them. It was the *Aucocisco*, barreling down past the west shore of Bailey at full steam, after a futile but record speed run from Portland to try to aid her stricken running mate. Ralph Bailey remembered: "It was a record run all right, but when we got there the *Merryconeag* had burned to the waterline and sunk. They had to dredge her up to salvage her boiler and engine later."

There was little for the crew of the *Auco* to do but stare at the still-smoldering ruin of the *Merryconeag* as their own steamer maneuvered into the fire-damaged slip. But here she was, all the same, in ample time to make the scheduled stops to Portland, which would never see the likes of the *Merryconeag* again.

The cause of the fire that Friday night was never precisely determined. Ralph Bailey held a view popular among the company's engine gangs after the fire:

I always thought that the fireman's smokepot which had oil in it and a wick coming off it, might have gotten tipped over. It was a small tin pot, about as big as a flask can and was used to light off the boiler. It would have been pretty combustible in a winter-heated engine space. Well, in those days, we didn't have electric lights around the pit and at night it was 'darker than a pocket' down there. Everything was oily, with valve oil and whatnot, of course, and that fire had probably no more than started and you couldn't have gone down below at all!

A native of Orrs Island, Judson A. Webber became a popular purser. Jud's brother-in-law was Captain Ed Archibald, founder of the Portland-Rockland Line.
Maine Historical Society

Withheld from both the press and government investigators at the time, a story surfaced much later of how a group of teenagers had been seen lurking at the wharf until the steamer was vacated that evening. Shoreside witnesses claimed to have heard a raucous party going on aboard the *Merryconeag*, but offered no evidence of involvement by the two crew members, who were supposed to be asleep below decks. A natural curiosity of youth as to the mysteries of a darkened engine room could have led to a nocturnal visit, and this scenario still fits like a glove with Ralph Bailey's opinion.

Veteran skipper Earl Stockbridge added a personal note on the demise of the *Merryconeag*: "I was on her the previous summer and early autumn as Mate. When she burned, I had been laid off and was working for the Grand Trunk Terminal as a stevedore, longshoring. I was usually laid off in winters back then. I lost my Mate's license in the fire because I left it aboard the *Merryconeag*, where I thought it would be when I went back in the spring!"

The first winter in years without the Merryconeag *to take the brunt of icebreaking finds the battered but unbowed* Aucocisco *doing her stuff to clear the channel in towards the Orrs Island Landing. It is the winter of 1918, and the old salt shed in the distance still serves Prince & Daniels Company.*
Robert and Grace Green

Some time after the fire, the *Merryconeag*'s salvaged boiler and engine were taken to Portland for scrap. The wreck remained visible for many years and generations of island boys were able to scurry over her at low water, cutting away fittings left behind or simply pulling out copper fastenings and nails to sell or barter. In fact, the old keel, many stunted ribs, and hard pine planking are there to this day, still discernible in the mud at dead low water, or under a seaweed covering out beyond the crown of ledge upon which the hulk grounded on that awful night.

In 1993, Bob Green, grandson of the Sebasco House Lodge proprietor who fought the fire with so many others of his townsmen 75 years before, told how the hotel moorings were obstructed by the wreck for decades. He and his father before him had labored to cut away individual ribs that blocked safe passage after stripping away planking. The problem existed through World War II years, and Bob himself cleared the last obstructing frames. Having hauled ashore some of the hard pine planking, still pegged securely

with treenails, he noted how sturdy it was after three decades of constant immersion. Curious, he had a quantity of it milled and dressed locally and was pleasantly surprised when the planking turned out was comparable to virgin timber, and still full of pine pitch. Excited at the discovery, he pursued the matter and it resulted in all the bottom timbers and the garboard strakes he needed to completely rebuild his Hampton-style lobster boat!

Because the *Auco* had been readied to run during the coldest months of 1918-19 anyway, the flaming loss of one of its better vessels was absorbed stoically by line officials, at least for the time being.

A familiar figure around Custom House Wharf during the C.B. & H. Lines years, the company's pretty secretary, Alice Flynn, was affectionately nicknamed "Mickey" by the steamer skippers and their crews. Mickey managed to brighten the premises for a decade, bringing sunshine to help light the gloom of gradual, inevitable decline. Still aglow with memories of what she called her happiest years, she remembered:

The South Harpswell Landing in June 1918. For a time in 1907 and thereafter, this was the South wharf, serving the Casco Bay Line, while the older Harpswell Line North wharf was used by the Sebascodegan, Aucocisco, *or* Machigonne, *only 150 yards away. As the newer structure, this South wharf was chosen for continued use by C.B & H. Lines.* Robert and Grace Green

In the wintertime, I used to go to Orr's on the *Aucocisco* about once in two or three weeks, I guess. I would take my typewriter and work back in the quartermaster's room. When it was time, the cook/steward would bring up my dinner. I used to love that! They fed on all the boats except the *Emita*. I don't think they ever had a cook on her. I remember how keeping accounts used to bother me, in the office, when a fellow might have his breakfast on one boat and then, for some reason, they'd switch him to the non-feeding boat! Normally, if a man worked on a boat with a cook/steward, then I'd have to deduct 15 cents a meal from his wages. Captain Charlie Morrill lived over the hill at Orr's Island and would walk up there if he could spare the time. Sometimes, in warmer weather, he would even bring me back a bouquet of flowers from his garden—until his wife got wind of it, anyway!

Along with young Carleton Morrill, only son of Captain Charlie, who grew up on the steamers and later became a quartermaster of the *Aucocisco*, many a hard-working crew member yearned to steer the big white steamboat on her courses. Another successful candidate of years ago, Lovell Sawyer of Portland, offered many favorable remarks about his years aboard her:

Becoming quartermaster was a deckhand's idea of becoming a really important person. You got to wear a cap with gold braid on it, to steer, to pull the engine room bell cord and the whistle cord. No more struggling with bags of mail and coal, and cans of milk and ice cream! No more swabbing decks and polishing brass.

Sawyer's sentiments matched those of many others who had stood their watches at the *Auco*'s big wooden-spoked wheel, both before and long after him. Some, like Cliff Hamilton, Bert Stockbridge, Carl Morrill and Warren Graffam, worked their way up to higher assignments and greater responsibilities on the steamboats. Other youths, such as George Linscott, Peter Schuyler, or Bailey Island summer resident Kimber DeHart, spent several summers in that lofty post, but were somehow content to satisfy later sea-going desire with seasonal sail yachting along the coast, if not commercial fishing. Onetime quartermaster Mike O'Reilly of Cliff Island eventually took his expertise to the cockpits and wheelhouses of successive Portland pilot boats where he served until his retirement.

Quartermaster Sawyer had more to say about life aboard the *Aucocisco*:

The soft heat from the boiler and engine, flavored with the clean smell of fresh valve oil, made the engine room a cozy spot at the end of the day, with picknickers returning from their outing, tired and undemanding.

Old deckhands can still hear the call, 'Let go the spring line!' and remember the summer sun, the evergreen trees of the islands, the gentle 'dong' from the engine room, the jingle bell for full ahead, the dull clank of the firebox door, the black smoke and soft 'snick, snick, snick' of the engine and the flat 'rumble bumble' of the propeller beneath the fantail. She was a queen, the *Auco*!

The Bankruptcy of 1919

Dark storm clouds were fast gathering for C.B. & H. Lines as the 1919 season opened. Though the war in Europe was over at last and great hope was pinned on the certain revival of passenger revenues, the company was still mired heavily in debt and sinking perceptibly deeper. However, a degree of optimism seemed justified by a report in the *Daily Eastern Argus* of July 5: "There was a great rush of travel to the islands yesterday, Peaks Island being visited by thousands. The *Aucocisco* put in most of the day on that run; she having capacity numbers on some of her trips.

Many took in the trip to Long Island and further down the bay. From all appearances the business this season will be the best for the line in many years." Perhaps, then, all would be well; optimists felt they had cause to cheer.

In the closing months of World War I, engine room difficulties had begun to dog the *Forest Queen*. Repairs for the ailing steamer ranked high among the Lines' woes, when the first lightning bolt came. The *Argus* of July 8, 1919, bannered its headline: Casco Bay Boats Stop Trips to the Islands at 10 o'clock Because of Libels Filed by Creditors. The article itself read:

It is said that bonds will not be filed and the boats will be sold at auction and service discontinued until some satisfactory arrangements can be made. Libels aggregating about $50,000 have been filed with the U.S. District Court in Admiralty against the six steamers comprising the fleet of the Casco Bay & Harpswell Lines by the lien creditors. The only names appearing on the six distinct libels are the A.R. Wright Company, coal dealers, and the Portland Company, marine engineers and shipbuilders . . .

The steamers *Emita* and *Maquoit*, and the lighter *Venture* had already stood idle since 3 p.m. the previous afternoon, when the first libels were served. Acknowledging the heavy flow of passengers and freight, the court held off serving further libels, naming the *Pilgrim*, *Aucocisco* and *Forest Queen*, until 10 a.m. the following morning. The *Argus* went on to say:

The greatest consternation prevailed among those depending on these boats in getting back and forth among the islands. . . .Thousands of summer and permanent residents of the islands in Casco Bay will be seriously affected by the actions of yesterday, to say nothing of the loss which would be suffered by the general business interests of the city if the steamers are put out of commission today. . . .While those living on Peaks Island can manage to get back and forth to the city on the ferryboat *Swampscott*, there are no boats in the harbor to take the place of the steamers of the Casco Bay & Harpswell Lines. The two small steamers [*Anna Belle* and *Tourist*] owned and operated by Captain Oscar Randall [are]. . .not of sufficient size to begin to accommodate the hundreds of people going to the other islands in the harbor and down the bay. It is a most uncomfortable situation and the solution is not in sight.

The despair of greater Portland could not match that of C.B. & H. Lines officials, not in a hundred years. The first word received by Manager Goding was a message passed along to him by a court newspaper reporter at about noon of that fateful day. Within hours the libel writs were served. It was an almost unbelievable shock. Here, at the start of the Lines' best season in over four years, the future prospects were to be dashed to oblivion. But the facts could not be disputed. One good season could mean the repayment of some debt, but the total amount owed was still insurmountable. To illustrate the tragic circumstances, some $32,000 in first lien claims were followed up by about $18,000 in second lien claims. The billing amounts against the *Aucocisco* alone totaled a whopping $14,000!

A specially selected city government committee hastily arranged to carry food to the Catholic orphanage on Diamond Island and to landings within the city limits, the trips to be made by the city fireboat *Engine No. 7* and Captain Randall's small steamer *Tourist*. Meanwhile, the frantic mood of the people was reflected in blistering editorials such as the following from the *Argus* of July 9:

Something Must be Done at Once! Portland has been dealt a cruel blow at the moment when she would feel it the most. Portland's thousands of summer guests have been treated with scant courtesy at the same time. . . .The lives of many babes at the islands have been put in jeopardy. . .traffic to the islands has been cut off when it was 60% greater than last year and increasing steadily [and] trading connection with the islands was the best in years. It is time for action and steps should be taken immediately for resumption of the island steamer service upon which so very much depends. It should be done at once, this morning! Delay is but dangerous and costly. . . .This is not the moment to discuss the merits of the case nor can the community afford to await a settlement by the slow process of the law. Portland must at once have its island steamer service restored and it is the proper duty of those who have the power and opportunity to act now!

The forces of the law had momentarily prevailed amidst much severe criticism and at 10 a.m. on Tuesday, July 8, the remaining libels were served by Deputy U.S. Marshal Eugene S. Harmon on the steamers *Pilgrim*, *Forest Queen*, and *Aucocisco*, after the first two were allowed to make their early morning trips to the upper bay. The *Auco* was seized when she arrived from Orrs Island shortly before 10 a.m. Federal keepers were immediately stationed aboard each steamer and the vessels were forbidden to leave their berths at Custom House Wharf.

The diminutive steamer Mary Jane *alone served eastern bay points and island stops through the long off-season of 1919-20. A pall of coal smoke drifts over the water and into the camera lens, as she departs South Harpswell, headed out toward Thrumcap Islet on her way back to Portland, in late autumn 1919.* Robert and Grace Green

Confusion and inconvenience now reigned, with cottagers and residents at islands in the lower bay being hurt most by the turn of events. Peaks Island residents were better off than most, however, as the ferryboat *Swampscott* remained in constant operation all day and well into the night. Thousands of passengers were carried, while Manager Edgar Rounds hurriedly searched for a second boat to accommodate the crowds. He could not find one for an emergency charter and the *Swampscott* continued her burdensome tasks alone. Captain Walter Kennedy's little steamer *Mary Jane* made her regular trips during the day to Mere Point and the inner side of Great Chebeague Island but her capacity was so limited that it was impossible for her to stop at any other landings. On the return of the *Tourist* from her Gurnet trip at 5:30 p.m., she made a run out to Little and Great Diamond Islands and other ports, followed by two more trips later in the evening. Many people were forced to rely on motor launches and fishing boats for transportation, although Manager Goding did succeed in chartering a powerful naphtha launch to carry the mails to the islands and landings around the bay on a twice-daily basis.

The editorials continued to flare at the stoppage of service, demanding it be resumed at once, without another hour's delay. While the creditors had every right to collect the money due them, the public stormed over the attempt to collect it at the expense of thousands of local residents.

Stirred to action by the demand of the local citizenry, Portland's Mayor Charles B. Clarke called a meeting for 9 a.m. on Thursday, July 10, inviting all parties concerned in the financial difficulties. A Chamber of Commerce meeting the previous forenoon had set the stage for this more important confrontation, though the Chamber members had made some positive headway in finding transportation alternatives. At the first meeting, Herbert Clay, local agent of the Eastern Steamship Lines, stated that his company's steamer *Mineola*, now tied up at Rockland, could be brought here at once for service in Casco Bay if necessary. A C.B. & H. Lines spokesman reported that the company had secured the steamer *May Archer*, of Port Clyde, and expected her to enter service immediately. He went on to say that she had run on the Portland-Rockland line for a short time in 1918, was quite speedy, and had a capacity of about 250 passengers. Line officials believed that she would fit in nicely. In actual fact, the ferry *Swampscott* continued to carry large crowds on its Peaks Island run; the Randall steamer *Tourist* was by now carrying freight and passengers for lower bay stops on her daily trips to and from Gurnet, while the little *Mary Jane* was making one trip daily to Cliff Island, South Harpswell, Bailey and Orrs Islands.

Mayor Clarke's City Hall conference was well attended by principal officers of the Chamber of Commerce, as well as representatives of the Kiwanis and Rotary Clubs, the A.R. Wright Company, the Portland Company, the special committee appointed by the city government, the Casco Bay & Harpswell Lines, and the Union Safe Deposit & Trust Company, holder of the mortgage on the steamer fleet. They were to spend all day in session with attorneys Sidney Larrabee and Wadleigh Drummond for Union Safe Deposit & Trust, and Gerry L. Brooks for the lien claimants, working well into the night to reach a compromise.

The effort was worthwhile. The final decree, signed by Judge Scott Wilson at 10:45 p.m., allowed that all liens be lifted on condition they would again be filed and served in the autumn, with C.B. & H. Lines to pay the two creditors' companies a total of $10,000 over and above its operating expenses to release the lien claim. This latter stipulation stemmed from the conviction of the creditors that the boats would bring a much lower price if auctioned in the fall instead of in prime season. The state courts promptly named Judge Edward C. Reynolds and Charles W.T. Goding as Receivers to operate the steamers. It would only be a short reprieve, for the court had not disavowed the death knell, already tolling for C.B. & H. Lines.

After a tie-up of almost three days to the minute, the Casco Bay & Harpswell Lines vessels resumed their runs on Friday morning, July 11, 1919. The newspapers, though, were looking ahead to the autumn months and continued their policy of hammering home the purpose and value

The Lookout Point House was the nearest accommodation to Harpswell Lookout Landing for steamboat passengers. It operates to this day as a popular bed and breakfast establishment known as the Harpswell Inn. Barbara D. Munsey

Posed aboard the Pilgrim *in the late years of the Casco Bay & Harpswell Lines consolidation, Captain Wilbur Gates stands at the center with Chief Engineer Harry Ricker beside him (at left). Purser Winfield Hodgdon stands at right.* Warren N. Graffam Collection, from Hilda Cushing Dudley

of the island steamboat service, through editorial and article. This outpouring lasted for several days and saw Mayor Clarke and others many times lauded for their commendable performance and public service. The editors always gingerly sidestepped the issue of blame for the incident and offered hopeful sentiments that somehow the steamers would remain in service, while warning, through innuendo, of the consequences to the city and region if the island fleet was not supported.

Steamer crews, idle now for days, arrived early on Friday morning to ready the boats for resumption of service. Some of the steamers, including the *Aucocisco*, had been moored with banked fires, which cut considerably the time needed for steaming their boilers. Passenger and freight traffic was heavy from the start and this must have gladdened everyone's heart at Custom House Wharf, which had known little cheer lately. Business became even better as word gradually spread that service was restored to the islands. It was back to near-normal now, but the press would let no one forget the perilous hours, as the *Argus* first observed: "Steamboats are good property now and are worth as much to Portland people as to anybody else. Don't let our island fleet go..." then sermonized, "Portland doesn't want to lose its island steamer service, Portland can't afford to lose its island steamer service, hence Portland must patronize its island steamer service."

The sudden legal tie-up of the boats was quickly remedied and a close-down forestalled, but not a single vessel escaped the net of financial and operational calamities of 1919. Luckier than some, the *Maquoit* was nevertheless libeled for almost $4,000 in repair and coal bills. The *Forest Queen* continued to be unfortunate, being taken off her run on July 15 in mid-season, to go onto the marine railway for repairs.

By July 16 Captain Morrill had noted that the *Auco* was not making good her time between courses, since annual spring overhaul had been postponed to save funds. The Receivers agreed that something should be done and as soon as the *Forest Queen* cleared the marine railway, the *Auco* was hauled off to have a very foul bottom cleaned.

The steam scow *Venture* was libeled with an unpaid coal fuel bill of $2,537.88, this sum being larger than those for any other steamer except the great *Pilgrim*. This amount resulted more from her frequent use than from extra operating expense.

Though a dark shadow was cast over steamboats and crews with the passing days and weeks, there was one light diversion for the *Aucocisco* this season, when on July 29 she carried to Portland a most unusual cargo. There, laid out side by side on a tarpaulin spread over the forward freight deck, were no less than seven large sharks. These gray marauders had worn thin the patience of Bailey Island fishermen by tearing up their nets and

An unusual aspect of this view is that the Aucocisco *is engaged in commercial service on the Kennebec River. Chartered for a daily run to Boothbay Harbor in early spring 1920, the proceeds helped pay the reorganization costs for the new Casco Bay Lines.*
Jane Stevens, from Captain James Perkins

gear to steal bait never intended for them. They had paid the supreme price and were now bound for transshipment to Boston, where they would net a good bounty from Boston fish dealers eager to pay high prices for every shark killed.

Now the *Forest Queen* again came to the forefront as an operational headache. On August 8, while leaving Evergreen Landing at about 3:30 p.m., she broke a steam line coupling and was towed back to Portland Harbor by the tug *Ben Hur*, which guided her into a berth alongside the Noyes Machine Works for further repairs. On Saturday, September 6, the *Queen* was in trouble once more, this time losing a propeller blade while coming up from Long Island. She was beached on the South Portland mud flats for repair, to prevent another ill-affordable charge by the South Portland yard, and the *Emita* went on the run in her place. Two days later, the *Forest Queen* returned for what proved to be her last active weeks in island service.

Much too soon, the summer season came to a close, and service, especially to landings below Long Island, was cut back with a revised timetable on September 16.

On September 24, Receivers Charles Goding and Judge Reynolds filed a petition in the Supreme Judicial Court to discontinue all Casco Bay & Harpswell Lines operations at the close of business on September 30, 1919.

In accordance with the court decree of July 10, it was duly accepted and authorized by Judge Wilson. One by one the steamers were laid off and tied up, their fires raked out and boilers allowed to go cold. Crews were sadly dismissed, but first instructed by Superintendent Locke and Charles Goding to watch carefully for future developments. Finally, only the *Forest Queen* and *Aucocisco* kept steam up. The closure date came, but it was evident that the creditors would not file in U.S. District Court until noon the next day. Receiver Goding decided to make the Wednesday morning runs before federal keepers were stationed aboard. Captains Morrill and Thompson were willing to remain with their crews, and made these trips without difficulty. By Wednesday afternoon, October 1, however, the gavel of the Supreme Judicial Court fell, and the reign of the Casco Bay & Harpswell Lines consolidation had come to an end.

Only the little Kennedy steamer *Mary Jane* departed Custom House Wharf, running one round trip daily between Portland and Orrs Island through the spring of 1920. In addition, Captain Oscar Randall kept his small steamers, the newly re-acquired *Gurnet* and her older sister ship *Tourist*, in operation all through the fall. Peaks Island remained well served by the ferry *Swampscott* for the duration.

PART II

THE INDEPENDENT ISLAND LINES

An excellent character study of kindly old Captain Horace Bartol Townsend, 1838-1907. A principal owner of the Freeport Steamboat Company, he skippered the Haidee *and* Phantom.

C. & N. Kitchen, from F. Garfield

CHAPTER 8

THE INNER BAY AWAKENS TO STEAM

Patent and Flushing

The pioneer efforts to offer scheduled steamboat service to residents of the northeasterly reaches of Casco Bay, consisting of the smaller Middle, Merepoint, and Maquoit Bays, but commonly known as the Inner Bay, included two separate experiments early in the nineteenth century.

The first was an 1825 endeavor by innovator and entrepreneur Seward Porter to run his coastwise steamboat *Patent* on a line from Portland to New Wharf on Middle Bay at Brunswick. However, after only a few trips, Captain Porter began steaming for Bourne's Wharf on the New Meadows River, which had better stagecoach connections to Bath. Even so, the line died in less than a year.

In 1846, an outmoded New York sidewheeler named *Flushing* was bought by railroad interests to run between the rebuilt New Wharf and Portland. Commanded by Captain Robert Chase, the *Flushing* ran until June 9, 1849, when the first train of the newly completed Kennebec & Portland Railroad reached Brunswick. An interlude of three decades followed the demise of this railroad steamer service.

Tyro and Harraseeket

The first steamboat to serve Freeport was the *Tyro*, built locally for Captain J.P. Weeman in 1860. Primarily a freight steamer utilized to haul raw materials and finished products between Dennison's Mill and Portland, the *Tyro* was soon a handy mode of transportation for travelers as well. Engineer Charles Craig had installed a novel hinged smokestack to allow the steamer to pass under a low fixed bridge just below the mill landing. This device was the key to a brisk business in grist and sawmill goods, but may have contributed to an 1861 fire which left the *Tyro* badly damaged and withdrawn from service. Replaced by the new steamer

Harraseeket, a vessel with better passenger accommodation, the *Tyro* remained laid up until sold in 1863 to the United States Army, which used her until 1867. As chance had it, the *Harraseeket* was the last steamer to ply between Mast and Porter's Landings. The fare for her river and bay trips was 50 cents.

The Freeport Steamboat Company

Haidee and Phantom

During the early 1880s, commercial steam navigation to Casco Bay's outlying islands flourished, but the Inner Bay shore and islands had remained strangely quiet. This evergreen wonderland did not see a regular steamboat until 1884, when the first venture, of what would eventually become a considerable network of small independent steamboat lines before the turn of the century, was spawned.

In the autumn of 1883 workmen employed by locally prominent sea captain Horace B. Townsend carried their axes and handsaws onto the lush timberland of Staples Point at Freeport. Their chore was to cut down enough sturdy oak trees to provide the keel and frames for a small steamboat, christened *Haidee* after Captain Townsend's daughter.

The *Haidee* began a new service between Freeport and Great Chebeague Island, with Captain Townsend himself serving as skipper. The new steamer was popular on the short crossing to Casco Bay's second largest island. Favored as the *Haidee* was among patrons, she did not cut deeply into the Harpswell Line's Great Chebeague revenues. The longer journey to the busy metropolis of Portland remained more customary for island travelers and as the novelty of crossing on the *Haidee* waned, so did her business.

Undaunted by this setback, Captain Townsend hauled the *Haidee* off the Chebeague run and readied her for a new route between Freeport and Portland, with an intermediate stop at Town Landing, Falmouth Foreside.

A rare view of the Freeport Steamboat Company's steamer Phantom *shows her taking shape on the builders' ways at South Freeport in 1887.* C.R. Thomas

Never noted for her beauty, the steamer Phantom, *seen at the South Freeport Wharf, was every inch a practical rig.* C.R. Thomas

Now calling his enterprise the Freeport Steamboat Company, he set about to recoup his loss of earnings.

Captain Townsend steadily expanded the route for a larger, more faithful following of customers. By 1886, the *Haidee* was hard pressed to meet the demands of increased passenger and freight business and the skipper began looking for a larger craft.

The problem was solved by Captain Townsend's alliance that year with Captain Horace B. Soule, also of Freeport. Under this partnership, a second steamer was soon under construction at South Freeport. When Captain Townsend brought out the *Phantom* in 1887, Captain Soule, in turn, took command of the *Haidee*. With the end of the summer season, however, it was certain that a two-boat service could not be sustained and the *Haidee* was laid up to act as spare boat on the line. Knowing full well that her sale price would pay the builder's costs for the *Phantom* in jig time, however, the Freeport Steamboat Company placed her on the block early in 1888.

The *Haidee* made her parting voyage from Casco Bay that spring, bound "down east" for passenger and excursion service at Machias. The many years left in her almost-new hull were destined to be spent far from Freeport, and she never returned to her home waters. More on the later career of the *Haidee* can be found in the Wayward Steamboats appendix.

The new *Phantom* was a fitting solution to the Freeport Steamboat Company's problem of limited capacity, and served trouble free for years, but she was dismally unattractive. Everything aft of her pilot house looked as if the builders had thrown it together as an afterthought. Among the Casco Bay steamboat fraternity, she was openly referred to as "a grotesque-looking thing."

In earliest years, Soule and Townsend had registered their steamers at Freeport, but had since shifted terminus and offices to the foot of Portland Pier. Following that move in 1887, Freeport Line vessels bore the legend "Portland" on their sterns. Still a fledgling organization when compared to the two older and larger bay lines, the Freeport Steamboat Company reached wider public notice through regular advertisements in the local press. One in the *Daily Eastern Argus* on March 10, 1891, typified off-season service: "Freeport Steamboat Company—Steamer *Phantom* will leave Portland Pier for Freeport, touching at Falmouth Foreside, Cousins, Great Chebeague and Littlejohn's Islands and Wolfe's Point, at 3 p.m. daily, Sundays excepted. Returning will leave South Freeport at 7:00 a.m., touching at all landings commencing March 16, 1891—H.B. Soule, Manager."

The schedule changed during the second week of June each year, and the *Phantom* would begin the day by leaving South Freeport at 6:40 a.m. and make all stops before reaching Portland Pier by 8:40 a.m. Then, after

The Phantom, *second vessel of the Freeport Steamboat Company, at an early island steamboat wharf.*
Steamship Historical Society of America

a pause to allow for breakfast and maybe coaling up, the ungainly steamer would depart for South Freeport and waylandings at 9:55 a.m. If all went well, the *Phantom* would tie up again at the South Freeport wharf by 11:40 a.m. After idling away the noonday, her engine gang would stir up the fires and raise her steam pressure for another trip to "the west'ard," leaving at 1:55 p.m. or thereabouts. This was the busiest and best patronized daily round trip, arriving at Portland by 4 p.m. About an hour later her whistle would blow to announce the *Phantom*'s last departure of the day from the city.

In order to travel the full distance to or from Portland, the *Phantom*'s passengers were faced with a five-mile carriage ride between the village and the South Freeport wharf. Most travelers took advantage of the company's horse-drawn vehicles, and tourists boarding at Portland could therefore take an excursion of 38 miles, including the five-mile drive, after spending only one dollar for the round trip. A one-way fare over the entire route cost 70 cents. Morning passengers bound for Freeport arrived in time to catch eastbound trains, while train passengers headed toward Portland could take a pleasant ride and then sail the rest of the way into Portland. But such inducement did not draw heavily from the ranks of time-conscious travelers, and this left general freight and local passenger trade as mainstays of the Freeport Line.

The *Phantom*, with sturdy derrick boom rigged on her foredeck, often proved more useful than other local passenger steamers in hauling freight. Among her steady accounts, wholesale clams shipped from Hamilton Brothers on Great Chebeague alone numbered several thousand barrels each year. Freighting was arduous work, and brute strength in a steamboat deckhand could be a real asset. Take powerful Dave Coffin, for instance, one of the hardier of the *Phantom*'s roustabouts. To this day, stories have been handed down telling how he could manhandle a full wooden barrel of clams off the deck, raise it to his chest and hurl it bodily to the top of a wharf at low tide.

In 1894, the owners, anticipating additional business, extended the *Phantom*'s route beyond the South Freeport stop to Bustins Island, Mere Point and Harpswell Lookout, opening a new era in steamer travel on this section of Casco Bay. Nevertheless, by 1895 the Harpswell Line with several new steamboats, the best schedules and personnel, and operating from the same terminal as the *Phantom*, had cornered the Great Chebeague passenger and freight business which was the Freeport Line's bone and marrow. As if this were not upsetting enough, rumors were circulating of a pending Portland & Yarmouth Electric Railway of trolley cars, planned to serve the communities along the Inner Bay shore as far as the Cumberland-Yarmouth town line.

The steamer Madeleine *at her Portland Pier berth. By the time this photograph was taken, the line had been extended northward as far as Yarmouth Foreside.*
Steamship Historical Society of America

What little notice the press took of the Freeport company's operations usually came as bad news. The August 24, 1904, issue of the *Six Town Times* stated:

What might have been a serious accident occurred at Bustin's last Friday afternoon. The signal used there for hailing the *Phantom* is a barrel and it is suspended in the air [on a pole] and as boys like to. . .know the why and wherefore, Master Chester Nichols of Cambridgeport was pulling up the ropes unnoticed and looking up to see the barrel and how it worked. Suddenly the barrel descended and struck the boy on the upper lip just below his nose. He was taken to Freeport to Mr. Ambrose Britt's home. The doctor was summoned and the boy cared for.

The Freeport Steamboat Company and its able if unattractive steamboat might have continued for decades to come, because certainly the islands of Cousins, Littlejohn, Bustins and Mere Point still needed service, as did loyal patrons at Great Chebeague and Harpswell Center. A desire had even been expressed for an added stop at Birch Island, on the leg between Mere Point and the Lookout. As it turned out, the imagination and courage required to go on were absent. The 1896 season was the firm's last and, at its close, the Falmouth Foreside Steamboat Company bought the *Phantom*.

The Falmouth Foreside Steamboat Company
The Portland, Freeport & Brunswick Steamboat Company
A "New" Forest City Line

Alice, Phantom, Madeleine, Vivian, Isis; and *Tremont*

The launching of the new Harpswell Line steamer *Chebeague*, in the spring of 1891, left the older Brewer-built steamboat *Alice* as surplus. Accordingly, her charter from the dormant Waldo Steamboat Company was quickly ended. Far from presenting any problem, this news brought an immediate offer of lease by the newly organized Falmouth Foreside Steamboat Company, whose terms were gratefully accepted.

Readying the *Alice* for service required only minor overhaul and painting. On April 15, she made her first trip between Town Landing and Portland Pier. Under command of Captain Ben M. Seabury, the crew had turned out hours before dawn to light off fires, get steam up and prepare for that initial 6 a.m. departure. At Portland, the *Alice* unloaded her none too numerous passengers and whatever small amount of cargo the line had been lucky enough to receive. Loading for the scheduled 7 a.m. trip back to Falmouth Foreside then began and the *Alice* left punctually. Business was nothing to crow about, but the owners realized it would take time for the route to develop.

The schedule continued with further departures from Town Landing at 8:55 a.m., 1 p.m. and 5 p.m. From Portland, additional trips left at 9:50 a.m., 3 p.m. and 6:15 p.m., with the nightly layover at Town Landing.

Within a month, the company extended its route to Yarmouth Foreside, with the line's terminus changed to Portland Pier and the schedule reduced to two trips per day. General Manager Albert Waite went to work preparing a new schedule effective on May 18. Thereafter, Captain Seabury daily backed the *Alice* from her Portland slip at 7 a.m. The stop at Town Landing was now preceded by calls at Mackworth Island (on signal) and Waite's Landing, Falmouth Foreside, then on past Broad Cove and Prince Point to Bucknam's Point wharf at Yarmouth Foreside. By 8:30 a.m. the steamer was turning southbound once more for Portland and waylandings. At 3 p.m. the *Alice* began her last round trip of the day northward. The homeward leg of this voyage commenced at 4:30 p.m. and she arrived back at Portland Pier about 6 p.m.

An advertisement in the June 9, 1891, *Daily Eastern Argus* further emphasized the reliance of Inner Bay steamboat lines on "Old Dobbin":

> On and after June 15th, connections will be made by carriage between Yarmouth Foreside and Yarmouthville. Carriages will leave the Royal River House, Yarmouthville for the landing at Yarmouth Foreside at 7:45 a.m., and 3:45 p.m. Through tickets can be procured of O.E. Lowell, Royal River House, Yarmouthville or of Captain Seabury on Board steamer *Alice*.
> —Albert H. Waite, Gen'l Manager

The overland connection became established, although offered only in summer. The *Alice* remained continuously on this route until the spring of 1893, when she served the Peoples Ferry Company cross-harbor service, in company with the Kennebec steamer *Winter Harbor*, until completion of the ferryboat *Elizabeth City* in April.

That the Falmouth Foreside line was a sound venture is aptly shown by events of 1892, when Portland shipbuilder Nathan Dyer was commissioned to design and construct a larger and more suitable vessel than the *Alice*. The result was the steamer *Madeleine*, built at Cape Elizabeth and launched in 1893.

Under command of Captain Seabury, the *Madeleine* immediately took up mainline service between Portland and Yarmouth, the intermediate stops unchanged except for the addition of Madockawando Landing as a flag stop. Certainly not the least of Dyer's creations, this latest vessel is detailed more fully, with notes on her builder, in the Fleeting Bygones appendix.

An "eyebrow" awning over her wheelhouse windows has recently been added as the Madeleine *calls at Falmouth Foreside in the summer of 1896. The company's business was still fine at this time, but such good fortune would not last.* Steamship Historical Society of America

The builders had adorned the *Madeleine*'s otherwise garishly decorated wheelhouse with a handsome carved and gilded eagle, one of only half a dozen to ever perch atop island steamer pilot houses. Others spread their wings high aloft on the *Emita* and *Forest Queen* of the Casco Bay Line, as well as the *Merryconeag*, and later the *Sebascodegan* and *Maquoit*, of the Harpswell Line. All these majestic golden birds disappeared eventually, replaced by searchlights necessary for night operation.

The *Madeleine* remained Captain Seabury's command during the busier late spring, summer and early fall schedules. But after the neighboring Harpswell Line laid up or leased its second steamer each off-season, the Falmouth Foreside Line was fortunate in having popular Captain Jimmie Long aboard the *Madeleine*. This left Captain Seabury free to take on an increasing share of the line's administrative chores, while occasionally working the *Alice* or *Phantom*. The *Madeleine*'s engineer was William H. Cook, a former towboat man, later to become one of the best-known long-tenure engineers on outside route island boats.

The former Freeport Line steamboat Phantom *ended her days in somber livery as a sardine carrier at Eastport.* Steamship Historical Society of America

The skeletal old Waldo Steamboat Company finally gave up its ghost and dissolved in 1895, after selling the steamer *Alice* outright to the Falmouth Foreside Line, which had successfully expanded its route to include Porter's Landing along the Harraseeket River shore and South Freeport, and in 1896 took over all the former Freeport Steamboat Company holdings.

Successful operations, which kept both the *Alice* and *Madeleine* reasonably busy in warmer seasons, with the *Phantom* bearing the brunt of winter operation, brought a brief term of welcome prosperity. A shuffling of officers saw Albert Waite ascend to the company presidency and Edmund R. Norton become treasurer and general manager.

The fortunes of the Falmouth Foreside Steamboat Company faded miserably after the 1897 tourist season. The 1898 opening of the Portland & Yarmouth Electric Railway line took the public's fancy, and left steamboat passenger traffic plummeting.

It was with crisis impending that Captain Seabury became general manager in early 1898. Undismayed by the bleak outlook, he surveyed the company's chances of survival and opted to keep operating, with funding aided by sale of the *Alice* to the Passamaquoddy Ferry & Navigation Company. The proceeds realized from disposal of this steamer were desperately needed, but provided only temporary respite for the ailing firm. Commencing with the acquisition of the unstable old Freeport Line, the beleaguered company was kept reeling with several major

missteps made by owners and management in rapid succession. Built to replace the *Alice* in 1898, the jaunty little steamer *Vivian* was launched at Portland for the firm's new affiliate, the Portland, Freeport & Brunswick Line, to quickly become an unhappy example of the directors' "too little, too late" policies. Closely resembling the Diamond Island Association's onetime steam yacht *Isis*, the 41-foot *Vivian* was a virtual copy of the former's improved commercial rig.

Another injection of funds arrived with the spring of 1899, when the Passamaquoddy Ferry & Navigation Company purchased the tired and homely *Phantom*, which joined the *Alice* at Eastport and Lubec.

The *Phantom*'s replacement on the roster became available when the Harbor Defenses of Portland came to occupy Great Diamond Island's most valuable acreage. Fort McKinley and its military realities (to be examined more closely in a chapter on military steamers of Casco Bay in a future volume) brought the demise of a major summer cottage colony, or at least its elitist attitudes. Captain Seabury's spirits must have soared again when it proved an easy matter to transfer title of the small steamer *Isis* from the Diamond Island Association to the Falmouth Foreside Steamboat Company, she having been retired from her exclusive service to the Great Diamond colony.

By mid-season of 1899, freight and passenger business was scarcely worth the effort, even considering an eleventh-hour addition of service to several more Inner Bay stops. Captain Seabury's enthusiasm had brought this new run to fruition under the affiliated firm officially chartered as the Portland, Freeport & Brunswick Steamboat Company. Using the Falmouth Foreside Line's formerly mainline *Madeleine*, along with the new *Vivian* for lighter periods and charter work, the revised operation was implemented by leaving the last shadow of the original shoreline circuit to the tiny steamer *Isis*.

The struggling Falmouth Foreside Line now offered extra excursions and more charters, which, for a while, brought heartening results. But tourists seemed more inclined to flock to the ticket offices of the well-advertised Harpswell Line or Casco Bay Line. Small wonder, when the *Casco Bay Breeze* lost no opportunity to herald steamers of the larger fleets, but somehow virtually ignored the services offered by the small Inner Bay companies.

The Portland, Freeport & Brunswick Line, which lasted less than three months of the 1899 season, offered a daily circuit from Portland Pier to Great Diamond Island (using the Association's old Casco Wharf, on the west shore), Waite's Landing and Town Landing (Falmouth Foreside), Prince's Point, Cousins, and Littlejohn's Landings, Hamilton's (Old Stone Wharf) at Great Chebeague, Chamberlain's Landing at Brunswick, and Lookout Landing at Harpswell Center.

The so-called Forest City Steamboat Company lifted a familiar but long-defunct identity to bolster its aspirations to provide Inner-Bay service. Its handsome Barbour-built Tremont, *however, lasted for only one season on Casco Bay.* Maine Maritime Museum

A notebook kept by Casco Bay's unofficial steamboat historian and general waterfront factotum, Warren Graffam, tells that the *Madeleine* was in operation on this extended route by May 15, 1899, and that Ben Seabury's ideas looked so good at the time that another firm immediately came on to compete with the Portland, Freeport & Brunswick Steamboat Company. In fact, on May 30, the trim, handsome Barbour-built steamer *Tremont* arrived to run for the self-styled "Forest City Steamboat Company" on its own Freeport and Brunswick run out of Portland. This so-called "Forest City Line" was not the historic firm described earlier in these pages but a small, independent and somewhat arrogant group, pompously taking for itself an honored title, disused for several years. An ill-conceived venture which was a resounding failure and extremely short lived, the pretentious little company went so far as to contract with a builder named Bennett to construct another wharf (on the site of ancestral New Wharf) near Brunswick, called Pennell's Wharf, in June 1899. Despite all efforts, the line died early in the season and the *Tremont* returned to her home port of Bangor.

The Graffam notebook indicates that the Falmouth Foreside/Portland, Freeport & Brunswick Steamboat companies fared no better that year with the steamers *Madeleine* and *Vivian*:

Vivian—Steamer owned by the 'Portland, Freeport & Brunswick Steamboat Co.' in 1899.
July 17, 1899—An attachment was placed on this steamer for $1,000. A keeper was placed aboard.
July 25, 1899—Steamer *Madeleine* is plastered by the crew to recover wages. They were Joseph C. and Eugene Thompson of Cumberland, Walter E. Johnson of Freeport, Harry E. Sawyer of Pownal, and George L. Burnham of Portland. Keeper put aboard the steamer at Portland Pier where she laid all day. Has been running on Falmouth Foreside route for the last six years and is considered one of the best steamers in the harbor.
July 26, 1899—Plaster removed as owners post a bond. [*Madeleine*] sold for $8,000 to run in Boston.
Aug. 27, 1899—Steamer *Vivian* discontinued service on run to Mere Point from Portland.

Leaving a trail of coal smoke drifting on a light southwesterly breeze, the steamer Madeleine *prepares to make the long, gradual turn which will take her between Fish Point and Diamond Ledge and on along the Inner Bay route toward the Foresides.* Maine Historical Society

Because a Dyer-built steamboat never stayed idle for long, the *Madeleine* soon steamed away and promptly went to work as a Boston Harbor excursion boat. More of her history away from the Maine coast appears in the Wayward Steamboats appendix, together with those of her fleetmates.

Try as it might, the Falmouth Foreside Steamboat Company was still no match for the efficient trolley car. Patronage was at record low, thanks to the Portland & Yarmouth Electric Railway Company trolleys, which now offered faster and equally comfortable travel and made any number of convenient stops along the way. The electric cars left Portland's Monument Square as early as 6:15, 6:45 and 7:15 a.m., then every 30 minutes until 11:45 p.m. each day for East Deering, Falmouth Foreside (including Underwood Springs Pleasure Park), and Cumberland and Yarmouth Foresides. Returning schedules into the city were just as convenient and numerous.

Incredibly, the steamboat company struggled on with an iron will, even taking the Portland & Cape Elizabeth Line passenger ferry *Josephine Hoey* on loan to augment the *Isis* and *Vivian* on the shoreline route. The diminutive size of these three passenger steamers, with virtually no adequate freighting space, hindered the company and caused it to face reality in the late autumn of 1899. It was voted to put the *Vivian* and *Isis* up for sale. The *Josephine Hoey* quickly reverted to the Peoples Ferry Company.

In a manner of speaking, the genealogies of six originally independent companies all came to be vested in the Falmouth Foreside/Portland, Freeport & Brunswick Steamboat companies. The books were forever closed when the steamers *Isis* and *Vivian* both became private yachts under new ownership in the early spring of 1900. Although this amalgamated enterprise did not win the race into the twentieth century, the day of the independent steamboat line on Casco Bay was far from over.

The Brunswick & Portland Steamboat Company's advertisement shows the Corinna *as she appeared when new.* Maine Historical Society

The Brunswick & Portland Steamboat Company

Corinna

Even though two steamboat lines, operated over similar routes, had already met with failure or financial difficulty, a third firm was organized to make a bid for success in 1899. This latest effort amounted to a pooling of interests by Captain E.A. Baker, Messrs. Brown and Swett, and others. Their new steamer *Corinna* was well under construction at Portland for the account of treasurer Wendall S. Wadsworth. When chartered as the Brunswick & Portland Steamboat Company, the new line had its headquarters on the west side of Portland Pier. The small scope of the venture is reflected in the dual role of Captain Ed Baker, as both skipper of the *Corinna* and general manager of the company.

First call for the *Corinna*, following each day's departure from Portland Pier, was an exclusive stop at tiny Clapboard Island, scantily populated in those days, and only later occupied in isolated splendor by a single 23-room summer mansion and a few estate outbuildings. From here the small steamer would navigate up the Inner Bay, making the old landings at Cousins, Littlejohn and Bustins Islands, then turn in around the southwest end of Bustins to make for the Harraseeket River entrance and the former South Freeport landing place of the *Phantom*, *Haidee*, and *Madeleine*. After an hour and a half luncheon stopover, the *Corinna* would cast off to make the return trip, including all stops, and arrive back at Portland Pier around 3 p.m.

While it was the intent of the company to serve Brunswick, as its name implied, arrangements fell through or were not made at all. Disagreement among ownership and management over the route soon became rampant. As it turned out, the problems over route expansion gave only a hint of the underlying obstacles at the close of the prime season. The enterprise was already so deep in debt that the steamer *Corinna* was seized and placed in the charge of a keeper. Offered for sale by the U.S. Marshal, the auction was set for 10 a.m., September 16, 1899.

In retrospect, the intensity of the 1899 competition over the Inner Bay route between Portland and Harpswell Center, waylanding at the mainland points of Freeport and Mere Point at Brunswick, in addition to all the island stops lying between, might be classed as a peculiarly frenzied episode. Since all three steamboat companies involved eventually suffered either outright defeat or at least had vessels legally impounded for debts, all the fervor defies reason. As with the Portland, Freeport & Brunswick Line, the principals of the Brunswick & Portland Steamboat Company refused to give up. Reorganized in time to be among the precious

The steamer Corinna *of the Portland, Freeport & Brunswick Line is shown laid up, probably following the company's failure in 1903.*
Steamship Historical Society of America

The Corinna *as she appeared in her final rig. Although a flattering copy of* Gurnet's *layout in this mode, she never saw Casco Bay service after her rebuild.* Frank Claes

few attending the auction sale, they were successful in funding a bid. The sale was recorded to W.S. Wadsworth of Delano Planing Mill for $1,850, together with bills which brought the total cost to over $3,100. This was less than the original $4,000 cost of *Corinna's* boiler, engine, and tanks, considered to be one of the finest steam plants of any harbor craft. The Brunswick & Portland Line was destined to be the sole survivor among the several adversaries, and the only one with steam up in the spring of 1900. Internal disagreements over management and route, however, soon cropped up again and would not disappear.

By the autumn of 1901, one ownership faction favored dropping the Freeport leg, following disappointing revenues at the end of the line's third season. The Brunswick & Portland Steamboat Company moved during the winter months of 1901 from its prime location at Portland Pier to a more economical berth at Long Wharf. At Captain Baker's stubborn insistence, however, the Freeport stops continued. As general manager, his views prevailed and he advertised his firm's existing Freeport route in the *Casco Bay Directory* of 1902.

When spring approached, the other shareholders adamantly advocated both the omission of Freeport service and the extension toward Brunswick. The bitter controversy rose to a fever pitch, as the divided parties split even further at the strong suggestion to drop all operations from Portland and remove to Brunswick on the upper reaches of the bay. The opinion seemed justified to those who felt that any success on an island route from Portland would only invite competition and eventual defeat by one of the larger bay lines. For Captain Baker, this latest twist of ideas bordered on sheer idiocy and he would have no more of it! To the mutual relief of everyone, he promptly sold his share of the business and stormed out on his own.

The remaining officials of the Brunswick & Portland Steamboat Company soon made the very changes they had proposed. A suitable landing and office were available at the Lookout, Harpswell Center, and the wharf was repaired at Mere Point, Brunswick. At this, the Long Wharf leasehold was closed out and the *Corinna* steamed away, bound for quieter surroundings. The company's principals had become so totally mesmerized by the visionary Inner Bay islands' cottage colonies they believed to be imminent now, that this relocation made sense to them.

Having succeeded Captain Baker in the office of general manager, P.C. Merriman launched the revised route schedule in June 1902. The timetable consisted of two daily round trips by the *Corinna* departing from Harpswell Center and touching at Birch Island, Mere Point, Bustins, Littlejohn and Cousins Islands and return. At first this line seemed to be catching on but, in truth, freight and passenger traffic rose from almost nothing to meager levels and then grew no more, despite false indicators such as an occasional crowd on the steamer's decks. Of the two mainland points served by the company, neither could offer much in the way of shopping and business services, or the usual city entertainments. Mere Point, although nearer to downtown Brunswick, was still a lengthy wagon or "horseless carriage" ride over tortuous roads. At any rate, the firm could never hope to prosper and events proved Captain Baker correct after all.

Refusing to admit its mistake, the company continued headlong into bankruptcy following the 1903 summer season. It had fervently persisted in hoping that the ambitious summer resort of Birchmont might still come to be on Birch Island, albeit belatedly. But it did not, and the hoped-for Upper and Lower Goose Islands and Frenchman's Island (later French Island) cottage colonies never got to the serious planning stage at all. Harpswell town selectman Thomas E. Skolfield was named principal Trustee in receivership and the *Corinna* was laid up in litigation. The steamer was out of commission until 1909, when at last a charter was arranged to the Devereux steamboat interests at Castine. At this point, *Corinna*'s Casco Bay adventure effectively ended, but her remaining years "down east" are noted in the Wayward Steamboats appendix.

The Freeport & Portland Steamboat Company

James T. Furber

No sooner had he freed himself from the Brunswick & Portland Line than Captain Baker organized another company to pursue the route he had championed with the *Corinna*. Papers certified, he went in frantic search of a vessel for his Freeport & Portland Steamboat Company, hoping to commence the season of 1902. Laid up at Saco, the diminutive steamer *James T. Furber* seemed exactly what he needed and Captain Baker purchased her from R.H. Ingersoll and associates.

Built on the river at Kennebunk in 1892, the *James T. Furber* served briefly on a run between that village and Kennebunkport. Initially owned by railroad-connected individuals, she was named for a notable superintendent of the Boston & Maine Railroad during the 1880s. Not long afterward, the little *Furber* moved eastward to the Saco River. The following items logged in an old Graffam journal shed some small light on her earlier activities:

James T. Furber represented Captain Ed Baker's best hope of eventual prosperity as a Casco Bay steamboat entrepreneur, but his efforts met with little success. Seen here in her earlier Saco River days, the Furber's hull was later painted dark gray. McArthur Library, Biddeford

July 3, 1897—Mentioned as going to Boston to carry visitors out to the battleship *Massachusetts*.
June 29, 1899—Mentioned as being towed to Portland from Saco by the tug *James Sampson* for repairs.

On the Saco for almost a decade before trade shrank and drove her out of business, the *James T. Furber* came to Portland for a new lease on life. She was seven feet shorter than the *Corinna*, her other dimensions also being smaller, and she had little over a third of the net tonnage of her predecessor on the run to Freeport. Her first season, 1902, established the popularity of Captain Baker's new line.

The 1903 season also represented a fair success, in Captain Baker's opinion, and there was reason for optimism. The new company had proved to his former associates that they were wrong on two counts. The older company's service from Harpswell Center was a losing proposition and, moreover, the Freeport run had continued to turn a reasonable profit. All the same, Captain Ed would soon share their sense of grievance.

The news that the Harpswell Line would in 1904 bring on the fine new steamer *Maquoit* was a stunning setback, for both Captain Baker and the Freeport & Portland Line he had labored so hard to make a success.

The large company's new South Freeport Division spelled the end for his firm, without a doubt. It was only a matter of time until the superior Harpswell steamer would dry up the independent line's trade.

The premier year for the steamer *Maquoit* was as much a success as conditions allowed. On the other hand, a dogged reluctance on the part of the small independent line to surrender gained nothing except debt for the *James T. Furber* and owner Baker. When at last Captain Baker did throw in the towel, he dissolved the Freeport & Portland Steamboat Company, and resorted to transient excursion and charter business. The defeated steamer's more casual role commenced in 1905, taking the small vessel on countless junkets, ranging over the wide expanse of the bay. An item illustrating this random service appeared in the Chebeague Island column of the *Casco Bay Breeze* on August 24, 1905: "The steamer *James T. Furber*, Captain Baker, conducted a moonlight sail to Peaks Island Saturday evening, where the entire party attended the Gem Theater. Thirty-eight passengers were carried from here and a large number went from Cousins and Littlejohn Islands. The party arrived home about midnight."

Some years later, on the retirement of Captain Ed, the *Furber* became the property of his son, Captain Charles H. Baker, who continued the general charter and excursion operation until the end of summer 1917. Then the steamer was beached, stripped and abandoned, as much a victim of reduced traffic as of old age.

Ironically, the little *Furber* lost her bid for regularly scheduled service three times in her career, twice being thwarted by electric trolley car lines and finally by a combination of trolley and superior steamer competition.

Later in his career, Captain Ed Baker operated the small steamer *Lottie and May* on the South Portland ferry line, but his dream of a steamboat line among the bay islands remained with him long after retirement, and as a very old man he still took daily walks between Fort Allen Park and Custom House Wharf. At times he would shake his head and declare that "Casco Bay Lines holds the key to Casco Bay, but doesn't know how to turn it!"

CHAPTER 9

ROUTES OF THE RIVALS
THE LONG AND SHORT OF BAY OPPOSITION LINES

Portland & Small Point Steamboat Company
The MacDonald Line

Percy V. (later *Anna Belle*) and *Pejepscot*

Many bay and island people in 1897 thought that the Harpswell Steamboat Company should not be the sole source of transportation across the bay. Residents of the eastern bay, unhappy that the Harpswell Line did not touch at many of their villages, felt deprived of a reliable direct water route to Portland, the region's only metropolis. These villagers found a forceful advocate in James H. MacDonald of Portland. The proprietor of MacDonald's Fish Market at 158 Commercial Street avidly desired to try his hand at steamboating and chafed discontentedly as, year after year, his vision of an ideal route lay untried.

The Percy V. *put in several years on the Kennebec River before coming to Casco Bay as the first steamer of the Portland & Small Point Steamboat Company, a firm that soon expanded as the MacDonald Steamboat Company.*
Jane Stevens, from Captain James Perkins

Being at least in the midst of waterfront life at Portland, if not in the forefront of it, he used the opportunity to ply endlessly in search of financial backers. His concept of a line to run the bold sweep of water toward the easternmost village at the tip of Cape Small had an attractive ring to many listeners. A few investors banded together with him late in 1897. With $25,000 raised in working capital, the Portland & Small Point Steamboat Company came into being on January 3, 1898. The combined position of president and general manager went, appropriately enough, to Jim MacDonald, the guiding force behind events. The secretary for the new firm was M.A. Wren, elected unanimously.

In attempting to obtain a steamboat, the new firm was remarkably unfortunate. A golden opportunity to acquire the Harpswell Line's fine *Merryconeag* slipped through its fingers because of delay in organizing. The veteran steamer *Alice* was up for sale, but to the company's credit it did not bid on this small steamer for use on such an arduous route. The old *Phantom* was also undesirable.

Then MacDonald learned of a steamer on the Kennebec, up for sale after replacement on the Bath-Popham Beach route. Hastening to Bath for an inspection, he and his associates found the *Percy V.* not too enthralling for their tastes. They came away disenchanted. Now the weeks sped on toward the beginning of the 1897–98 winter season, and nothing more in the line of steamboats offered, at least none superior to *Percy V.* Forced to take action, the company renewed talks with the Bath & Popham Beach Steamboat Company and eventually MacDonald's firm purchased the *Percy V.* for $3,000. The Kennebec years for this vessel are detailed in the Wayward Steamboats appendix. Months before the formal legal processes of organization were completed, Jim MacDonald impatiently slapdashed his steamer in triweekly service, actually under the auspices of MacDonald's Fish Market.

The daily route begun in the late spring of 1898 by the 15-year-old steamer left from the east side of Portland Pier, traveled the inside route to stop at the wharves on Cousins and Littlejohn, then crossed to call at Hamilton's Landing (Old Stone Wharf) on Great Chebeague. With this last

The steamer Percy V. *came to Jim MacDonald's fledgling Portland & Small Point Steamboat Company as an older boat, but not greatly changed from Kennebec River days.* Frank Claes

stop her usefulness to islanders of the inner and central bay ended until much later in the day, as her captain swung the wheel to round Chebeague Point and make the long transit to Lowell Cove, on the east side of Orrs Island. Leaving tiny Goosenest Rock on the starboard hand, the *Percy V.* puffed her way between Stockmans and Whaleboat Islands, on past Little Birch Island, well north of Ministerial and Bates Islands, between Upper Flag and Eagle Islands (the latter Admiral Peary's summer home), inside Little Mark Island with its conical monument and shelter, around Jaquish Island to skirt the eastern shore of Bailey Island, westward of Pond and Ram Islands and on to Lowell Cove Wharf. All this distance and not one revenue stop between Great Chebeague and Orrs!

From Lowell Cove Landing, adjacent to Orrs Island village, the *Percy V.* made her way out between Ram and Oak Islands, past numerous treacherous ledges and the secluded summer haven of pastor and author Elijah Kellogg (which later passed to poet Edna St. Vincent Millay) on Ragged Island, before arriving at the mainland resort village of Sebasco. Leaving Sebasco, the steamer journeyed southward to Small Point village at the extreme eastern limits of Casco Bay and then doubled back to make a second (flag) stop at Sebasco, before steaming to the end of the line at Cundy's Harbor. After a brief stopover, the MacDonald steamer started the long trek back toward Portland, making all waylandings named above. Although revenues were only modest in the first weeks of service, the Portland & Small Point Steamboat directors forged ahead with a stout will to succeed.

The chilly days of Indian summer in 1898 saw an expected fading of patronage, but it became clearly evident that Sebasco and Small Point stops were destined for summer-only business. People there simply did not care about a year-round link with far-off Portland and preferred to travel the shorter overland distance to Bath. Within weeks, the line officials rescheduled the *Percy V.* to steam directly from Lowell Cove at Orrs Island to Cundy's Harbor and return.

As the cutting edge of the 1898-99 fall and winter weather set in on the region, sinking the mercury to new depths and stirring the open expanses and fetch of bay waters into furious chop, it proved folly to run an open steamer over the exposed route between Great Chebeague and Orrs. Numerous cancelations of trips, especially during November, which brought the famous ''*Portland* Gale'', forced the company to cut back service until the line stretched only to Cousins, Littlejohn, and Great

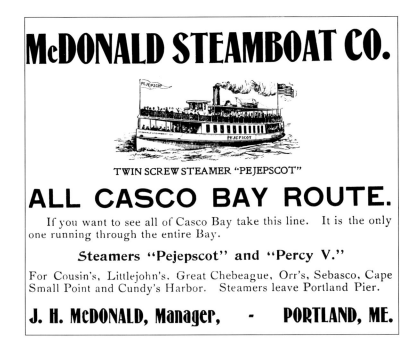

The MacDonald Line was at the height of its brief reign when this advertisement first appeared, but had not yet extended the route to include Gurnet. Maine Historical Society

The swift twin-screw, triple-expansion flyer of the MacDonald Line turned many a head when she arrived on the scene. The Pejepscot is shown at Gurnet Landing during the 1900 summer season. Willis H. Ballard

Chebeague Islands. More than just a letdown for the people of East Harpswell, this move placed the fortunes of a still-fledgling steamboat firm squarely in the back yard of the two major lines. In order to survive until spring, the *Percy V.* and her owners had to live on left-over scraps at a time when island business was lean anyway. Jim MacDonald's dream had suffered, but this only made him more determined as he pondered the future with his associates in their office, adjacent to the fish market.

The following spring, the *Percy V.* lost her key role to the company's new flagship, the *Pejepscot.* Engineer William H. Cook, who had kept the *Percy V.*'s machinery in above-average condition, stepped up to a better position on the powerful new steamer. Relieving him on the *Percy V.* was acting engineer Harry Hill, a young man who continued Bill Cook's efficiency in the engine room. No longer achieving the easy 12 knots, on only 80 lbs. of steam, that she did in her earlier years, the older MacDonald steamer continued to make occasional cross-bay runs whenever the *Pejepscot* ran special excursions, or extra trips as far as Chebeague as spare boat.

Even though 1898 had been a year of setbacks for the Portland & Small Point Steamboat Company, it was thought that an improved steamer, better suited to severe year-round demands of a trans-bay schedule, was the answer. During the long 1898-99 winter, Jim MacDonald learned of a five-year-old steel-hulled steamer, subject to U.S. Marshal's sale at public auction at New York City, after failure of the Hudson River excursion line which had her built. Following a trip to that city, MacDonald and company sat in at their fish market office for serious discussion. The steamer they had viewed would easily outclass, for speed, comfort, and general performance, anything else that Casco Bay had to offer. She seemed well worth their high bid, but this meant that a further amount of capital had to be raised. The company chose to get it by reorganization and additional stock subscriptions. When this plan did not meet with quick enough response to suit Jim MacDonald, he immediately staked all his other business holdings as collateral. His stepped-up attempt to acquire the *Pejepscot* was finally successful, and she steamed into Portland Harbor to become queen of the reconstituted and renamed MacDonald Steamboat Company.

The Pejepscot *makes a special excursion trip to the battleship U.S.S.* Indiana *at Portland Harbor anchorage. Interest in naval men-of-war remained at a peak for several years after the turn of the century, due mostly to invasion scares born of the Spanish-American War.* Maine Historical Society.

The MacDonald Line's Pejepscot *is shown laid up for the winter of 1901-02 at Portland Pier. The* Percy V., *just astern, is still active on a cut-back route.* Peter T. McLaughlin, from Warren N. Graffam

The Portland & Small Point Steamboat Company had become better known as the MacDonald Line when its flagship Pejepscot *was photographed in 1903 at Hamilton's Landing (Old Stone Wharf) on the west shore of Great Chebeague Island, her first revenue stop out of Portland.*
Warren N. Graffam Collection, from Hilda Cushing Dudley.

With its new steamer on the spring and summer schedules, the MacDonald Line gained popularity and began to make its mark on commuting habits. Its stops at Great Chebeague and Orrs Islands became a grave threat to the Harpswell Line, whose directors became wary indeed of the unfamiliar new flyer. The MacDonald Line soon had either the *Percy V.* or *Pejepscot* handling the schedule alone, and the unoccupied boat serving as back-up and available for excursion charters. This opened the door for extended special dinner excursion runs all the way to Gurnet Bridge, a trip handled best by *Pejepscot*. Round trips to visiting warships anchored in "the Roads" were also in vogue, owing their popularity to the sweeping Spanish-American War naval victories.

On the whole, MacDonald Line business seemed improved, but profits from special excursions consistently did more to bolster the company's coffers than did schedule revenues. Total income, after fuel and maintenance costs, did not allow Jim MacDonald to recoup his investment or cover the company's loan repayments. In the *Pejepscot*'s big engine space, Engineer Bill Cook had taken charge of a pair of matched triple-expansion engines, each turning one of the steamer's twin screws. She was the first and last of this breed in service to the Calendar Islands and

the reason was obvious. While *Pejepscot* was a sterling performer on the water, she was no bargain in economical operation. The demands of her twin triples made her a real "coal hog."

Over its lifetime, the MacDonald Line enjoyed no more increase in business to the eastern bay, though management stubbornly refused to acknowledge defeat. Finally, though, in the late autumn of 1902, bankers grew impatient with the struggling firm's indebtedness. Their challenge of the MacDonald Steamboat Company's right to continue brought the roof crashing in on the dreams of James MacDonald once and for all. In the opinion of former Casco Bay Lines advertising manager and purser Warren Graffam, "Jim MacDonald's strenuous efforts were doomed from the start. It wasn't a line that would ever pay. The *Pejepscot* was good-sized and a nice comfortable steamer. She was fast too, with those triple-expansion engines—faster than even the *Aucocisco*, I'll tell you that! Even so, the venture wasn't successful. MacDonald just couldn't make a go of it."

As part of the liquidation proceedings, the old *Percy V.* was sold north, to be registered at Rockport in 1903. The Wayward Steamboats appendix describes her Penobscot years in more detail. It was 15 years before the *Percy V.*, renamed the *Anna Belle*, returned to Casco Bay. We meet her again in later pages, on the rosters of two more local companies. The powerful *Pejepscot* went south, purchased by New York businessmen, and steamed back to her original surroundings on the Hudson River. With the departure of both its vessels from Portland Harbor in the dawning weeks of 1903, the MacDonald Line became history. More on the *Pejepscot*'s later years away are covered in the Wayward Steamboats appendix.

The Old Orchard Steamboat Company

Samuel E. Spring

In 1880, most people involved in steamboat service to the Casco Bay islands considered it thoroughly well developed. And there, for a while, matters came to rest. But one related idea—combining rail and steamboat transit—did surface in this same year. The lion's share of the route was via special excursion train, for vacationers or daytrippers, over the Boston & Maine Railroad's Portland to Old Orchard Beach trackage. Travelers might then board open-air "steam dummy" coaches of the Old Orchard Beach Railroad for the Saco River steamboat wharf. From Biddeford and Camp Ellis on the banks of the Saco, the envisioned steamboat line would run down to the sea at Biddeford Pool, a resort of growing importance which already boasted several inns and large summer hotels.

The S. E. Spring *was one of the last of her size and type to be launched as a sidewheeler. The choice her owners made did not hamper an active career, and their steamer always performed well.* The Peabody Museum of Salem

In due time a steamer took form on the ways of the George Russell yard at East Deering and a launching ceremony was held on July 1, 1881. Christened *Samuel E. Spring*, she was named in honor of Portland's sulphur match king, a noted railroad and shipping magnate who was also one of her principal owners. The new boat was a sidewheeler, with modest but adequate accommodation for her river shuttle. Each day, for the balance of summer, *Samuel E. Spring* waited to take rail passengers on to Biddeford Pool. While the day trip was popular, a longer stay might easily be booked at perhaps the Highland House or Yates House, these being among the best hostelries at "the Pool."

Both the Portland, Little Chebeague & Harpswell Line and the Saco River Towboat Company held shares in the Old Orchard Steamboat Company, and it was the Saco firm's trusted Captain Daniel Goldthwait of Biddeford who first took command of the *Spring* and brought her down from Portland to Saco. Registered at Portland, the sidewheeler was afterward enrolled as No. 8 on the Saco Customs Register of January 21, 1882.

The annual *Portland Directory* described the company simply as "owners of steamer *Samuel E. Spring* and running on the Saco River from Biddeford, connecting with the Old Orchard Beach Railroad and to Biddeford Pool—James L. Rackleff, Treasurer." The *Spring* continued her river run for nearly a decade, with little noteworthy change until July 21, 1888, when skipper Goldthwait was relieved by Captain John Fisher, Jr. Captain Fisher remained in command of her until August 10, 1889, when he left to join the Casco Bay Steamboat Company as master of its steamer *Cadet*. His successor on the *Samuel E. Spring* was Captain W.J. Craig.

The following year the Old Orchard line steamer was re-registered as the *S. E. Spring* of Saco, logical since that name form was the only one the vessel ever carried on her paddleboxes.

The 1890 season was financially unsuccessful for the company and its steamer, largely because "the Pool" had failed to equal Old Orchard Beach as a favorite summer resort. The steamboat line was never able to advertise a lower-priced combination fare from Portland or Old Orchard, and the lack of real support from the railroad had helped to erode the river line's trade. What finally doomed the water route, without a doubt, was the onset of regional trolley line construction. With its fate so clearly sealed, the river line was abandoned at the close of the tourist season.

The steamer Greenwood *is shown departing Weeks Landing about 1890 on another of her 14 shuttle runs to Portland Pier each summer day.*
Steamship Historical Society of America

During its lifetime, the Greenwood Garden amusement park was chiefly responsible for the creation of several successive shuttle steamboat lines and also improved the financial picture of the mainstay Casco Bay Line.
George E. MacGowen, Jr.

The Greenwood Garden Steamboat Line

S. E. Spring (ex-Samuel E. Spring) and Greenwood

The end of the Old Orchard Steamboat Company in 1891 brought the steamer *S. E. Spring* back to Portland Harbor on lease to the Greenwood Garden Steamboat Line. Operating between Portland Pier and Jones Wharf on Peaks Island, she worked the harbor crossings for the remainder of her years in Maine waters. The origins of the Greenwood Garden Line lay in an ill-considered charter of the steamer *Emita* to the Weeks family at Peaks Island by the Star Line, begun but soon terminated in June 1886. The Star Line and second Forest City Steamboat Company consolidation followed in the spring of 1887. If the resulting second Casco Bay Steamboat Company could have had its way, the merger would have ended all competition on the lucrative run to Peaks Island. But such was not the case.

While the Star Line and second Forest City Steamboat Company were still only talking about amalgamation, the rebuffed Captain Freeman N. Weeks, still smarting from the abortive *Emita* charter, was busy translating his personal ambitions into action, and quietly contracted with Nathan Dyer's Portland yard for construction of a light-tonnage steamer. At the same time, wharf builders went to work to improve Weeks Landing, not far from either Forest City Landing or the Greenwood Garden Amusement Park. By the time the little steamer *Greenwood* made her appearance, the calculating Captain Weeks had renewed an agreement with Greenwood Garden owners Captain Charles H. Knowlton and John B. Griffin to provide frequent service between the island park and the mainland. By 1884, Captain Knowlton had relinquished his interest in the first Casco Bay Steamboat Company, being succeeded by local chewing gum manufacturer and towboat owner John B. Curtis. No doubt remorseful at his folly in selling, Knowlton was now merely insuring that an exclusive route to Peaks Island would be denied to "Gummy" Curtis and his Casco Bay Steamboat Line.

The *Greenwood*'s 1887 schedule called for as many as 14 shuttle trips daily between Portland Pier and Weeks Wharf. The new steamer rapidly built up a hefty trade in tourists and city dwellers to the regions's miniature "Coney Island" at Greenwood Garden. Via the combined round-trip steamboat fare and admission to the Garden, for only 25 cents per adult and 15 cents for children, Captain Weeks prospered.

Those golden days of live theater entertainment and amusement thrills on Peaks Island were in full swing now as native-born Bart McCullum packed the Pavilion House to its canvas sides, both daily and nightly at the Park. A talented actor and shrewd entrepreneur, "Mac" brought an

An early study of the sidewheeler S. E. Spring, while on the Saco River Line to Biddeford Pool, reveals that her decorative paddlebox paintwork was altered several times.
McArthur Library, Biddeford

atmosphere of Broadway to Peaks and increased revenues for all concerned. Greenwood Garden Line co-sponsored open-air vaudeville, with acts such as ''Professor'' Carlyle's trained dogs; the European Musical Clowns; or ''Prince'' Leo's breathtaking balloon ascent of 1,000 feet into Maine skies, an event always climaxed by a death-defying parachute descent!

Still another performer, ''Professor'' Oldwie, a much-heralded crackpot, was advertised as able to walk on water. And certainly he did, every day, aided by ''boat shoes'' (which better resembled two covered miniature rowboats) strapped to his feet. But the crowds loved it all the same. Oldwie also engineered miniature mock naval battles with toy warships and skillfully placed fireworks. The battle plan never varied. It always called for a single American warship to boldly and heroically defend the island against an entire invasion fleet of foreign ships. Fuses were touched off by the professor, with throngs cheering from both shore or small craft. Carefully timed shots would ring out, singly at first, then rise to a crescendo as the larger supply of fireworks on the foreign vessels went off, to simulate destruction by the lone American man-of-war.

Other island attractions served to heighten the atmosphere of cotton candy enchantment, as the Forest City rink, built in January 1884, beckoned to youthful lovers of roller skating and also offered dancing, to the music of Welcome's Band, while the nearby Greenwood Opera House produced matinees and Broadway favorites, usually light-hearted musicals.

Passenger traffic for the new Greenwood Garden Steamboat Line grew

until the little *Greenwood* could no longer handle all the volume. The anathema of sacrificing passenger overflow to the Casco Bay Line caused Captain Knowlton and John Griffin to purchase the *Greenwood* and Weeks Wharf at the end of the 1890 season. The thrust of the bargain with Captain Weeks was their argument of financial ability to expand operations and a hint that otherwise they could not see fit to continue the combination ticket so attractive to patrons. The *Greenwood*'s new owners promptly placed her up for sale, with hopes of garnering enough funds for a new and larger boat. This decision soon found the *Greenwood* steaming toward Eastport, just another of many local steamers which eventually made their way to Passamaquoddy Bay. Her career there seems to have been short, for the *Greenwood* last appears in the *Merchant Vessels of the United States Register* of 1893.

Knowlton and Griffin were anxious to obtain a new steamboat, but chanced to cross paths with old rival George Westcott, former president of the Harpswell Line. He, together with business partner John S. Morris and others, had always been associated with the Old Orchard Steamboat Company, and now their smaller secondary seasonal line had come upon hard times. From the joint Harpswell Line/Old Orchard Steamboat offices at 22 Exchange Street, Westcott's immediate proposal was that Captain Knowlton charter that organization's *S. E. Spring*, in lieu of building an expensive new vessel. The *Spring* was of ideal size for the island shuttle run of the Greenwood Garden Line, so Captain Knowlton seized upon the idea and any new construction plans eventually died.

With charter of the sidewheel steamer confirmed, plans to rebuild Weeks Wharf, enlarging this old former Jones Hotel landing at Peaks, went ahead. The name reverted to Jones Wharf, it now being more similar in size to Forest City Landing.

Commencing June 28, 1891, the *S. E. Spring* began running from Portland Pier, leaving for Jones Wharf as early as 6 a.m. and making the round-trip shuttle on an almost hourly basis each weekday until 9 p.m. Then, if the weather was stormy or foggy, the crew of the *Spring* tied up and banked fires for the night. If the evening was fine and clear, however, the old sidewheeler made one more trip to Peaks, leaving at 9:30 p.m. and returning to her berth at about 10:30 p.m. On Sundays, service was offered at near-hourly intervals between 9 a.m. and 6:50 p.m., with no late evening runs scheduled. This year, in addition to the usual round-trip adult fares of 25 cents, the Greenwood Garden Line introduced a "17-ride commutation ticket good on steamer or admission to Garden" for only one dollar. The firm's greatest assets were the commutation and combination tickets, as well as scheuled frequency of trips. These factors offset the disadvantage that *S. E. Spring* landed her passengers a bit farther from the amusement park than the Casco Bay fleet at Forest City Landing.

The Greenwood Garden Line remained successful through the holiday rush of September 1893, but old Captain Knowlton decided that a newer vessel was needed and withdrew the *S. E. Spring*. Unwilling to face termination of a profitable charter, George Westcott began a frantic search for another vessel and thus acquired the steamer *Jeanette*. Then he turned his attention to finding a buyer for the *S. E. Spring*, and the Old Orchard steamer was sold down the coast.

Registered at Boston in 1895, the *S. E. Spring* was altered to increase passenger and freight capacity, and placed on a route from Boston to Baker's Island and Salem for two seasons. When the Baker's Island line acquired a new screw steamer, the old sidewheeler was laid up at Cunningham & Banks Wharf, at the foot of White Street in East Boston.

At the time of the *S. E. Spring*'s Boston layup, an interesting sidelight occurred. Months after the idled *Spring* had been left to rock quietly at her moorings, her old Portland rival, the *Forest City* (ex-*Gazelle*), steamed into Boston Harbor and tied up alongside the former Old Orchard steamer. For several days the *Forest City* lay over at the C. & B. Wharf, on her way to service at Baltimore.

At this point, enter young Chelsea schoolboy, Ernest C. Metcalf. Restless yearning for a seagoing career often led him to haunt the waterfront when he ought to have been in class. Laughingly "hired" on this particular morning by a gruff old captain, amused at the boy's endless questions and avid interest in his lumber schooner, then loading for ports in the South, Ernie took the bait. Rushing home, he secretively packed a black handbag, and was off to boast mightily to all his buddies in the schoolyard about running away to sea! It felt great to be "man of the hour" at noon recess, until a bell-ringing teacher appeared, forcing him to steal off quickly and await "getting underway" that afternoon.

When the sailing hour was near, he proudly threw his black bag down onto the deck of the schooner, amidst the wondering looks of a half-dozen sailors. Ernie then climbed down the wharf ladder, as dignified as his pounding heart and excitement would permit, but only moments later caught a glimpse of his black bag in mid-air going in the opposite direction and landing with a thud on the wharf above! Something was amiss here. Then followed a din of laughter which failed to drown out the loud oaths and curses of the ship's bucko mate, whose big work shoe connected squarely with the seat of Ernie's pants and sent the bewildered lad right back up the wooden ladder! "Ya take that little black bag with ya and get to hell outta my sight, ya damned little ragamuffin, and don't ya come back here no more!"

The words rang in the youngster's ears as he tried to fathom matters. There was no going home ever again, he thought, only to face laughing and gesturing friends who would tease him endlessly. He was broken, crestfallen, and needed solitude. Two old steamboats seemed to beckon him as he passed Cunningham & Banks' dock in the gathering dusk, desolate old hulks to match his feelings and a place to spend the night. Ernie chose the closer steamer after he noticed signs of life aboard the larger craft lying outboard. His free "hotel" was very old and he considered her as dying, just like his own soul. The nameboards proclaimed this haven to be *S. E. Spring*, but he thought little more about the aging steamer.

The evening grew steadily colder, for the winter was not yet past and the steamer's houses were chilled and drafty. Curled up on a bench in the main deck cabin, his misery intensified with the squealing and scurrying of water rats in the hold below. Teeth chattering from the cold and from fear of the noisy rats, he crept topside to the pilot house and tried settling himself into one of its dark after corners. Still he could not sleep and the prospects of spending another hour on the old *Spring* were too much, so the young seafarer beat a hasty retreat homeward. Crawling into his room over the usual roof-top route and through an attic window, the exhausted lad found his bed and promptly forgot his sea career in deep slumber.

Happily enough, the way of the sea did not evade Ernie Metcalf much longer and in later life he rose to take command of the steamship *North Land* on the New York to Portland route of the Eastern Steamship Lines.

A shade less than 45 feet in length, the little Isis *was one of the smallest of all the island steamers, running on the snobbish private line to Great Diamond Island until 1899. This later photograph shows her in service at Boothbay Harbor.* David Crockett

By 1939, Captain Ernest Clifford Metcalf was head of the Maine School of Navigation, thence becoming Executive Officer of the Maine Nautical Training School at Castine, which later became the Maine Maritime Academy.

The *S. E. Spring* left East Boston when the aged and badly deteriorated steamer was purchased for New York Harbor service to City Island in 1901, arriving there under her own steam. Following the 1903 season, the old paddlewheeler was laid up in a Staten Island backwater at Kill van Kull, set afire and burned to retrieve scrap metals.

The successor to the *S. E. Spring* on the Portland-Peaks Island shuttle route was the steamer *Jeanette*, a fairly new boat from the deep South, described in later pages.

The Diamond Island Transportation Company

Isis

Prior to the 1880s, Portland Harbor's Great Diamond Island was populated only by families of itinerant fishermen and a few hardscrabble farmers. Most open land was left to grazing livestock or used solely for the annual harvesting of hay. This placid existence was terminated in 1882, when a half-dozen prominent Portland citizens banded together, believing that the island's shores would make an ideal spot for secluded seaside summer

homes. They were led by E.G.P. Smith of Portland, who first conceived an exclusive summer community "free from objectionable contacts." Inviting James P. Baxter, J.H. Johnson, Seth L. Larrabee, H.W. Noyes, S.L. Lyford, and Edward H. Elwell into his confidence, Smith succeeded in stirring them with his dream. The elite Diamond Island Association was organized to purchase over 200 acres of Great Diamond, finally acquired for about $20,000.

In the spring of 1883, six stockholders built cottages and the Association had an improved channel dredged to old Farm Landing, on the shore facing adjacent Peaks Island. The island had previously been accessible to steamers of the Forest City Steamboat Company only at high water. However, the Association made it known that the summer colony was reserved and that any uninvited strangers were persona non grata. High standards and controlled land sales were strictly enforced. One island store was permitted to do business and one farm family was employed to supply cottagers with fresh milk and vegetables, and also to tend the storage outbuilding filled with preserved ice, an essential summertime luxury. The seasonal club and restaurant, which served as a community social hall for the well-to-do islanders, rounded out the facilities.

The less tolerant among Great Diamond high society frequently complained to the steamboat company of "annoyance from objectionable fellow passengers en route to other islands." Association members, indignant at supposed inaction on their behalf, finally took matters into their own hands. Funds were set aside to establish the membership's own

Diamond Island Transportation Company in 1884, and expensive dredging and construction on the island's inner shore resulted in the private Casco Wharf, a steamboat landing some 400 feet long. Looking to acquire a suitable steamer for the exclusive service, the Association membership was asked to vote on the small, four-year-old yacht-like steamer *Isis*, from Thomaston. Most members were unimpressed with her size and performance, plus the suspected impending need for modification and renovation, but lack of any other available craft that year found them granting grudging approval to purchase.

Those fears of dollar-conscious members of the Association were well founded, and the costly reconditioning was necessary to open the 1887 season. However, in her updated condition, the *Isis* gave good years of service on the Association's shuttle line between Portland and the western shore of Great Diamond. The best description of the company's scheduled service appeared in the *Eastern Argus* of June 9, 1891. The Association's ironclad rules against uninvited guests had relaxed a bit by this time, but perhaps only to aid its boat line, restaurant and store in the matter of survival. The advertisement read: "Diamond Island Transportation Company—On and after Monday, May 20, steamer *Isis* will leave Burnham's Wharf for Great Diamond Island daily (except Sundays) at 6, 6:30, 7:45, 10 a.m., 2:15, 4:30, 5:15 and 6:10 p.m. Returning leave Casco Wharf at 6:25, 7:30, 8:15, 10:30 a.m., 2:45, 5:45, 6:30 p.m. Arrangements for evening sailing parties can be made on board.—J.P. Webber, Captain."

Though busy during summer months, the *Isis* was usually hauled up each autumn, one notable exception occurring with a charter to the Peoples Ferry Company during fall and winter of 1892-93. With the passing years of the nineties, the Diamond Island Association lost much of its former aloofness, and as its social taboos were relaxed, the importance of maintaining a private steamer line diminished. Service by the Casco Bay Steamboat Company to the harbor islands had improved markedly and Great Diamond was included in its schedules, using the improved Farm Landing. Its enforced and protected patronage no longer guaranteed, the Diamond Island Transportation Company was finally reduced to defeat when the Casco Bay Line introduced half-hourly service to the islands for the summer of 1899. The line was abandoned in September and the *Isis* became the property of the Falmouth Foreside Steamboat Company.

In 1901 the *Isis* turned up at Damariscotta, running river excursions before her owner took her to Boothbay Harbor where tourism was more lucrative. Finally converted into a steam fisherman, the *Isis* labored offshore until 1909, when the former "high society" steamer was beached and abandoned to salvage.

The steamer Island Belle *gave the Temple Bros. "5-cent Line" its finest hour in the vain struggle for profits among competing lines to Peaks Island.*
Steamship Historical Society of America

The Temple Brothers "5-cent Line"

Jeanette, *M. & M.*, and *Island Belle*

First brought to Portland under the auspices of George Westcott, to satisfy desires of Captain Knowlton and associates for a better vessel than the old *S. E. Spring*, the *Jeanette* was a bit sturdier, but a smaller vessel. The replacement craft fell short of Captain Knowlton's expectations, and he refused to renew Westcott's charter agreement. This caused Westcott to despair and surrender his lease on the Boston-registered steamer and, with it, his interest in local steamboating expired.

The *Jeanette*'s lease was promptly taken up by the Temple Brothers of Portland, who entered into an agreement with the actual owner, Captain Charles W. Howard of Peaks Island, to put the steamer into shuttle operation. Captain Howard, an ardent steamboat man of considerable genius, was only lately warming to the idea of a local service. Already known as the "father of Rangeley Lakes steamboating," having built and launched the first two steamers in that northern region, Captain Howard and family migrated south each winter, to operate steamboats on the

ANDS.

Both the Eldorado *and* M. & M. *had been outclassed by other vessels in the Casco Bay island fleet well before this photgraph captured them together on the Bath waterfront. Though the* Eldorado *had stayed on for some years, the* M. & M.*'s tenure on the "5-cent Line" to Peaks Island was brief.*
Jane Stevens, from Capt. James Perkins

St. Johns River in northern Florida. Summers were spent in Maine where the family held considerable real estate. They added the Bay View House at Peaks Island as one of their first Casco Bay properties and this brought Captain Howard's nautical talents to the new scene in due time.

While wintering in Florida, Charles Howard first viewed the steamer *Jeanette*, still building on the river bank at Norwalk in 1893. The lack of funds by defaulting owners brought action, as the skipper envisioned a business sideline on Casco Bay. When he bought the new boat and sailed her all the way home to Maine that summer, it was in the face of such adverse sea conditions that the first crew quit and he was forced to hire another at the next coaling stop north of Cape Hatteras. For the *Jeanette*, excursions filled the bill until Captain Howard stumbled onto a better opportunity.

A neighborly alliance with Greenwood Garden interests brought a lease and contract with Temple Bros. Company and the future of the Peaks Island shuttle service seemed assured. With the 1894 season, the new operators began their "5-cent Line." For the 1895 season, however, poor Captain Howard was left "standing on the dock." In fact, his only continuing participation now was in the lease of his Bay View Wharf to the Temple Bros. firm.

The *Jeanette*'s love affair with the "5-cent Line" management was a short one. The Temples felt that they must locate a larger and faster craft if they were to compete against the Casco Bay Line and fortunately they found a boat to meet their requirements in time for the 1895 season. The rugged and speedy *Island Belle* soon arrived, after ill-starred Lake Erie ownership, and her appearance in Portland Harbor saw the end of the *Jeanette*'s charter and her lease as well.

Captain Charles Howard's most misbegotten opportunity sailed through his fingers when the Jeanette *departed the Peaks Island shuttle trade for the St. Croix River. She eventually became the* Kingston *and remained in Hudson River service to the end of her days.* The Mariners Museum

Swift and sturdy, the Island Belle *is shown leaving Bath as a member of the Eastern Steamship Company's connector fleet on the Kennebec River. When she lost favor, Eastern sold her to the Island Ferry Company at Portland for return to Casco Bay.* Jane Stevens, from Captain James Perkins

Another brief and unfortunate contender in the Peaks Island competition was the steamer *M. & M.*, a wayfaring stranger along the Maine coast for decades, odd-jobbing wherever her owners could find a toehold. Built in 1886 at Thomaston for local owners, she came on to be outclassed beyond hope by both the *Island Belle* and the fleet of the Casco Bay Line. Low capacity, at 100 passengers, was the detractor and not speed, for the *M. & M.* could thrash out a remarkable 14 knots without the least effort. Before a season had passed, her operators had learned their lesson and the *M. & M.* retreated to the Kennebec River where she fared better. Eventually she became the *Stockton* of Penobscot Bay and River, long based at Bucksport. Owned by Bennett & Kerst, she was used to start the infamous steamboat rate war against the Blue Hill Line.

The *Jeanette* by 1896 was registered at Calais and operated by the Frontier Steamboat Company on the St. Croix River. The year 1904 saw her sold south to Salem, Massachusetts. Her later history is related in the Wayward Steamboats appendix.

Arrival of the high-stepping *Island Belle* for the "5-cent Line" service was a triumph greatly marred by simultaneous acquisition of two Lake Erie near-sisters by the rival Casco Bay Steamboat Company. Nevertheless, the Temples carried on, counting heavily on the fact that the competition was obliged to service eight different island stops, to their own single landing at Bay View Wharf. But hopes only grew dimmer as Casco Bay Line service excelled, much aided by the smart and comfortable ex-lakers *Eldorado* and *Pilgrim*.

Already subjected to a loss of public support, the "5-cent Line" finally yielded to the superior half-hourly schedule directed by Casco Bay Line's general manager, Charles Goding. With the autumn of 1898, the two brothers abandoned the line and sold their *Island Belle* to the Eastern Steamboat Company of Bath. Off to an interim career on the Kennebec, the *Island Belle* was to return to Casco Bay, for good, some 13 years later. Her story will be resumed in a following chapter.

The Comet *appeared more dignified with her forecastle decked over and a raised pilot house, but her career on the bay ended too soon. Her New York owners later returned the wheelhouse to its original position on the second deck.*
Steamship Historical Society of America

The steamer Alice Howard, *never beloved during her short stay on Casco Bay, appears neglected at South Portland, while awaiting a purchaser in 1901. The seemingly clever use of two old steam sawmill engines, paired to form her homemade compound, proved a serious handicap.*
Steamship Historical Society of America

CHAPTER 10

MORE ROUTES OF THE RIVALS
GREENWOOD SHUTTLES TO GURNET GAMBITS

The Peaks Island Steamboat & Amusement Company

Alice Howard and *Comet*

The "5-cent Line" had no sooner settled its accounts and slipped into limbo than a new organization was formed by the Howard family of Peaks Island and several other individuals. Notably, one of the firm's principal officers was Edgar E. Rounds, who later became a living (and stentorian) legend around Portland with his sidewheel ferryboat *Swampscott*. At this time, Rounds was 43 years of age, and perhaps the island's leading businessman as well as the consummate politician. A visionary also, he was a founder and president of the Peaks Island Water & Light Company. Captain Charles W. Howard managed the family's large Bay View House, a leading summer hotel, and was also proprietor of Howard's Wharf, which gave the new concern an instant landing place on Peaks Island. While Ed Rounds ironed out a leased wharfage arrangement at Portland Pier, the ingenious Captain Howard had a marine railway jury-rigged on the beach adjacent to his wharf and laid a keel for the new company's steamer, relying completely on his own ideas and initiative.

Islanders watched with keen interest as the new steamer daily took shape on its temporary slipway, while the inventive skipper also installed in her a passable home-made compound engine. A cloud of anxiety had formed for curious brass hats at Custom House Wharf, as the homely but seaworthy steamer was launched on May 17, 1899, to a chorus of cheers from crowds along the island shore. Christened after Captain Howard's daughter, the *Alice Howard* soon began the latest of the Peaks Island-Portland shuttle lines. Captain Howard had pursued pre-season charter work, while also handling a temporary U.S. Army service with trips between Long Wharf and Diamond Cove interspersed in the daily schedule.

As homespun as its beginnings may seem, the Peaks Island Steamboat & Amusement Company meant business. Immediately it resorted to the notorious nickel fares that had so enraged the Casco Bay Steamboat Company during the Temples' "5-cent Line" years, an old specter revived once again.

There was business enough to warrant the new company's efforts all right, but the *Alice Howard*'s home-project engine was a heartache. The steamer was no speed demon, but the real thorn was her stubborn crankiness, being hard to fire or steam evenly. For the time being, the owners swallowed their disappointment as their steamer handled the convoluted schedule adequately, if not with the greatest dispatch. At times, it became necessary to substitute Captain Howard's privately owned steam launch *Princess*, held under auspices of the Bay View House, to free the *Alice Howard* for other runs or charters as he and Rounds aggressively sought extra business.

Due to substantial cost savings credited to Captain Howard's personal construction of the *Alice Howard*, the Steamboat & Amusement Company turned a profit in its first season. In October the owners indulged in considerable backslapping as their steamer was prepared for winter hauling-out on her island railway.

The *Portland Directory* of 1900 carried the advertisement: "Peaks Island Steamboat & Amusement Company—5c. Fare—Leave Portland Pier hourly—See daily papers for full timetable—Steamer *Alice Howard*." The company's second season was another success story, although for her part the *Alice Howard* resorted to chronic bad behavior. At summer's end, in 1900, a company meeting found everyone agreeing that Captain Howard should lay down a new, improved steamer. This time, though, a contract would be signed with the Portland Company to build and install the steam plant.

Weeks later, the *Alice Howard* was rudely deprived of her snug winter cradle and floated to a berth at Howard's Wharf. With slipway free, the captain supervised a work gang in laying the keel of his second steamer.

The new vessel was ready for service early in 1901. With two boats, it seemed logical that the Peaks Island Steamboat & Amusement Company might extend its service to include other nearby islands, but such was not the case. The company showed its displeasure with the *Alice Howard* by placing her up for sale.

There were no bids from local parties, too well aware of the steamer's bad reputation. Even so, an interested group from southern Maine and

The Alice Howard *was much better received by the public during her many years on the Piscataqua River ferry crossing from Portsmouth, New Hampshire, to Kittery, Maine.*
Frank Claes

Captain Charles W. Howard and his wife Jennie were well known as proprietors of Peaks Island's Bay View House. The skipper's ownership of the Alice Howard *and* Comet *insured a good flow of tourists to their hostelry.* Howard E. Mosley

New Hampshire showed up to look her over. Days later, the locally rejected steamboat cruised past Portland Head toward a remarkably successful career on the Piscataqua River. More about her later years appears in the Wayward Steamboats appendix.

Completed in ample time for the summer tourist invasion of 1901, Captain Howard's proud little steamboat *Comet* seemed to have everything the poor old *Alice Howard* had lacked. Well-powered for her size, the *Comet* was a trim and perky rig. Captain "Cliff" Randall recalled: "I thought she was going to be a towboat when Captain Howard first built her. She just had the good lines and look of a little towboat!" The Peaks Island Steamboat & Amusement Company's flagship was so named to clear the firm of its old "show boat" image with travelers, and in honor of the 1892 and 1899 passages of Holmes's comet, a newly discovered heavenly phenomenon, observed and studied by Captain Howard from his favorite rocking chair on the Bay View's veranda.

Business for the steamboat lines increased steadily now as the Casco Bay islands, and particularly Peaks, enjoyed their greatest popularity. This local mecca of tourism attracted not only the masses to its 21 hotels and boarding houses, but literary and theatrical luminaries, some near the zenith of their national celebrity and others in the ascendancy toward future fame and fortune. Horatio Alger, Jr., author of stories for America's youth which often appeared in bestselling periodicals such as *Munsey's Magazine* (published by a native Mainer) and many books, summered on Peaks. Broadway producer George M. Cohan cut his theatrical teeth with plays at the Gem Theater, while the same edifice provided early employment for later Hollywood motion picture director John Ford. Actor Sidney Toler, subsequently the Charlie Chan of countless mystery movies, also appeared in many productions on the old Gem's stage.

Events of 1907 saw major reconstruction and enlargement of the *Comet* by the Steamboat & Amusement Company. According to Captain Randall, "They hauled the *Comet* up on the beach down here at the foot of Centennial Street [Peaks Island] and cut her in two. When this was done, they hauled half of her up the beach for 20 feet and rebuilt her with a new 20-foot mid-section and also added sponsons on her." The entire task of cutting the *Comet* in two for lengthening was laboriously done using a simple crosscut saw. The project added a deck over the forecastle, and the *Comet*'s pilot house was lifted aloft and pegged on the boat deck for better visibilty.

In her stylish new mode of dress the *Comet* enjoyed success, but there was a new scheme afoot by several businessmen to enter into a Portland-Peaks Island ferry service of their own, using a larger craft and better facilities. Rebuilding the *Comet* represented the Steamboat & Amusement

Company's best effort to forestall such a development, but did not allow for the tenacity of the new group. Many weeks before the opening of the 1908 resort season in Maine, the new Island Ferry Company completed its steel-reinforced slips, both at Peaks and at Portland Pier. Following on the heels of these events, the formidably large double-ender passenger ferry *Swampscott* arrived in Portland from her former home port of Boston. The rhythmic cadence of the *Swampscott*'s great paddlewheels as she entered ''the Roads'' figuratively played a swan song for the *Comet*'s Peaks Island shuttle service.

Since the ferry line also charged a nickel fare for foot passengers, there was little left for Captain Howard and associates to do but withdraw from competition and attempt to come up with an alternative service. In response, the *Comet* commenced in June to offer frequent daily trips from Portland Pier to Trefethen's (Casino) Landing, farther northeast along the Peaks shoreline, and then on to Long and Cliff Islands. This new run proved satisfactory for a while and greatly pleased the residents at these points. The little company had apparently survived its first round in the battle against oblivion. Long Islanders, especially, were happy with the renewed service to Cushing's (West End) and Marriner's Landings.

But the new schedule was not all that successful financially. Although Captain Howard held that things might work to better advantage in 1909, Manager Edgar Rounds could see no future, in view of service already rendered by the combined Casco Bay & Harpswell Lines. After much dispute over a future course, the two disgruntled principals dissolved the Peaks Island Steamboat & Amusement Company, divided assets and went their separate ways. Ever afterward, Ed Rounds and Captain Howard remained sworn enemies.

When the outspoken Rounds, longtime city councilman, and political ''boss'' of his ward in Portland, just happened to pass the Bay View House at Peaks one day, he roared a few sarcastic remarks up to the sweating Captain Howard, who was re-shingling the hotel roof. The discussion soon reached a fever pitch of obscenities, until, in a fit of rage, Captain Howard reached for the loosened bundle of cedar shingles nearest him and pitched it down on unsuspecting Ed Rounds! The air was momentarily filled with raining shingles, tools and whatever improvised missiles could be hurled at a quickly sobered Rounds, soon out of harm's way down the street, but muttering darkly and shaking clenched fists at his adversary.

It was not surprising that the *Comet* should remain in the hands of Captain Howard, for he had always been the principal owner and more closely associated with the steamer in his duties as skipper. The captain had another plan, revealed in the *Casco Bay Breeze* of June 24, 1909: ''They're talking of running the *Comet* down to Gurnet Bridge via the

The Fairview Casino, built out over the Great Island shore of Gurnet Strait on pilings, shared greatly in the good fortune and revenues stemming from the three steamboat landings close at hand. Its pavilion prospered especially during the years that the Harpswell Line steamers landed next door, and the Comet *helped it survive it even longer.* Stewart P. Schneider

inner route through Merriconeag Sound. If they can come it with the *Comet*, they can do more than the fishermen can always do in motorboats when they get into the tortuous channel northwest of Sebascodegan Island. Perhaps the channel has been dredged.'' The seasonally oriented *Breeze* staff may be excused for not being aware that the small Prince Gurnet passage had been worked over by a steam dredge at the forceful application of Captain Howard.

However, the proprietors of both the Gurnet House hostelry and its neighboring establishment, the cavernous Fairview Casino & Pavilion, just across the Gurnet Bridge on Great Island, had long known of Captain Howard's latest plan and eagerly awaited commencement of the new service. Each of these amusement and tourist-oriented businesses had suffered two seasons of lesser profits and nagging uncertainty after the 1907 consolidation of the two competing steamboat lines landing in opposition at New Meadows River wharves on both sides of Gurnet Strait. For them, the doomsday cake had seemed further iced by abandonment of the remaining line in 1908 and the sale of C.B. & H. Lines' *Sebascodegan*.

Soon afterward, the *Comet* began the Portland to Gurnet route and for many years it was to be her regular run on Casco Bay. This lengthy shore dinner trip became a famed institution, continued in later years by Captain Oscar Randall's small steamers, and finally by Casco Bay Lines.

The well-liked Comet, *second vessel built for the Peaks Island Steamboat & Amusement Company, is shown in her earliest form at Bay View Wharf, Peaks Island. Later she was the first steamer to run on schedule to Gurnet via the inside route through Ewin Narrows.* Captain Carleton R. Morrill

The Peaks Island Steamboat & Amusement Company's greatest assets were Captain Howard's steamer Comet, *which is beached in front of her owner's Bay View House near Jones Landing. At this time, the* Comet's *principal run was the seasonal shore-dinner route Portland to Gurnet, via Ewin Narrows.* Warren N. Graffam Collection, from Hilda Cushing Dudley

By 1910, the *Comet* shifted her home berth to Custom House Wharf. Although control by C.B. & H. Lines was suggested, that firm's secretary Alice Flynn Davis revealed: ''The *Comet* was around then, but Casco Bay & Harpswell Lines never owned or operated her at any time.'' Continuing the route exactly as it had been established two seasons ago, Captain Howard would cast off and back his trim white steamer into the channel daily at 10 a.m. Bound for Gurnet Bridge, he would make two regular stops, at Peaks and South Harpswell, avoiding Great Chebeague and Cliff Islands, but stopping at other landings on a flag signal from the wharf. When the *Comet* made her transit of Merriconeag Sound, left High Head to port and entered the narrow upper reaches of Harpswell Sound, Captain Howard would usually make a stop at Town Landing, North Harpswell, at the entrance to Ewin's Narrows.

Some distance upstream from this wharf, the skipper would signal to the dining room staff of the large Gurnet House inn on the steamer's whistle, sounding one short blast for every ten persons aboard desiring a shore dinner at the hotel. At Buttermilk Cove Landing, passengers climbed the steep slope, by way of a series of graduated and easy staircases, to the imposing wooden Gurnet House. Here a stopover of about two hours was made for dinner and walking tours of the wooded grounds or along the bank for a view of the tide race beneath the old Gurnet Bridge, connecting Harpswell's upper reaches with the New Meadows River. Some ''through'' passengers made motorboat or land connections for New Meadows, Brunswick, or Bath, but most boarded the *Comet* for the trip back over the bay, usually docking again in Portland by 5:45 p.m.

It was as certain as the sudden winds of a summer squall that the *Casco Bay Breeze* would do its best to encourage Captain Howard's steamboat line, since it meant an increase in tourism to the eastern bay. The newspaper's attitude is reflected in an item from the issue of July 25, 1912:

Steamer to Gurnet Running—A 30-mile sail with a shore dinner, and a good one, at the end is attractive enough, but when you add the features obtained on the famous Gurnet trip, the winding through Casco Bay's innermost reaches, the picturesque shores close by, the [innumerable] homes and cottages passed, and the rushing tides of the upper channel before Gurnet is reached, then the charm of the sail becomes irresistible. Take this trip. . . .You will thank us after you have taken our advice.

The summer of 1914 brought brief competition for the *Comet* from a grandiose organization which called itself the Portland, Bath-Casco Bay Rapid Transit Company. We'll delve into its history and adventures later,

Under ownership of the Pearsall Line in her final form and only marginally maintained, the Comet *was photographed on July 19, 1936, near Riverside Drive, New York City.* R. Loren Graham

but the net effect of the whole affair on the *Comet*'s patronage to Gurnet Point was practically nil. At first attempting a cross-bay service over Captain Howard's already established route, this firm had started running the smaller steamers *Tourist* and *Gurnet* to the same Gurnet House landing. On the New Meadows side of the old fixed bridge, the Rapid Transit motor vessel *Alpine* awaited each steamer arrival and then departed in a connector service to the New Meadows Inn at West Bath. The new company's horn-blowing fanfare over a selfless ''People's Line'' was a trip into unreality. It surprised no one when the new line failed before June had run its course.

The following summer, 1915, was a stand-off contest as plans to run the *Tourist* as an independent Gurnet line steamer went ahead, with Captain Oscar Randall at the helm. Captain Howard showed his ire by refusing to bow out of the running. That season the larger *Comet* still carried many more people to and from their shore dinners than the better-advertised, but scandal-tainted, Randall line steamer.

It was said that Captain Charles W. Howard had never had a sick or feeble day since the date of his birth at Readfield, 69 years before. Time caught up with him, however, when on April 17, 1916, he was felled suddenly by a stroke, while busily at work in Frank A. Howard's Portland Pier machine shop, overhauling the *Comet*'s steam engine for another season on Casco Bay. His widow, Jennie, promptly sold the *Comet* to their nephew Frank and the steamer was tied up at the old South Portland dry-dock wharf. Then, in mid-November 1918, a slow-leaking *Comet* filled and sank. It took many unsuccessful attempts before the crew on the tug *Ben Hur* were able to pump her out for repair ten days later. Moored again at her lay-up berth, the *Comet* was soon towed across to the east side of Portland Pier for overhaul at Howard & Horne's shop berth.

The old Howard steamer's boiler and engine were hastily reconditioned by the machine shop staff and shortly thereafter she steamed away to a new career on the Hudson River and New York Bay. The Wayward Steamboats appendix follows up on her New York years.

Although never a true steamer, the motor passenger vessel Alpine *was the first boat to be operated by the Portland, Bath-Casco Bay Rapid Transit Company.*
Steamship Historical Society of America

Captain Oscar C. Randall, whose vision produced the well-intentioned but short-lived Portland, Bath-Casco Bay Rapid Transit Company, stands beside the wheelhouse of that line's first steamboat, the Tourist, *whose forecastle is still not decked over.* Walter T. Randall

The Portland, Bath-Casco Bay Rapid Transit Company — The Randall Line

Tourist, Gurnet and *Anna Belle*

A first step toward creation of yet another steamboat company on Casco Bay was quietly taken in the year 1909. At this time, Captain Oscar C. Randall, a boatman hailing from Peaks Island, invested in an 11-ton motor vessel. The four-year-old *Alpine* had been a gasoline screw yacht owned by the Deering P. Merrill family of Portland, but now became a workaday craft stripped of finery. Captain Randall used the *Alpine* as a charter party boat, at least until 1913 rolled around. By this time he had been able to charter his motor vessel to the New Meadows Inn at West Bath for use in a private hotel passenger service. Her summer operation between the old steamer *Comet*'s terminus at Gurnet and the riverside inn further upstream led Captain Randall to plan a sweeping takeover of the entire route between Portland and New Meadows. He reasoned that his own firm might quickly supplant Captain Howard's *Comet* through superior equipment, gained by public sale of stock, and an operating policy distinctly slanted to favor patrons of the line.

In the process of forming his organization, Captain Randall associated himself with George Winfield Brown. Although employed as a bank messenger, Brown also headed the Diamond Island Casino and swimming-pool complex, located at the Little Diamond Wharf. "Windy" Brown, as he was known to those who disliked him, had a feel for money matters and a careful eye peeled for the quick buck. He proved just as apt at psychology. Along with the usual blocks of shares for sale to investors, he placed an additional large number of shares in escrow for a unique future dole to those customers who best patronized his freight and passenger service.

Aided by Harry L. Cramm, both Captain Randall and Brown superintended the sale of bonds, commencing in mid-1913. His most enthusiastic buyers were islanders from the Diamonds and Long Island, although purchasers included a representative number from all across the bay. By early November, their treasury reached $100,000, and the new company was incorporated as the Portland, Bath-Casco Bay Rapid Transit Company. Having rented an office in the First National Bank building on Exchange Street, president Captain Oscar Randall, treasurer Brown, and secretary Cramm next were faced with securing additional tonnage, more substantial than the company's lone motor passenger boat *Alpine*. Though the Rapid Transit officials had near-utopian plans, they first chose to have one small steamer constructed on a trial basis and go ahead on a second vessel if the first met expectations.

Veteran steamboat engineer Ralph Bailey of Falmouth remembered:

When they had the *Tourist* built, I went down to Boothbay Harbor with Oscar Randall. The Reed Brothers shipyard people there told him the hull by itself would cost $1,800 with regular lumber, or he could pay an extra $100 and pick out the lumber himself! Well, we picked over all the oak timbers to insure there was no cross-grain stuff. Even at that time he talked to them a good deal about having another one like her built in just a short while. Anyway, those yard people got to figuring ahead, I guess, so when Oscar called up about a second boat, they had the *Gurnet* already built and waiting. Now you know they'd gone and built her out of all that lumber we rejected from the *Tourist*! And she cost more to boot!

By the time the steamer *Tourist* arrived at the company's dock on the west side of Portland Pier, it was too late in the year to launch the intended cross-bay route, so the new boat was placed instead on a shorter interim service, competing with C.B. & H. Lines as far down as Long Island. The speedy 12-knot *Tourist* quickly gained acceptance.

In spring 1914, the *Gurnet* joined her sister in the limited island service. Although the *Gurnet* had been completed somewhat larger in dimensions and tonnage, and could muster additional horsepower over the *Tourist*'s steam plant, her "built from odds and ends" stigma left the *Tourist* widely considered the better craft. Captain "Cliff" Randall, retired C.B.L. skipper and nephew of Captain Oscar, recalled that "the *Tourist* and *Gurnet* were both good little rigs when they first came to the bay. They had no decks over the bow then, only a narrow walkway around the pilot house. On the chunky side, maybe, but sturdy, and with all the hard usage they got over the years, they had to be just that!"

The summer season of 1914 was intended to be a stellar one for the Rapid Transit Company, and began with a burst of advertising and editorial fanfare from the accommodating pens of the *Casco Bay Breeze* staffers, though a portion of half-truth can be credited to George "Windy" Brown.

An advertisement appeared in the *Casco Bay Directory* of 1914-15 (issued by the publishers of the *Breeze*):

The New Steamboat Line for Casco Bay is distinctively the People's Line—and is being run in the interests of the people. The steamers of the Portland, Bath-Casco Bay Rapid Transit Company will ply regularly between Portland & New Meadows (or West Bath) via Gurnet Bridge...taking the inside route through the New Meadows and Gurnet Rivers. It has or will have landings at Portland Pier; Forest City and Trefethen's, Peaks Island; Little Diamond Island; West End [Cushing's] Landing and Doughty's, Long Island; Cliff Island; Chebeague; Harpswell; Bailey; Orr's; Gurnet Bridge; and New Meadows. Excursions will be run daily to Gurnet and New Meadows where ample time will be allowed to secure one of those now-famous shore dinners and connect with Kennebec, Bristol and Boothbay boats, by electric and steamcars to Bath, Rockland, Brunswick and all points on the Maine Central Railroad. This sail from Portland to New Meadows is one uninterrupted stretch of panoramic beauty and grandeur, unsurpassed by anything of the kind in New England. This company owns 3 fine boats: The *Tourist* of 225 passengers capacity is fast, staunch and beautiful; the *Gurnet* of 250 passengers capacity is the same model, only 2 feet wider. These 2 boats and the *Alpine* having a passenger capacity of 125, will be at the service of the people of Casco Bay continuously. Fast times and frequent trips will be the order. The company contemplates the building of two larger boats, 100 feet in length, 400 passenger capacity, each with an ability to speed 15 to 16 m.p.h. They are to be named *City of Portland* and *City of Bath*. No freight is to be carried on these passenger boats when its handling will interfere with the passengers' service...baggage and express handling...only, at landings other than terminals.

As might be guessed, the advertisement was duly signed by George W. Brown, Treasurer.

Brown insisted on referring to his plan of profit-sharing as "the great secret of success of this new line," whereby passengers might share in profits they themselves produced. The primary gimmick was the commutation ticket. Purchasers of these $1, $10, or $100 tickets were given a bonus of 10 percent of the ticket price in preferred stock. Bondholders, as well as preferred stockholders, would receive a firm 10 percent yearly on the investment value, but in commutation tickets rather than cash.

Wherever possible, Brown attempted advance payments in these tickets to avoid the 6 percent interest rates then established. There was only a vague promise of year-end dividends when earned and payable.

The Rapid Transit Company was not able to achieve the all-encompassing route it had ambitiously announced in the *Casco Bay Directory*. The expected landings at Forest City, Great Chebeague, Cliff Island, Harpswell, Bailey and Orrs Islands failed to materialize, stymied by growing lack of confidence in a company so incredibly unrealistic.

Starting on Saturday, June 27, 1914, the Rapid Transit Company inaugurated its first full summer schedule. With Captain Randall handling the *Gurnet* and Captain Walter Kennedy at the helm of the *Tourist*, one of these steamers would leave Portland Pier each morning at 6 a.m. to touch at Little Diamond Island, Fort McKinley Wharf on Great Diamond, as well as West End and Doughty's Landings on Long Island. Again at 7:45 a.m. a steamer departed, this time omitting Fort McKinley, which was not picked up again until much later in the day. Similar departures from Portland were made at 9:45 a.m., 1:30, 3:30, and 5:30 p.m., this last one again calling at Fort McKinley. P.B.-C.B. Rapid Transit opted for a night service to island landings, an arrangement always shunned by Casco Bay & Harpswell Lines and its predecessors. Two such runs were made, daily and Sundays, at 9:30 and 11:20 p.m, making all stops mentioned above and adding Trefethen's Landing at Peaks Island.

The company's intended mainline service to Gurnet, New Meadows and waylandings finally emerged on July 1 as merely a non-stop 9 a.m. shore dinner trip to Gurnet each Sunday with connection from there to New Meadows via the *Alpine*. It seemed a poor alternative to the daily line still run by Captain Howard and the *Comet*. The fortunes of July and August set the trend—a downward spiraling which immediately threatened company survival. The end came suddenly, climaxed in scandal when George Brown, more aware than anyone of the impending collapse, packed up all available funds from the enterprise and hurriedly left town for parts unknown! This stunned the two remaining officials as much as the victimized investors and hurled the Rapid Transit Company headlong into bankruptcy and seizure by the United States Marshal. The steamboat line which had proclaimed "everybody a stockholder and a friend" had left its loyal investors grinding their collective teeth!

Taken aback by disastrous events and personal loss of some $15,000, Captain Randall paced through the essential legal processes, refusing to believe that his dream was dead. In an attempt to salvage enough floating equipment to establish a limited operation, he was aided by his brother-in-law, Walter S. Trefethen, also of Peaks Island. When the U.S. Marshal's sale at public auction was held in the autumn, the two bid successfully

Except for a more enclosed main deck, this view of the Gurnet *renders some idea of her original rig. She is seen here off Scituate, Massachusetts. The steamboating dilemma on Casco Bay in 1919 prompted her return to Maine waters.* Willis H. Ballard and Steamship Historical Society of America

A passenger on the Tourist *snapped a photo of Captain Oscar Randall as he toured the decks. The well-known skipper always poured his heart and soul into steamboating on Casco Bay.* Walter T. Randall

on the *Tourist*. They watched with little sentiment as the *Alpine* went to Captain Walter Kennedy, who intended using her in bay charter and excursion work. What crashed down on their hopes was finding themselves vigorously outbid on the steamer *Gurnet* by a Massachusetts party boat operator.

After a long winter lay-up, the *Tourist* emerged in the spring of 1915 for another crack at the local route. Meanwhile, the *Gurnet* had made her way to Bay State waters and a second career of excursions and party fishing from Scituate and Plymouth harbors. No effort was made to rename her either, particularly as daily runs frequently took her past famed Gurnet Rock Lighthouse off Plymouth. Only a strange set of circumstances some five years later would reunite these two Randall steamers in island service from Portland Pier.

Offering service as far "down bay" as Long Island with the *Tourist* from late spring all through the summer season of 1915, the revived Randall venture scored successfully. Poor maintenance and upkeep had rendered the opposition C.B. & H. Lines' *Maquoit* in sad shape and "slower than cold molasses," as her crew bemoaned. Her schedule called for her to arrive at Long Island by 7:30 a.m., after departing Harpswell at 5:15 a.m., but it proved impossible to get there on time. Consequently, the little *Tourist*, which now made a nightly layover on the southwest side of Cushing's Landing at Long Island, was waiting there to take on the entire Diamond Roads crowd of island working people bound for the city. With this sort of encouragement, it was decided to run the *Tourist* year-round.

Unfortunately for Captain Oscar, the *Maquoit* had been brought back to peak performance for the 1916 season, and he could no longer make severe inroads into the C.B. & H. Lines passenger traffic. That government officials favored the Randall line as a reliable transportation link to Casco Bay military fortifications was small consolation.

The *Tourist* finished up in autumn with earnings substantially down, forcing Captain Randall to think about a renewed daily Gurnet line, now abandoned by the Howard interests. Then the *Tourist* could resume a Portland to Long Island and waylandings circuit each long off-season, adding a bonus of island night service.

By July 1917, Captain Randall had scheduled a new routine for his steamer. An advertisement which first appeared in the *Casco Bay Breeze* during June and was repeated weekly tells it best:

The Famous Gurnet & New Meadows Route—Effective July 1st—steamer *Tourist* leaves West Side, Portland Pier at 9:15 a.m., touching at Forest City Landing and Trefethen's, Peak's Island; Ponce's and Doughty's Landings, Long Island; Chandler Cove [fish wharf], Great Chebeague; Wilson's Landing, Orr's Island; and North Harpswell arriving at Gurnet 12:20 p.m.; connecting with boats for New Meadows Inn. Returning, leave Gurnet at 2 p.m. touching at all above landings arriving in Portland in ample time to connect with steamers and trains. Circuit trip by boat and trolley: $1.50; Round trip by boat to Gurnet: $1.00 Captain O.C. Randall, Manager.

At long last, the Gurnet line worked favorably for Captain Oscar and became the summertime forte of the *Tourist* for a considerable span of years. The captain soon had his financial affairs back in order, to the extent that, in early 1918, he bought out the remaining interest in the *Tourist* from Walter Trefethen. Then, with an itch to get back into the nearer island trade, which had eluded him in summer while the *Tourist* ran to Gurnet Bridge, he set out in search of a second steamer. This brought back to Casco Bay an aging, but thoroughly rebuilt, *Anna Belle* (ex-*Percy V.*) of the old MacDonald Line. With the newly acquired vessel he re-entered the Portland-Long Island fray against a none-too-pleased Casco Bay & Harpswell Lines.

Of all Casco Bay steamers, the *Tourist* was allegedly the first to sound her whistle in a long salute to victory and peace on Armistice Day at the end of World War I. Three weeks later Captain Oscar had less cause to celebrate as he became blinded by a bright beam of light directed at him during his landing at Government Wharf, Little Diamond Island, and the *Tourist* smashed head on into the dock, claiming a substantial section of wharf timbers, knocking off the vessel's stempost nearly to the waterline and otherwise damaging the bow. The *Tourist* was unharmed below the boot-topping and took no water, but her 200 passengers were obviously shaken.

Meanwhile, Captain Randall became displeased with the elderly *Anna Belle*'s performance. She served him mainly as a spare boat, spelling the *Tourist* for repairs or bunkering while he continually scouted the coast for a better craft. The only nugget of progress was his successful ten-day charter of the Damariscotta steamer *Tourist* (later *Sabino*) on Monday, December 16, 1918, to run until his own *Tourist* was permanently repaired.

The July 8, 1919, legal tie-up of C.B. & H. Lines should have been a golden opportunity for Captain Randall to place his two steamers into the sudden breach in island service. But the *Tourist* had been doing impressive business on Gurnet shore dinner trips while the Long Island and waylandings route of the *Anna Belle* had been curtailed for several weeks after chronic boiler and machinery trouble forced Captain Oscar to lay up the old steamer. He did his best to aid stranded islanders, short of making chaos of his own business. That afternoon, when the *Tourist* returned from Gurnet, he made three additional trips to nearer bay island stops before banking fires for the night. Then on that same Tuesday evening, members of a special Portland city government committee paid him a call and succeeded in arranging cancellation of his Gurnet trip the next morning. Instead, the *Tourist* ran a special 9:15 a.m. trip from Portland Pier carrying food to all island stops on the C.B. & H. Lines route.

On Thursday, July 10, the *Tourist* commenced carrying freight and passengers for Cliff Island, South Harpswell, Bailey, and Orrs Islands en route to and from Gurnet Bridge. In the evening, Captain Randall took three shorter trips as far as Western Landing, Great Chebeague Island, and return. The next morning C.B. & H. Lines got underway again, propped up by receivership, but late fall and winter operation of the libeled fleet was out of the question. Captain Randall set his sights on all the extra passenger and freight trade that would be his if only he could obtain another reliable steamer.

In late August, the tide of fortune turned with news that the *Gurnet*'s Massachusetts owner, Captain Edward E. Edson, had passed away. His widow had left the former Randall steamer idle and up for sale. The matter was reported in the *Daily Eastern Argus* of September 2, 1919:

Passenger Steamer *Gurnet* Coming Back to Portland—Portland is to have another passenger steamer. Captain Oscar C. Randall having purchased the smart little steamer *Gurnet*, formerly owned by him but which was sold from here some 5 years since to go to Scituate, Massachusetts. . . .The *Gurnet* is now undergoing clean-up and painting for return to service here. She was built for the Portland to Gurnet route and will probably return to that run another season as she is a speedy little craft [and] just what is wanted on that route.

Captain Randall left for Boston by train on the night of Monday, September 15, taking an engineer and deckhands, and returned up the coast with the *Gurnet* late the next day.

With two dependable steamboats in a roster of three, the captain resumed his commuter line by placing the *Gurnet* in service to Long Island. Keeping the *Tourist* in the profitable Gurnet excursion trade for another week, he took fullest advantage of the fair weather remaining. Then the *Gurnet* continued alone, while the *Tourist* tied up at the Williams Brothers float for a quick overhaul. After the scheduled demise of C.B. & H. Lines on September 30, Captain Oscar placed both steamers on island runs to the bankrupt company's landings, but this arrangement ended with lay-up of the two vessels before winter weather set in. He had rid himself of the troublesome *Anna Belle*, selling her to an eager Peaks Island Ferry Company, which promptly overhauled the elderly craft for extra Peaks and nearer islands service.

In 1920, the Randall steamers came on early but the rejuvenated firm at Custom House Wharf, now named the Casco Bay Lines, was ready to get underway by April, and this meant a return to normal operation for the *Tourist* and *Gurnet*. With both the Gurnet Bridge line and the local island business doing nicely during the warm summer months, Captain Randall enjoyed substantial profit over the 1920-21 period, thanks particularly to the shore dinner long popular with Maine coast vacationers. A typical dinner of this time included lobster stew or fish chowder, both steamed and fried clams, a lobster (or two, if desired), rolls and butter, pickles, and a hot or cold beverage. The meal was topped off with a dessert of ice cream, usually referred to as ''frozen Danish,'' and layer cake. The cost of the entire meal ranged from 75 cents to $1.25.

An engineering characteristic of Captain Randall's two steamers was the open boiler/engine space, allowing the same man to tend the boiler and operate the engine. One feature especially favored was the keel condenser, employed in place of the hated contraption pre-cast on the engine frame of larger island steamcraft. Said retired engineer Ralph Bailey:

Enjoying an excellent reputation for its shore dinners, the Gurnet House was served daily in season by direct steamboat lines from Portland. Photographed about 1909, the Gurnet House was destroyed by fire just before World War II. Barbara D. Munsey

Factual and informative, a 1915 advertisement for the steamer Tourist *gives the passengers all the information they need for a delightful day afloat.* Maine Historical Society

While the Tourist *went over to Casco Bay Lines soon after the demise of Captain Oscar Randall's steamboat services, the* Gurnet *remained laid up for sale. Eventually, she too joined the Casco Bay Lines fleet.*

I was with Oscar Randall on the *Tourist* for quite a while and, although those keel-pipes were simpler affairs, we had to guard against them freezing up when the sea water got real cold during the winter. We used to take and mix up a bucket of pickle [sea and feedwater combined] and take it into the discharge line by the vacuum suction. This was called 'salting the condenser.' We did this at night and then when we got the plant going again in the morning, the first thing we did was pump this 'pickle' overboard so not to get it into the system.

Oscar Randall hadn't always been lucky in the steamboat business and, after being strapped for cash more than once, he tried every way he could to keep his costs down. One thing he did was go over to Maine Central coal docks often as he could to buy cheap coal dredged off the bottom or cleaned up around the loading areas and sold cut-rate by the dory load. But the trouble was that, besides colliers, the sulphur ships used to come in there to discharge every so often.

Well, this dory-coal was sometimes full of sulphur chunks the size of a lemon. Now when we fed this coal into the boilers on the *Tourist* and *Gurnet*, that sulphur would burn and melt and

cause the worst and biggest clinkers you ever saw! I've seen them almost as big as a small suitcase! I'd have to be working steady to break these things up in the firebox and what a nuisance that was! Whenever I could, I used to take and shovel a batch of this coal out of the bunkers and onto the floor plates and wash it down with a hose to get the sulphur out of it and then discharge the mess out the ash ejector. I finally got mad enough to go over there and tell off old Frank Trott, the guy that sold dory-coal. I said to him, 'Don't you leave any more of that stuff in there! We want half-decent loads of coal for those boilers.'

Captain Oscar's nephew, George "Cliff" Randall, came to work for him and took over one steamer while his uncle commanded the second boat. Captain "Cliff" was a welcome addition to the personnel, but with this one piece of luck came two bad strokes. First, the *Gurnet* became hard to steam, and both her speed and efficiency sank to a point where she was a grave nuisance, much as the old *Anna Belle* before her. Second, Captain Oscar had contracted rheumatoid arthritis and it took firm hold, causing considerable pain and lameness. After much urging, the skipper was finally convinced that he should forego his life on the water.

After a round of negotiation with C.B.L. president Edward B. Winslow in early autumn 1921, Captain Randall closed a fair deal by selling the steamer *Tourist*, with rights and franchise to routes. The *Tourist* was at once incorporated in the Casco Bay Lines fleet, but Winslow displayed little immediate interest in the *Gurnet*, so the slightly larger Randall steamer was laid up at her Portland Pier slip.

Captain and Mrs. Randall used the proceeds of the *Tourist* sale to buy a farm at Scotter's Hill, near Scarborough, and the following spring they began raising raspberries. But Captain Oscar's condition worsened enough to prevent him from working his crops. Realizing that both he and his wife Nellie might do better in a warmer climate, in 1924 he again went to Winslow and pressed Casco Bay Lines' principal owner to purchase his steamer *Gurnet*. This time Ed Winslow was sympathetic to Captain Randall's arguments and within days the *Gurnet* was on the marine railway for repairs and reconditioning and the C.B.L. fleet had again increased by one more steamboat.

For their part, the Randalls then sold the Scotter's Hill farm and purchased a fine central Florida home with several large citrus groves, where Captain Oscar remained until his passing. Born in Boston, but a resident of Peaks Island from infancy, he had played and worked on the water from the earliest opportunity. Later he fished for a living, and made many winter merchant sail trips to Cuba and the West Indies as seaman or cook and eventually as mate. Ownership of a succession of sail fishing and party vessels finally led Captain Oscar to invest in his first powered vessel, the 35-foot launch *Tourist* (I), a namesake of his later steamboat. It was said of him: "Captain Randall knows the sea in all its phases. . . loves and fears its tremendous power. . . never overstepping the bounds of good judgment. He will not take a back seat for any of the old sea dogs in nosing his way around in a fog; he just intuitively chugs his way into the desired location."

With steam up, the Neptune *gets underway from T-Wharf on another harbor sightseeing tour. The East Boston waterfront forms the backdrop on this hazy summer day in pre-Depression times.* The Peabody Museum of Salem

CHAPTER 11

LESSER LINES
SOME LEFTOVER REMNANTS AND
STEAMERS OF THE EVENING

The Steamer Lines of Captain Kennedy

Mary Jane (later *Neptune*)

Another of Casco Bay's lesser yet significant steamboat ventures owed its inception to a spring 1890 launching at Noank, Connecticut, of the little steamer *Mary Jane*. Designed for the Long Island Sound oyster fishery, the *Mary Jane* spent only a short time in this trade before being sold in 1893 to Captain William H. Kennedy of Portland. The new owner wasted no time converting her into a lobster smack by adding a large open saltwater well in the stern for the carriage of live lobsters.

The lobstering industry suffered several poor seasons along the Maine Coast in the late 1890s, and when meager catches were coupled with a sudden slackened demand during the Spanish invasion scare of 1898, Captain Kennedy decided to keep profits alive by moving to New Brunswick waters to obtain smack business there, placing the *Mary Jane* under British registry. Her operation along the Fundy coast ended with a return trip to Portland in 1900, the elderly owner himself at the helm, following purchase by the Burnham & Morrill Company. Continuing her smack duties, she also performed towing chores in the area of the company's plant at the entrance to Back Cove. In 1904, the *Mary Jane* was sold outright to Canadian operators and left the local scene for more than twelve years, again registered as a British vessel.

Meanwhile, Captain Kennedy's son, Walter, had been actively employed by Captain Oscar Randall's Portland, Bath-Casco Bay Rapid Transit Company during its brief interlude on the bay. His experience ranging from deckhand to both engineer and skipper, he served with enthusiasm until the firm's collapse in 1914. Then, arranging a loan, he was able to post the highest bid on the motor vessel *Alpine* at the United States Marshal's sale. With this boat, he carried on a brisk charter excursion business. Because his earliest working days had been on his father's little *Mary Jane*, Captain Walter always thought highly of the old steam smack,

keeping track of her whereabouts. Thus, when he learned in 1917 that she was up for sale, he made his offer and brought the *Mary Jane* back to Portland once again.

To make use of her in his passenger operations, the younger Captain Kennedy rebuilt the *Mary Jane* with a second deck and a boat deck, planked over the old lobster well, raised the pilot house to the new second deck and extended the main deck house forward. However, the old smack lacked cabin space and her pilot house had the look of being set a bit too far aft. Her new profile found numerous island people referring to her as the "Old Boot."

Once the *Mary Jane* was readied, Captain Kennedy commenced a regular run from Custom House Wharf to the old Sunset and Hamilton wharves on Great Chebeague Island and thence to Mere Point. Flag stops were also made at Mackworth Island, Cousins, Littlejohn, Bustins, and Birch Islands. From the beginning, Captain Kennedy and his steamer operated trips that Casco Bay & Harpswell Lines (and later Casco Bay Lines) did not want, due to poor patronage. Because of her small size and capacity, the *Mary Jane* was ideally suited for this "clean-up" business. On this particular run, the former steam smack supplemented the ever more curtailed schedule of the larger *Maquoit* on the Inner Bay route. In order to round out earnings and carry his business in spite of slow days on the regular freight and passenger schedule, Captain Kennedy ran charter excursions in the off-hours during seasonable weather. For a time, Kennedy's steamer found regular employment during the off-season by taking the C.B. & H. Lines' lower Peaks and Long Island service each November, whenever the *Merryconeag* was transferred to the Orrs Island winter run.

No doubt the *Mary Jane*'s greatest claim to fame came with the traumatic summer season of 1919. When the legal embargo of Casco Bay & Harpswell Lines suddenly took paralyzing effect, the Kennedy Line was burdened with more passengers and freight volume than it could safely handle. On the day immediately following the tie-up at Custom House Wharf, Captain Kennedy ran his usual route, but found it impossible to

The tiny steamer Mary Jane, *sole guardian of the cross-bay run to Bailey and Orrs Islands through the autumn and winter of 1919, is shown as she appeared during her last year on Casco Bay as the* Neptune. R. Loren Graham

call at any additional nearer island stops. The next day, however, other emergency arrangements had been made and the *Daily Eastern Argus* of July 10, 1919, stated: "Captain Kennedy's little steamer *Mary Jane* is now making one trip daily to Bailey's, Cliff, Orr's and other points in the lower bay, carrying down great quantities of provisions and other supplies in addition to passengers." With a temporary settlement of the C.B. & H. Lines dilemma assured, the *Mary Jane* made one more trip to Orrs Island and waylandings on Friday morning and then returned to her normal Inner Bay schedule in the late afternoon.

A little more than two months later, as the Tuesday, September 30, deadline marking the official end of C.B. & H. Lines operations neared, grave public uncertainty arose as to whether any sort of organized service would be offered to the more remote Casco Bay islands. Since Captain Kennedy's steamer line was in no way connected with the larger bankrupt company, and by coincidence ran from the same terminus, the *Mary Jane* was in the best position to become a temporary transportation link.

Until the assets of the old company could be bought up and reorganized under a new corporate title, Edward B. Winslow himself became vitally interested in an interim steamer to handle the needs of the eastern bay, but with his own hands legally tied could do little or nothing to remedy the problem. Knowing that the ferry *Swampscott* would bring

Peaks Islanders through the crisis handily and that Captain Randall's steamers would continue covering the old stops as far as Long Island, Ed Winslow offered Captain Kennedy his private support and abundant persuasion. The details were soon ironed out and the *Mary Jane* was overhauled and prepared to provide the necessary run to the outside route stops beyond Long Island. When that infamous Tuesday finally arrived, the *Argus* reported: "Following the layoff of the C.B. & H. Lines steamers, the only vessel which will depart from Custom House Wharf will be the little *Mary Jane* which will make one round trip daily between Portland and Orr's Island."

Very few old Casco Bay steamboat men were richer in stories and memories than Ralph Bailey of Falmouth, who spent his youth on Little Chebeague, growing up in a world where these old craft were the indispensable backbone of communication. He made them his life's work, laboring down below in the engine spaces and fire rooms of virtually every island steamer from the old *Merryconeag* on down the roster to the tiny *Admiral*. Of the smaller vessels he worked on, he vividly recalled Captain Kennedy's steamer. In a most entertaining 1969 conversation, he went on about her:

I started in firing on the *Mary Jane* the winter of 1919, when she ran in place of the regular boats. Captain Kennedy ran her. When I first went on there, the engineer was John Cross. He was a brother to the governor. Well, he took sick after a while and that's how I got that job. I could tell you a story about that boat! She had an upright boiler in her and she didn't carry too much water. She carried enough to get down to Orr's Island and back, though, easy enough. But a lot of times we used to like to blow the boiler down and clean it, you know. Well, you'd eject about enough water to get up steam again the next morning. That winter they were cod fishing there at Orr's—some at Bailey's, but mostly at Orr's—and we loaded 27 barrels of codfish on *Mary Jane*'s upper deck. Well, she was just an old steam lobster smack that had been rebuilt and this was too much cargo for such a small boat.

Well, we left and went to Mackerel Cove, then started across to South Harpswell. It had been an old smoky sou'wester blowing, you know. Well, Captain Kennedy kept her head to as long as he dared to but, gosh, he had to bring her off in order not to run down on Haskell's Island. Just about as he started to bring her round and make for Potts Harbor, two or three big old waves come in there and she rolled down to her guards and came back all right. Then she rolled down more the second time and about that time

Later to become the Sabino, *the steamer* Tourist *sports her original rig in this early photograph at the South Bristol docks.* Steamship Historical Society of America

those barrels of fish took to sliding and shifted on the upper deck. The third time she rolled down far enough that water came down the companionway from up topside and she just hung like that! I'd already reached in and shut the throttle down—I never thought she'd make it! I grabbed a life preserver and I was going out through a window on the upper side. Well, somehow that son of a gun came back onto her feet! I never thought she'd make it, but she came back all right. She still had a hell of a list, but we got those barrels back in place and distributed all right.

Only one thing about that whole affair struck some of us as comical. Walter Kennedy had a bureau down forward, same as you'd have in your bedroom, where he used to keep his clean clothes. We also had down forward one of those old-fashioned wick oil burners to cook on. I happened to go down and look and two of them bureau drawers had come out with his clean clothes in them and dumped into a pile on the deck—and that oil stove was right bottom-up on top of the business! Kerosene had soaked right down through everything. Boy, didn't he dance and rave over that, he was so mad!

We used to go down to Orr's and, once we got everything done and shut down, we'd go up the hill to John Boyce's little pool parlor. That was the only place to go on Orr's in the winter. Old John, he sold ice cream. He used to get it from West End Dairy and we took it there on the boat, all packed up so to keep it from

melting. The dairy didn't advertise it as ice cream, they called it 'frozen Danish'—to be more stylish, I guess. The only trouble with John's place was he didn't have any hot water to wash dishes with. He'd take a dirty dish and 'souzle' it down in this bucket of cold water, then fill it with ice cream and pass it to you. It cost a dime a dish, you know. Well, after awhile the water in that bucket would get so thick you could stick your finger in it and leave a hole! Kennedy and I would go up to get some ice cream and he'd say, 'C'mon now, John, take that bucket on over there to the well and fetch a fresh bucket of water and then we'll have some ice cream. Otherwise, we won't have none!'

All that autumn and throughout the winter of 1919-20, the *Mary Jane* ran regularly on the Orrs Island line. The following April, a newly reorganized Casco Bay Lines resumed the eastern bay run and the *Mary Jane* was laid off for repairs and painting. By reason of its declining patronage, C.B.L. hedged at reopening the Inner Bay line service until the height of the summer season. It then became a seasonal run only, and remained so until 1923. Captain Kennedy was standing at opportunity's door this time and didn't even have to wait to knock! Immediately, he put the *Mary Jane* back on her old run, but on an expanded schedule which saw her operating all the way to Harpswell Center landing and neatly substituting for the lack of service by Casco Bay Lines. From then on, Captain Walter and his steamer did well during most of the year, but

The Williams Bros. steamer Admiral, *soon after her conversion from naval steam launch, approaches Jones Wharf at Peaks Island, while in service on the Cape Cottage-Cushing Island-Peaks Island run.* Peter T. McLaughlin, from Warren N. Graffam

suffered marginal returns when the much larger *Maquoit* came on the run each summer. The fact was, the *Mary Jane* was never very popular among island folk, who were leery of her because she was so small and narrow of beam. The inevitably well-spread story of her near-capsizing in Merriconeag Sound certainly won no friends for the little vessel.

In an effort to improve his steamer's reputation and make her more attractive for summer business, Captain Kennedy made numerous alterations, then changed the *Mary Jane*'s identity for the 1922 season. The old boat reappeared bearing the more innocent name of *Neptune*. This ploy did not work and the Kennedy line experienced another bad summer. The long off-season months that followed were nothing to brag about, and when spring approached in 1923, Walter Kennedy had had enough of attempting to build a prosperous steamboat line by struggling against the strongest tides of fortune. He abandoned service and sold the *Neptune* south, to the Dixon Steamship Company of Boston. This placed a burden of responsibility on Casco Bay Lines to provide some sort of service and, the company put its steamer *Maquoit* on the run several weeks early to fill the needs of year-round residents. That autumn, C.B.L.'s *Tourist* came on the run, sometimes briefly supplemented by other boats such as the *Gurnet*, *Sabino*, or *Nellie G.*, and later the motor mailboat *Edward B.*

Employed next as a Boston Harbor excursion vessel, the *Neptune* ended her days as a fishing party boat out of Boston and finally Scituate Harbor on the South Shore; she was abandoned in 1941. The Wayward Steamboats appendix contains more on her Bay State career.

The Williams Brothers and Island Evening Lines

Admiral *and* Sabino

Following the end of World War I, two Portland brothers, well established in marine repair work, decided that a small steamboat business might provide them with a profitable sideline. This notion prompted Harry and Fred Williams to purchase a 13-year-old naval steam launch at a government surplus sale. Cradled on the dock near their float landing and machine shop at Custom House Wharf, the small craft was altered and enlarged.

When relaunched and christened *Admiral*, in deference to her U.S. Navy service, the owners had widened her beam by adding sponsons, extended fully to the stempost, and had spliced on a new six-foot fantail stern section. A squat, boot-heel pilot house and a canopy deck from stack to stern lent her as much of a passenger steamer appearance as could be mustered.

Commencing with the summer of 1919, the Williams Brothers steamboat line offered daily service from Cape Cottage to Cushing Island (which satisfied a contract with the islanders' cottage association), then continued on to Forest City Landing at Peaks. Connections with steamers from all across the bay tapped into tourist crowds wishing a day's outing on Cushing or at the extremely popular Cape Cottage Park. Located on a rocky shore at the entrance to Portland Harbor, this ''trolley park'' was adjoined by both Fort Williams and the historic Portland Head Lighthouse. Visitors could enjoy a delicious shore dinner at the Cape Shore Inn (originally the Cape Cottage Casino) while admiring a beautiful panoramic view of the Casco Bay islands and the open sea beyond. A fine bathing beach and spacious park grounds enhanced the spot even further. The passage from Peaks to the park contributed most to the *Admiral*'s success in her first season of summer operation.

Early that September, the *Admiral* made her last run of the season and tied up at Custom House Wharf, but her owners soon placed her in temporary service on the South Portland ferry line, while they installed a larger compound engine in the regular ferry steamer *Lottie and May*. On the morning of Thursday, September 14, 1919, the *Lottie and May* took up her run once again and the *Admiral* returned to berth, idled for the winter.

The line from Cape Elizabeth to Cushing and Peaks Islands waned in popularity as years passed, continuing a decline which had virtually ended mainline steamer stops at Cushing Island since the great fire that destroyed its famous Ottawa House in 1917. No new hotel had replaced this huge rambling old mecca, so greatly favored by generations of well-to-do Canadian vacationers. Casco Bay & Harpswell Lines had naturally opted to cut back its schedule, forcing Cushing residents to contract with Williams Brothers for regular service.

The early 1920s brought discontent and disagreement between the *Admiral*'s owners. Captain Harry, who had taken the lion's share of interest in the steamboat line and skippered the *Admiral* for much of the time, held ambitions of expanding this end of the business. Fred, on the other hand, preferred to tend to the machine shop and chafed against diverting their attention away from the profitable marine service they had started in 1908. When in 1921 Oscar Randall chose to sell off his steamboat company's rights and properties, Captain Harry urged a takeover, but brother Fred opposed it firmly. Both Randall steamers eventually joined the Casco Bay Lines fleet and the opportunity for Williams Brothers to get into steamboating on a larger scale was lost.

By 1924, the *Admiral* was doing poorly on the Cape Cottage-Cushing-Peaks Island route, mostly because of superior summer schedules by Casco Bay Lines and the ferry *Swampscott*. Cape Cottage could be reached indirectly by larger, more comfortable steamers, if islanders decided to ride one of the regular fleet in to Custom House Wharf and then take a trolley or motor car.

The bleak outlook only caused Fred Williams more disenchantment. Captain Harry could sense futility also, but he had hatched out another steamboating plan. The new scheme failed to impress brother Fred and discord reached its peak, so the two men divided their interests, with Captain Harry taking the *Admiral* and steamer line. Fred acquired the entire Williams Brothers machine shop business, which continued to prosper and even survived into the 1980s as a division of Gowen, Inc. on Maine Wharf. Sold by Gowen owner Joseph Schmader in the mid-1980s, the firm became a division of the Brookline Machine Corporation, and was still a going concern in 1993.

Captain Harry began his so-called Island Evening Line and discontinued the original service in face of great displeasure among Cushing Islanders. While Captain Williams's Evening Line still made three Cushing stops each Tuesday and Friday, residents were left to find their own regular daily transportation. This situation was eventually rectified when Captain Williams chartered the small gasoline motor vessel *Paul* to become the chief link with the mainland, and later purchased this ex-naval liberty launch to fulfill island cottagers' association needs exclusively. In 1925, having acquired the old Randall office space and wharfage rights on the west side of Portland Pier, Captain Williams transferred his firm there. What he now operated was essentially the same old night line once

It is an August day in 1924 as the smart little steamer Sabino *approaches the wharf at Popham Beach. Her new layout was most becoming until tampered with later at Portland.* Willis H. Ballard

run by the Randall steamers to Little Diamond Island, Trefethen's and Evergreen Landings at Peaks, Fort McKinley on Great Diamond, and Long Island's Ponce's Landing. Casco Bay Lines still had not chosen to serve any of these stops during the evening hours.

As part of his expansion plan, the captain purchased and reconditioned the former South Portland steamer *Lottie and May* to handle charter excursion work and act as a standby vessel. This proved timely when almost immediately the little *Admiral*'s 19-year-old Navy standard compound engine and boiler wore out. Captain Harry and Fred cooperated long enough to reach a solution, something almost unheard of. After removing the *Admiral*'s faulty engine and boiler, they unpacked from its shipping crate the first marine diesel engine ever used on the Portland waterfront. A Bessemer three-cylinder model, it was carefully installed in the *Admiral*, and the news caused many a head to turn as the dieselized steamer rumbled across the harbor on trial runs.

On Captain Williams's night line, trips normally departed Portland Pier at 7:15, 9:15, and 11:15 p.m., the fare to Long Island being 50 cents and to all other islands 25 cents one way. Its boat still usually referred to as "Steamer *Admiral*" at this time, the line prospered for more than

The Island Evening Line just a memory now, Captain Cliff Randall backs the Sabino *slowly away from her new berth at Custom House Wharf as the* Maquoit *precedes her down the harbor channel. It is August 4, 1935, and the* Sabino *has been owned by Casco Bay Lines for only 12 days.* R. Loren Graham

a decade to come. Now Captain Harry's fine success allowed him to hire a second skipper to help operate the *Admiral*. Captain George "Cliff" Randall, already a veteran on bay steamers, spent his earliest working years as a fireman on the ferryboat *Swampscott*, then went on to serve as deckhand, mate and skipper of the *Anna Belle, Tourist* and *Gurnet* while employed by his uncle, Oscar Randall.

A robust program of charters and regular excursions filled most morning and afternoon "lag" time prior to the *Admiral*'s three regular evening trips down toward Long Island. Now a year-round business, daily low-patronage trips in place of larger steamers to Peaks Island over the cold months kept the line active, thanks to cancelation from the schedule by Casco Bay Lines. Night line business kept right on booming until the 1927 season proved that one steamer could no longer handle all the passenger volume alone.

Due to narrow beam and limited passenger capacity, the *Sabino* was hard pressed to meet the greater demands of the Portland operation, so she was rebuilt for the 1929 season by adding hull sponsons and creating a narrow main deck walkaround outside the original house and hull line. The upper deck retained its older contours, helping to spoil the *Sabino*'s proportionate lines, but the alterations made her more profitable during subsequent seasons.

Captain Williams's charter business played an active role in the company's success in the late 1920s. Captain "Cliff" Randall recalled:

I had the *Sabino* back on the Kennebec during the visit of the frigate *Constitution*, making special trips out there to "Old Ironsides." We stayed there three days, running from Bath City Landing down through the bridge to the anchorage, chartered out to a Mr. Jackson. On the last day of the charter, we were all having lunch on Front Street when Harry called up. He was having real trouble lately handling traffic with only the *Admiral*, so he told me to get going and get the *Sabino* back to Portland for the 11:15 p.m. trip. By gorry, we made it, though! When I came out of the river to go out by Seguin it was in the middle of a thunderstorm. I headed her for Portland, but before I'd gotten off Fuller Rock, it began to shut in thick afog and I never saw another thing till I got to Portland Head Light! It was the cussedest time I ever had with her! She was the handiest little boat, though, because I could throw 150 lbs. on her boiler and go anywhere.

Captain Harry now needed two crews to handle the *Sabino* throughout each long summer day, so he moved the younger Captain Randall to the night shift and hired Captain William Cushing, former skipper of the ferryboat *Swampscott*, to handle daytime trips. Captain Randall remembered that it usually fell to his crew to bring the *Sabino* over to A.R. Wright Company's dock and coal her up whenever necessary after the last run at night.

On Thursday, March 1, 1928, the *Admiral* began an unusual week-long charter to Casco Bay Lines under Captain Bert Stockbridge, in place of the crippled steamer *Tourist*. Purser Willis Ballard remembered:

> In the last week I was with C.B.L. we had the hard luck to wind up a lobster warp in the wheel as we left Little Diamond and had to be towed to Bennett's Wharf at South Portland to beach out. As a result, Captain Bert and I had to take over the Williams Brothers' *Admiral* for our trips, with one of the brothers at the engine. It seemed as though it was low tide all that week, as the little boat was always practically under the wharves and at times I had to set up a short ladder instead of a gangplank! What a change when I left her for my billet as Purser aboard the steamship *Jefferson* at New York, on Eastern's Old Dominion Line to Norfolk!

The bitterly cold Wednesday morning of January 16, 1929, with jammed pack ice all over the harbor, found the *Admiral* running close in toward the west shore of Peaks to find any signs of open water, when she struck and ran hard aground. The risk of being battered by the ice was ever present, but little damage occurred before the steamer floated free on a later tide.

With two vessels in service, the Williams operation was known informally as "Steamer *Admiral* and *Sabino*" until 1934, when it officially became the Island Evening Line. For the next two years, though business remained good, costs rose and the *Sabino*'s numerous alterations to suit traffic demands cut deeply into profits and caused Captain Harry considerable worry. Feeling the pinch financially, he decided to surrender the business, keeping only the *Admiral* for himself, and the Island Evening Line properties and franchise were transferred to Casco Bay Lines ownership on Tuesday, July 23, 1935.

The next adventure for the *Admiral* was conversion into a fishing boat in 1936. Captain Harry had taken an interest in fishing and the role apparently suited him well. He probably would have maintained his ex-steamer as a fishing craft indefinitely, had the United States Army not requisitioned the *Admiral* in 1941. Used as a shuttle ferry and supply boat between the Army's Custom House Wharf depot and harbor island forts, the *Admiral* donned dark gray paint for the next four years of war service, as did her much larger cousin, the steamer *Aucocisco*. At war's end, when the *Auco* came back to Casco Bay Lines, the company also purchased the little *Admiral*, intent on placing the dieselized steamer right back on her old night line runs.

The Falmouth Foreside Transportation Company

Nellie G.

As unpleasant as the depression years were to most people on a national scale, they were all the more dreary a time for the cottagers and residents of many Casco Bay inner route islands. The once very profitable South Freeport Division, established by the Harpswell Line in 1904 and then carried on by both C.B. & H. Lines and Casco Bay Lines in their turn, had disintegrated into a seasonal and irregular service. The indifferent service prompted a Falmouth father-and-son team to take action. Already proprietors of the Falmouth Foreside Garage and a small bus line, Captains Oren R. and Walter E. Swett set out to remedy the islanders' plight. In the autumn of 1932, they purchased the tiny steamer *Nellie G.* and added her to the assets of their Falmouth Foreside Development Company, originally formed in 1925.

Far from a new boat, the *Nellie G.* was a veteran of both Kennebec River and Boothbay Harbor service and more about her earlier years appears in the Wayward Steamboats appendix. Skippered by one or the other of the Swetts, the *Nellie G.* began running from Town Landing at Falmouth Foreside in May 1933, and calling at the steamboat landings at Cousins and Littlejohn Islands, then finally the Old Stone Wharf

Before coming to Casco Bay to run for the Falmouth Foreside Development Company, the Nellie G. *had served as a logging towboat and a shuttle ferry. Seen here in the 1920s, she carries a capacity crowd between Boothbay Harbor and the posh resort haven of Squirrel Island.*

The Falmouth Foreside Transportation Company's Nellie G. *is en route from Great Chebeague back to the Foreside in a view taken from the deck of the regular Casco Bay Lines inner route steamer.*

(Hamilton's Landing) on the west side of Great Chebeague Island. The 75-passenger *Nellie G.* returned over the same route to the Foreside. She ran regularly to Great Chebeague, with waylandings, until her little compound engine and boiler gave out later in 1933 and was removed at Handy Boat Service, Falmouth Foreside. With the early spring of 1934, after spending the winter months afloat, and frozen-in since January at her mooring off Handy Boat Service, a menacing crush of ice was seen to be threatening the *Nellie G.*'s safety as it slowly swept seaward with wind and tide. Alarmed at the prospect, her owners notified the Coast Guard at Portland, resulting in a mercy dash to the area by the cutter *Harriet Lane.* Freed by maneuvers to create open water around her, the *Nellie G.* then followed the *Lane* to Portland on a towline, rendered by the government in deference to her currently engineless state. Snatched from harm's way and deposited along side the Williams Brothers machine shop float, the *Nellie G.* had her first thorough reconditioning at Custom House Wharf. Then, in place of the old plant, the Swetts had a 40-horse-power gasoline engine installed and put the *Nellie G.* back in the seasonal service without delay. Her formerly black smokestack, retained in conversion to allow a dry exhaust system, soon received a "sunrise buff" paint job with a wide black topband, a custom borrowed from the Williams Brothers' own dieselized *Admiral*, not to mention Casco Bay Lines' *Emita* and *Gurnet.*

The *Nellie G.*'s island route was augmented, incidently, by the Swett bus line, which provided a convenient service between Town Landing and the Portland Bus Terminal at 616 Congress Street, using a pair of 7-passenger jitney "busses."

Over the decades of the 1930s and 1940s, many other local skippers shared the *Nellie G.*'s tiny bootheel wheelhouse with Captain Walter Swett (Sr.), as Captain Oren grew older and resorted to the management chores ashore. Among them were old-timers like Captains Warren Doughty, Clinton and George Cleaves, Alfred H. Hamilton, and former long-time steamer *Maquoit* skipper, Captain Prescott Taylor.

Few changes in the *Nellie G.*'s appearance took place other than a 1938–39 winter facelift caused by raising the pilot house out of the cockpit. The cockpit was decked over and the wheelhouse built up to adequate height for the helmsman. Not only a handier arrangement for making landings, the change presented the tiny vessel with a more proportionate layout. The opportunity to do this presented itself during an East Boothbay hull reconstruction project performed on the *Nellie G.* by boatbuilder Paul Luke. Here was a re-building finally made necessary by the honestly basic and informal maintenance program of a hands-on operation that was economy-minded for survival. Improvements to the dieselized steamer's passenger cabin, at the same time, were also well-received by patrons when *Nellie G.* re-entered service the following spring.

In August 1938, the old Development Company became Falmouth Foreside Transportation Co., Inc., under Captain Walter Swett and Captain Alfred H. Hamilton, and service was augmented that summer by the *Victory*, a wooden gasoline-powered vessel of similar size and layout, purchased that spring at Bar Harbor. While more detail on this firm's later, exclusively "oil screw" operations will be set down in a future volume of this chronicle, suffice it to say here that by the spring of 1946, the new *Nellie G. III*, a wooden diesel-powered vessel had been completed at Friendship that year. This new craft, named by the Swetts in unusual deference to the old *Nellie G.*'s former owners (who already had a 1930s-built *Nellie G. II* in service on their Squirrel Island ferry line) at Boothbay Harbor, took immediate prominence on the Casco Bay route. *Nellie G.* was forced into spare-boat status and her condition went downhill until she was hauled out for survey and lay-up in the autumn of 1951.

The following spring, Captain Walter, with sons Walter Jr. and Paul, were unpleasantly surprised to find that their old steamer's stern section had pulled away from the main body of her hull as they attempted to tow her free of the lay-up cradle in the cove just east of Handy Boat Service. The stunning evidence of weakened structural integrity, especially in light of *Nellie G.*'s declining importance to the Swett operation, spelled doom.

Although sold on the spot, supposedly for local freighting duty, in May 1952, the little ex-steamer lay dormant. The new owner, Theodore Taplin of Falmouth Foreside, finally floated her to Underwood Landing. Deemed, by now, to be of no further use, the *Nellie G.* was stripped down and then burned to retrieve her remaining scrap metal.

Following a remarkably brief sojourn on the Peaks Island route in the mid-1890s, the steamer Louise *next offered the traveler a unique round-trip excursion from the Portland waterfront to Riverton Park at Westbrook, via the Presumpscot River.* Willis H. Ballard

Queen of the Presumpscot between Pride's Bridge and the Lower Falls was the Santa Maria, *which connected with the Presumpscot River Steamboat Company's line from Portland Pier.*
Willis H. Ballard

CHAPTER 12

STEAMBOAT COURSES INTO LIMBO AND MORE STEAMBOATS EAST OF HARPSWELL

The Presumpscot River Steamboat Company

Louise, Santa Maria, Sokokis

In 1895, another steamboat venture was established at Portland Pier. With dockage on the west side, officials took delivery of their steamer *Louise* in June. Constructed at South Portland, the slender, cabin-enclosed two-decker was lighter than most bay boats and resembled a steam yacht.

The new line commenced scheduled shuttle service to Peaks Island in the face of overwhelming odds and was soundly trounced in one season. But the stubborn owners held firmly to the Portland Pier facility and their unlucky steamboat. Knowing that the new amusement park at Riverton would be opened the following year for its premier summer season, and aware of an upriver steamer operation already in existence, they evolved a plan for a three-segment Presumpscot River line.

With the *Louise* ready to handle the lower river, harbor and bay run, the Presumpscot River Steamboat Company was incorporated in the autumn of 1895 and ordered a second boat. Built as a link between river dams and townships, and considered a pioneer in her mid-river portion of the trade, the new steamer was given the historic name *Santa Maria*.

On June 20, 1896, Riverton Amusement Park opened its gates and the steamboat *Louise* provided a pleasant alternative to carriage or electric trolley car. Then, to further promote travel via the scenic Presumpscot River, the middle route commenced on July 4, as reflected in an *Eastern Argus* advertisement:

Presumpscot River Steamboat Co. Steamer *Santa Maria* will leave Cumberland Mills, foot of Warren Avenue dock, Sundays included, for Prides Bridge (Riverton Park), West Falmouth and Lower Falls and Pleasant Hill at 10 a.m. and 2 p.m. To make close connections with the steamer, take Westbrook electrics leaving Preble Street at 9:10 a.m. and 1:10 p.m. Leave Riverton Park for

all landings downriver at 10:30 a.m., 2:30 p.m. and 4:30 p.m. [making] close connections with Riverton electrics, leaving Portland at 9:30 a.m., 1:30 p.m. and 3:30 p.m.

Passengers coming upriver aboard the *Louise* could transfer to the *Santa Maria* and cruise from Prides Bridge to Cumberland Mills. There, at the lower dam, carriages transported them another mile to a wharf above the upper dam at Dana Warp Mills, where the launch-style steamer *Sokokis* waited to take them on a five-and-a-half-mile journey as far as Mallison Falls, below South Windham village. The river circuit made by two cooperating companies, one somewhat removed from Casco Bay's salt-water steamboating, soon combined in the parent Presumpscot River Steamboat Company.

The operation began with Captain Joseph H. Haselton, original owner of the *Sokokis*, who started the upper river Westbrook-Mallison Falls line in 1893. The *Sokokis* had been built at Portland that year, with a hull of finely varnished cypress wood, crafted at the waterfront yard of shipwright Joseph Dow. Built-in seats around the open-air hull cockpit perimeter, augmented by camp chairs in the center of this surprisingly roomy welldeck, allowed a capacity load of 125. The trip to the river's edge was made on skids pulled by struggling ox-teams.

Maine's noted street railway historian Charles D. Heseltine offered a plausible explanation for the attempt to make steamboating up the far reaches of the Presumpscot a business success:

We presume that the citizens of Pleasant Hill and West Falmouth areas would make use of the *Santa Maria* for shopping trips to Westbrook's retail district in the nineties, because there was no street railway for convenient transportation into Portland. Same applies to *Sokokis* for those living in the Little Falls area of Gorham or at South Windham, hence these small river steamers might have been of considerable value.

Photographed at the old Mallison Falls pavilion, the Sokokis *was the third steamer in the chain of Presumpscot River connecting vessels.*
Steamship Historical Society of America

The *Sokokis* survived eight years of operation over her 11-mile route, making three trips daily except Sunday, often brushing against the dense growth of trees only a foot or so off the banks of the winding stream as she made her way to and from the upriver landings at the Falls proper and the pleasure pavilion. Old Captain Haselton and son Joseph Jr. were noted for their ''seat of the pants'' navigation of the unlighted amd unmarked waterway, through even the darkest night or densest fog. Whenever dances at the pavilion required special round trips or moonlight sails, piloting was done by ranging on familiar trees, aided by searchlight. All the river runs were limited to the warm months, since year-round service through ice and harsh elements was beyond the capabilities of the unprotected river steamers.

In 1897, both the *Louise* and *Santa Maria* were withdrawn in the face of trolley competition and sold. Each was hauled overland by ox teams, and (reportedly) then by railway flatcars to Sebago Lake for Captain Charles Goodridge, the Lake Region's leading steamboat entrepreneur. The *Sokokis* continued to operate the upper river segment, however, for another four years, until the extension of the electric railway from Westbrook to South Windham ended her popularity.

Charlie Heseltine recalled:

I always wondered if old Captain Joe Haselton might have been some distant relative of mine—twenty-third cousin or some such thing—but what I found so very interesting in the defeat of the river steamboat trade by the street railway electric cars was one jocular little fluke I remember from quite awhile back. No doubt, many trolley employees had pleasant memories of riding on steamers like the *Santa Maria*, and oddly enough this boat was at least informally celebrated when the Portland Railroad roster turned up a maintenance-of-way utility sand car christened 'Sandy Maria'!

At Sebago Lake Station the *Santa Maria* and *Louise* were placed in service to the Songo River across Sebago Lake, then through Songo Lock, across the Bay of Naples (Brandy Pond), thence the length of Long Lake, making waylandings as far north as Harrison. Not long afterward, each was rebuilt and enlarged, with wide sponsons and sheathed guard rails adding to their formerly slender beam. Still later, main deck cabins were enlarged and pilot houses raised aloft to the second deck. The *Louise* was renamed *Longfellow* until 1901, when she was hauled out to sacrifice boiler and engine to the new lake steamer *Songo* and abandoned. The

The Presumpscot River Line's Louise, *one-time Peaks Island opposition boat, attained considerable popularity after she went to Sebago Lake. After two rebuildings she eventually emerged as the* Longfellow *and is seen approaching a retractable drawspan across the Songo River.*

Peter T. McLaughlin, from Warren N. Graffam

Santa Maria would appear to have taken the name *Hawthorne*, but this possibility and her exact fate is uncertain, although her demise probably occurred by 1912. The *Hawthorne* is known to have been dismantled that year, to provide a boiler for the new steamer *Goodridge* of 1913.

For her part, the *Sokokis* was sold and again moved overland, skidded in a cradle over the frozen snow-covered ground of early spring in Maine, right through the downtown streets of Westbrook. Supervised by Lorenzo Knights, the labor took no less than four pairs of horses and twelve teams of oxen, working almost two days, to drag her to the water's edge at Back Cove. Following a season as an excursion boat, then lay-up at Widgery's Wharf in Portland Harbor, came a stint of fishing excursions, running daily parties to the cod grounds, ten miles out to sea. The local career of the *Sokokis* ended one bitterly cold winter night when she suddenly capsized at the wharf under the weight of tons of snow and ice. Raised in the spring of 1905, she was sold for ferry and towing duties out of Perth Amboy, New Jersey. In 1913, her harbor chores at an end, the *Sokokis* was abandoned, to disappear within the huddle of many another old wreck beneath the tidal backwaters of Staten Island.

The Stroudwater Steamboat Company

We Two

Certainly a short-lived enterprise, the Stroudwater Steamboat Company fielded its tiny launch *We Two* in the mid-1890s. The owners did indeed mean business, in spite of the shallow waters of their rural river route and an even shallower level of patronage. The company's advertisement for its schedule, commencing on the first of May 1895, stated that its steamer would be "daily (Sunday included) making a round trip every hour from 9 a.m. to 6 p.m., giving you one of the most beautiful sails of 10 miles for 25 cents. Take streetcars to Stroudwater from Post Office, Munjoy Hill, and all steamer landings and railroad depots."

Of the standard open steam launch type, the *We Two* departed from a canoe club landing just above the old Stroudwater dam. The little vessel's statistics were never listed in MVUS Registers and are lost in the obscurity of time. An estimate would place the company's tenure at no more than two seasons, that of 1895 and perhaps 1896.

The name of the Lilliputian steamer We Two *commemorated the owner-partners shown seated aboard her. They ran their Stroudwater Steamboat Company in earnest, but lack of public interest left them sadder and wiser men.* Willis H. Ballard

Placing the Mineola *on the Bailey Island-Gurnet route took great faith on Captain Ed Archibald's part. He was largely influenced by family ties on Orrs Island, chiefly the encouragement of Harpswell Line purser Jud Webber. The line proved to be a sentimental folly, after all.* Frank Claes

In common with several minor lines, the career of the Stroudwater Steamboat Company was brief, but wherever an apparent gap in service existed, various steamboat concerns attempted to fill the void. In the eastern bay, for example, the collapse of the MacDonald Line in 1903 did not end the desire of residents for regular service beyond Orrs Island. The first such venture seemed as sound and well-equipped as any on Casco Bay. Others were far less a match by any measure, and one steamboat company never got past the planning stage at all.

The Gurnet Steamboat Company

Mineola

An endeavor headed by Captain Isaac (''Ed'') Archibald of Port Clyde, the Gurnet Steamboat Company began auspiciously by using Captain Ed's own spare Portland-Rockland steamer, the *Mineola*. Since the new route was merely a connector with the Harpswell Line at Bailey Island, the limited business between this tiny village and Gurnet, with waylandings, found the *Mineola* too large for the route. At the time, she outclassed any other steamboat on Casco Bay.

The new company was first heralded in the July 7, 1904, issue of the *Casco Bay Breeze*:

> Sunday last, the *Mineola* of the Gurnet Steamboat Company made her first trip of the season, leaving Mackerel Cove at 7:40 a.m. This new line will make two round trips, taking in Gurnet Bridge, North Harpswell, Orr's and Bailey Island. With such a fine steamer as the *Mineola*, we see no reason why this water route should not in time, be a success. The schedule is as follows: Leave Gurnet Bridge daily at 10:15 a.m. and 6 p.m. Leave Bailey Island at 7:40 a.m. and 1:30 p.m.

The *Breeze*, always loyal to steamboat men, threw its full support behind the Gurnet Steamboat Line. Its charitable observations aimed at boosting the new firm but there was really precious little more it could say. The effort of the Gurnet line was a good study in the possibilities of running the tortuous route above Ewin Narrows and through Prince Gurnet channel (marked only by bush stakes) with a sizable vessel. There were intricacies involved in navigating this stream, even with the aid of sound local knowledge, to the little wharf on Buttermilk Cove at Gurnet Point. The experience was not lost in the later ventures by Captains Charles

A gasoline engine has supplanted the neat little steam plant she once had, but this view still gives a fair idea of the Jule's *appearance while she served two successive New Meadows line firms.* The Peabody Museum of Salem

Howard and Oscar Randall. The last feeble reference to the line appeared in the July 21 issue of the *Breeze*, under the Bailey Island column: "Mr. & Mrs. Chester Sinnett, with their son Chester, enjoyed a sail on the *Mineola* to Gurnet Bridge Tuesday last."

By the end of July, the *Mineola*'s operation had proved such a dismal failure that she was promptly removed from service. With the Gurnet line abandoned, Captain Archibald sought to recoup his losses. He immediately chartered the *Mineola* to the Portsmouth-Isles of Shoals line for the balance of the 1904 season and the entire summer of 1905.

The New Meadows Steamboat Company

Jule

As the 1905 season neared, Captain Ed Archibald showed interest in a steamboat service for the easternmost portion of Casco Bay, but was much wiser after his Bailey Island-Gurnet folly of the previous year. He had since acquired the ex-steam yacht of famed actress Julia Marlowe at Boston and had the craft rebuilt for passenger service. Retaining her original name of *Jule*, this little steamer was set to begin service in early summer for the captain's newly formed New Meadows Steamboat Company. The objective, at first, was to provide connector service from Bailey Island to the eastern shore of Orrs Island, then to Cundy's Harbor, Sebasco, and Gurnet Bridge.

The new business was feasible because of the *Jule*'s small size. As usual, the *Breeze* did its best to promote prosperity with an entry in its June 8, 1905, issue: "The New Meadows Steamboat Company are having their steamer put in readiness for the summer travel and will soon be running on scheduled time. They will surely be welcomed and, we hope, well patronized, so that the efforts of the company to please and accommodate the public may be given the appreciation they are due." The New Meadows Line was to enjoy success, although both ownership and basic route were altered a number of times.

Following its first change of ownership, the New Meadows Line suffered a setback in 1907, when both the Harpswell Line and Casco Bay Steamboat Company extended service to the area. The little *Jule* could offer no competition against the through-service steamers *Merryconeag* and *Sebascodegan*, so a rescheduling of her run was made forthwith. That year she began a connector line from Gurnet to Small Point, with waylandings at Cundy's Harbor and Sebasco. To this was added a novel and ambitious foray of another nine miles around Small Point and on to the Kennebec River entrance, where the *Jule* landed at the Eastern Steamship Wharf with its long boardwalk leading to the massive Hotel Rockledge, her passengers' usual destination, overlooking the sands of Popham Beach.

This run proved a suitable alternative during the brief reign of the *Merryconeag* and *Sebascodegan*, but 1909 editorials of the *Casco Bay Breeze* could only lament the larger vessels' absence, while chafing for someone to take up the Portland route once more. Its voice did not fall on deaf ears, for the owners of the *Jule* were game to try their hand at a once-daily trip to Portland across Casco Bay, the most arduous service the little ex-yacht ever attempted. The morning run would begin on the lower New Meadows River and arrive back there late in the afternoon.

Prudence Johnson of Bailey Island fondly remembered her passage on the *Jule* during the summer of 1912. Then a little girl, she boarded the "cute little steamer *Jule*" with her father at Cundy's Harbor. At about 8 a.m. the steamer, having already come from Sebasco, cast off and steamed to the southward. Once the calls at Lowell Cove, Orrs Island, and Mackerel Cove at Bailey Island had been completed, the *Jule* then headed across Merriconeag Sound with about 20 passengers bound for the port city. Mrs. Johnson remembered with some humor that while her own "sea legs" stood her in good stead that day, most of the women became very seasick as the little steamer rolled and pitched into a stiff wind and choppy seas. Much to their relief, they reached Portland and made a landing at Long Wharf by 10:45 a.m. Most of the passengers seemed very happy to take leave of the little *Jule*, despite dead low water and a steep gangplank, as well as the doubtful footing of a sloping, irregular walkway on the old wharf. Allowing a three-hour stopover for shopping or errands, the captain of the *Jule* blew his two-blast departure warning and backed the steamer clear at about 1:45 p.m. Mrs. Johnson recalled that the steamer touched at the same landings on the return voyage and that she and her dad were ashore once again at Cundy's Harbor in good time for an ample supper of her mother's good old-fashioned country cooking.

During the *Jule*'s Portland line service, the New Meadows Steamboat Company also continued its seasonal run between the New Meadows Inn,

Sebasco, Small Point and the Hotel Rockledge at Popham Beach, using the trim motor cabin launch *Allequippa*, built at Bristol in 1902 and first operated on the Damariscotta River. A gasoline screw vessel, the *Allequippa* was highly popular with guests of the old New Meadows Inn.

Years before being sponsored out and reduced to odd-jobbing as a passenger and freight boat, the *Jule* was documented at Boston in 1900, then at Damariscotta from 1910 and at Rockland from 1915, even though operating that year on a cross-Casco Bay service route from Portland's Long Wharf for the successor Sebasco Transportation Company. In 1925, the registered home port shifted to Portland, despite ownership by Warren P. Fassett of Bristol. In 1927, the *Jule* became the property of the Ethridge family, surrendered her old steam plant for a new gasoline engine, and went over to the Boothbay Harbor-Pemaquid line. Here, she lived to honorable old age, being finally abandoned in 1941, more than four decades after her launching in 1899 at Weymouth, Massachusetts.

The Peoples' Steamboat Company—
Ghost Line of Casco Bay

Strong misgivings kindled the emotions of Harpswell people over the steamboat consolidation of 1907, uniting their favored and highly successful Harpswell Steamboat Company with the nearly bankrupt Casco Bay Steamboat Company, an indication that bay travel would never again be as efficient and accommodating as it had become since the turn of the century. The tide of dissent, strengthened by cutbacks in C.B. & H. Lines schedules for 1908, produced action. In the August 20, 1908, issue of the *Casco Bay Breeze*, a solution was published:

Peoples' Steamboat Company Organized At Harpswell—New Line Elects Officers And Applies For Charter—Plans Being Made For Summer And Winter Service To Casco Bay Islands—In a month's time, a new steamer line may be running in Casco Bay if the plans of the recently organized Peoples' Line at Harpswell are perfected without delay. The movement has been on foot for several weeks and a great deal of quiet work has been done on many islands.

The final meeting was of considerable interest. It was held at Seaside Hall, Orr's Island, last Thursday evening at which officers were elected and organization papers applied for at Augusta. The capital stock of the company will be $50,000. . .with a par value

The rugged steamer Mineola *of the Eastern Steamship Company fleet, soon after the Portland-Rockland Line was sold out by Captain Isaac Edson Archibald.* Steamship Historical Society of America

of ten dollars and it has been announced that one or two fast steamers will be immediately procured and, if possible, the line would begin operations in two months or less, giving winter and summer service.

The officers elected Thursday were as follows: Dr. Leon L. Hale, Chebeague—President; John E. Osborn, Orr's Island—Treasurer; John B. Keough, Portland—Clerk; Directors: Dr. Hale; John Osborn, Henry Allen, Orr's Island; Almond A. Quimby, Chebeague Island; William L. Purington, South Portland. To these will be added Lendall M. York and Everett E. Sinnett of Bailey Island, and Thomas F. Flaherty of Cliff Island.

Early in the evening there was a mass meeting in which about one hundred were present, and when it was asked how many of these would support the line, all were said to have stood up. It has been announced that the sale of stock has been excellent and that shares unsold are readily disposed of as the company propose to run safe, fast, and comfortable boats between every island below Long and as far as Orr's, making the necessary number of round trips to Portland daily. It has also been said that freight rates would be cut and passenger fares reduced, the line being run to accommodate the people of the lower bay and giving best possible service at rates sufficient only to pay dividends on the capital of the company.

The new company will have to charter its steamers at first, with the option of buying if they are satisfactory. Or, in case proper boats cannot be obtained, new steamers specially suited to the needs of the lower bay service will be built. The Portland terminus will probably be Portland Pier, where the boats of the Harpswell Steamboat Company formerly landed, but no lease has been entered into as yet. Stock was quite freely subscribed to at the meeting after the company had been organized and also, it is said, that a great many shares were engaged during the preliminary canvas of the bay which will now be taken up by buyers.

Proponents of the Peoples' Steamboat Company had been impressed with the size and performance, if not the patronage, of Captain Ed Archibald's *Mineola* when she ran locally in 1904. The general feeling was that an acquisition of this vessel, and the smaller but equally able *Tremont* of Castine, would stand them in good stead to compete with Casco Bay & Harpswell Lines. The fact is, the Peoples' Line was an emotionally charged brainstorm which reflected—and vented—much local anger, bitterness and defiance of the moment. Once the degree of effort, plus the field of obstacles to be surmounted, were recognized, it did not take long for regression and apathy to drain life from the project. With its organization floundering in a sea of setbacks and a lack of real loyalty, the Peoples Steamboat Company was finished before it really began and the trumpeting *Breeze* story of August 20 might just as honestly be called an epitaph.

Other Steamers Among the Isles

Besides the scores of better-known scheduled steamboats plying harbor and bay island waters in the early 1900s, there were a number of much smaller launch-type steamcraft. Usually classed as yachts, a few were placed briefly in commercial service. Some of these open-air canopied steamers have already been mentioned in light of their scheduled service, such as the *Sokokis* and *We Two*. But there were others, devoted almost entirely to charter excursions.

The tiny steamers *Pauline* and *Princess* operated at least during 1903 and 1904, and did not escape mention in the pages of the *Casco Bay Breeze*. As much of Pauline's story as can readily be told comes down to us in the *Breeze* of July 30, 1903, which carried an advertisement:

Steamer *Pauline*, Merryconeag Wharf, South Harpswell, Maine. This fine new steamer can be engaged by parties by the day or hour. Accommodates 30. Fine cushioned seats and carpeted floor. Will carry parties to any location desired. Offices at the Merryconeag and Ocean View Hotels. Address: F.S. Purrington, South Harpswell, Maine.

The Ocean View Hotel mentioned was located at South Harpswell and not connected with the smaller but equally well-known Ocean View hostelry at Bailey Island. That the *Pauline* was not strictly alone in the charter business is brought home by the existence of the *Princess*. This steam screw passenger boat was owned for a time by Captain Charles W. Howard of Peaks Island. He did not include her in his regular Peaks Island Steamboat & Amusement Company operation, but maintained the diminutive *Princess* for special charters. Even so, she certainly saw shuttle service on particularly poor business days not requiring larger vessels, and also substitute work at the Gurnet Bridge connection to the New Meadows Inn. Steam launches of this type soon gave way to the more efficient gasoline launches, which had grown steadily in number since the late 1890s.

Steamboat Data/Log

The following table contains principal dimensions, tonnages and vessel particulars not necessarily included within the chapter text. Most of the information may be verified by reference to *Merchant Vessels of the United States* annual registers published since 1868. Vessels noted with an asterisk (*) pre-dated the establishment of the U.S. Government official numbering system, but do appear in the "Lytle-Holdcamper List": *Merchant Steam Vessels of the United States*, a volume listing a majority of the steamcraft in existence prior to 1868. Those vessels jointly listed in both of the above sources, or not listed and never documented, are so indicated.

Official Number	Vessel Name(s)	Type	Tonnage (Gross & Net) Principal Dimensions (Length, b.p.; breadth; depth; in feet)	Year Built (Year Rebuilt)	Where Built (Where Rebuilt)	Engine Steamplant Particulars; Notes & Remarks	Crew
Unlisted	*Kennebec*	sidewheeler	Unknown (converted from sail)	(1822)	Bath, Maine	Double-oblique beam engine.	
(*)	*Experiment*	screw propeller	61 tons 60.4' x 12.7' x 9.0'	1844	Pittston, Maine	Two engines, early twin-screw application.	
Unlisted	*Antelope*	sidewheeler	Unknown 55.0' x 8.0' x 2.5'	1850	Portland, Maine	3-horsepower rating.	
5019 & (*)	*Casco*	sidewheeler	43 tons 75' x 12' x 4'	1852	Portland, Maine	Horizontal-type engine. Two 12" cylinders & 2' strokes. Re-engined 1863.	
9452 & (*)	*Favorite*	sidewheeler (later screw propeller)	96 tons 100' x 14' x 6'	1861	Portland, Maine	Steamplant inherited from *Casco*; geared up at 3:1 ratio (see above).	
24442	*Tiger*	screw propeller	69 tons	1852	Philadelphia, Pa.		
25092 & (*)	*Uncle Sam*	screw propeller	78 tons	1855	Portland, Me. (?)		
26642	*Warrior*	screw propeller	16 tons	1863	Portland, Maine		
90284	*Magnet*	screw propeller	23.6 gross, 11.8 net 58' x 11' x 5.3'	1871	Deering, Maine	25-horsepower rating.	
145054	*Tourist* (I)	screw propeller	10.3 gross, 5.2 net 37' x 16' x 3'	1871	Portland, Maine	30-horsepower rating.	
(*)	*Island Queen*	sidewheeler	71 tons	1856	Portland, Maine		

Official Number	Vessel Name(s)	Type	Tonnage (Gross & Net) Principal Dimensions (Length, b.p.; breadth; depth; in feet)	Year Built (Year Rebuilt)	Where Built (Where Rebuilt)	Engine Steamplant Particulars; Notes & Remarks	Crew
Unlisted	*Gipsy Queen*	sidewheeler	(unkown) A larger boat than predecessor *Island Queen*	1859	Portland, Maine	Steamplant inherited from *Island Queen*.	
4917 & (*)	*Clinton*	sternwheeler	43 tons 83.2' x 16' x 3.5'	1851	Gardiner, Maine		
(*)	*Teazer*	sternwheeler	87 tons 118' x 17.4' x 4.4'	1852	Gardiner, Maine		
Unlisted	*Lily*	screw propeller	79 tons	1868	Portland, Maine		
10609 & (*)	*Gazelle* b *Forest City*	sidewheeler	163 tons 105' x 18.6' x 6' (125' x 18.6' x 8')	1865 (1873)	Portland, Maine	Flat-bed "walking beam" engine with 2' cylinder and 4' stroke; 100-horsepower rating.	
8716	*Express*	screw propeller	38.6 gross tons 70.1' x 13' x 5.3'	1871	Philadelphia, Pa.	High-pressure engine, 15x1¼ single cylinder. Boiler rated at 120 lbs. p.s.i. Note: Old A.L. Archanbault 9¼x5 foot boiler replaced by Portland Co. model in Feb. 1885. 50 indicated horsepower.	3
91125	*Minnehaha* b *Minnie*	screw propeller	18.5 gross, 9.2 net 50.6' x 16.5' x 4.1' (As rebuilt in 1915: 34 gross, 18 net)	1879	Portland, Maine	30-horsepower rating. Repowered with 65-horsepower steamplant in 1915.	3 to 4
13193	*Josephine Hoey*	screw propeller	12 gross, 5.6 net 48.0' x 19.8' x 4.0'	1865	New York, N.Y.	Two 7x5" high pressure reciprocating engines; steamed by a single boiler of 4½' diam. and 6½' height, rated 80 lbs. p.s.i. and 9 (nominal) horsepower.	2
90644	*Mary W. Libby*	screw propeller	21 tons 47.1' x 13.5' x 4.2' (27.5 gross, 13.8 net 54.1' x 19.5' x 4.9')	1874 (June 1881)	Cape Elizabeth, Maine (East Deering, Maine; Merrill Bros.)	12 x 10" non-condensing reciprocating engine steamed by vertical boiler 8' high x 4' diam. Design pressure 100 lbs. p.s.i. and rated at 22 horsepower.	2
125728	*Cadet*	screw propeller	65.6 gross, 48.8 net 88.6' x 16.6' x 6'	1879	Newburgh, N.Y.	Compound reciprocating engine fired by lake-type boiler.	
135431	*Emita*	screw propeller	99 gross, 76 net 84.0' x 23.6' x 5.9' (as dieselized: 111 gross, 89 net)	1880 (1894) (1901)	Athens, N.Y. (Portland, Me.)	120 horsepower McEntee & Dillon compound; lake-type horizontal boiler. Converted to diesel of 230 h.p. Feb.-April 1928. Replaced by a 260 h.p. 6-cylinder Cooper-Bessemer diesel in 1940.	5 to 6

Official Number	Vessel Name(s)	Type	Tonnage (Gross & Net) Principal Dimensions (Length, b.p.; breadth; depth; in feet)	Year Built (Year Rebuilt)	Where Built (Where Rebuilt)	Engine Steamplant Particulars; Notes & Remarks	Crew
85582	*General Bartlett* b *Atrato*	screw propeller	115.2 gross, 72.1 net 96.7' x 22.5' x 5'	1879	East Boston, Mass.	75-horsepower rating.	
120557	*Florence*	screw propeller	36 gross, 18 net 56.0' x 15.0' x 7.0'	1883	Boston, Mass.		4
120689	*Forest Queen*	screw propeller	138 gross, 69 net 100.8' x 22.2' x 7.2'	1887	Athens, N.Y.	Compound reciprocating engine fired by lake-type horizontal boiler. Portland Co. reconditioned the compound engine and retubed lake-type boiler in spring 1909. This plant rated at 180 horsepower.	
136349	*Eldorado*	screw propeller	96.7 gross, 68 net 73.2' x 17' x 6.4'	1893	Buffalo, N.Y.	Compound reciprocating engine fired by lake-type horizontal boiler.	6
150524	*Pilgrim*	screw propeller	261 gross, 209 net 113.7' x 26.0' x 7.9'	1891	David Bell Shipyard, Buffalo, N.Y.	Lake-type horizontal boiler and compound reciprocating engine rated at 200 nominal horsepower. (Circa 1912) Repowered with a Portland Co. Scotch boiler and original 14" x 30" and 20" compound upgraded to 350 horsepower. Later years, received replacement Almy watertube boiler of 150 lbs. p.s.i. capacity. Each piston utilized an extended, guiding "tail rod" within the cylinders, a local steamboating rarity.	9 to 11
161911	*Verona*	screw propeller	149 gross, 101 net 110.3' x 28.1' x 8.0'	1902	Brewer, Maine	Compound reciprocating engine, fired by Scotch boiler.	9
125307	*Charles A. Warren* a *C.A. Warren* c *C.A. Warren* d *Casco*	screw propeller	41 gross, 26 net 76.8' x 16.8' x 6.8'	1873	Kaighns Point, New Jersey		
95350	*Henrietta*	screw propeller	45 gross, 22.5 net 62.9' x 16.1' x 6.5'	1875	Portland, Maine	Single flue-type boiler, keel-condensing, reciprocating 16" x 16" engine. Rated 100 horsepower at 97 lbs. p.s.i. working pressure.	5

Official Number	Vessel Name(s)	Type	Tonnage (Gross & Net) Principal Dimensions (Length, b.p.; breadth; depth; in feet)	Year Built (Year Rebuilt)	Where Built (Where Rebuilt)	Engine Steamplant Particulars; Notes & Remarks	Crew
115469	*Gordon* a *Sea Flower*	screw propeller	45.1 gross, 30.4 net 71.8′ x 13.8′ x 5.0′ (45 tons)	1876 (1883)	Clark's Island, Maine (Portland, Me.)	Rated at 40-horsepower.	
106277	*Alice*	screw propeller	12.1 gross, 7.0 net 53.2′ x 14.1′ x 4.3′	1884	Brewer, Maine; Barbour Works	Vertical boiler rated at 100 lbs. p.s.i.; and reciprocating 8-14x12″ compound (condensing) engine.	
92012	*Merryconeag*	screw propeller	165 gross, 82 net 95.8′ x 22.5′ x 8.9′ (Not readmeasured; superstructure modified)	1888 (1899)	East Deering, Maine; Geo. Russell Shipyard (Rockland, Maine; Cobb-Butler Shipyard)	Portland Co. firebox boiler 15″ x 26″/18″ compound reciprocating engine. (1899) 92″ x 168″ firebox-type replaced by Portland Co. Scotch boiler of 116″ x 144″ with design pressure of 130 lbs. p.s.i.	9 to 10
126716	*Chebeague* b *Engine No. 7*	screw propeller	47.7 gross, 23.8 net 71.1′ x 17′ x 6.6′ (Not readmeasured; superstructure modified)	1891 (1895)	Portland, Maine; Nathan Dyer d/b/a (doing business as) Portland Shipbuilding Co. (Portland, Maine; as above)	(1895) fireboat conversion: older Portland Co. Scotch boiler replaced by improved higher capacity 74″ x 132″ Portland Co. vertical-type boiler. Compound reciprocating engine.	
116671	*Sebascodegan* b *Commander*	screw propeller	160 gross, 90 net 103.8′ x 24.8′ x 8.9′ (Not readmeasured; superstructure modified)	1895 (1909)	South Portland, Maine; Nathan Dyer d/b/a Portland Shipbuilding Co. (New York, N.Y.)	Portland Co. 117″ x 144″ Scotch boiler; 15″ x 28″/18″ improved compound reciprocating engine. Rated 150 horsepower.	5
107286 Later, Federally documented & Off.No. 107286	*Aucocisco* b U.S.S. *Green Island* c *Aucocisco* An error in spelling in the MVUS Registers from 1897-1902 finds this vessel listed as *Ancocisco*. The listing is correct for 1903 and thereafter.	screw propeller	167 gross, 94 net 107.8′ x 24.9′ x 8.9′ (Not readmeasured; superstructure modified)	1897 (1907)	South Portland, Maine; Nathan Dyer d/b/a Portland Shipbuilding Co. (South Portland, Maine; as above)	Portland Co. 116″ x 144″ Scotch boiler of 130 lbs. p.s.i.; 15″ x 30″/18″ improved compound reciprocating engine. Rated 150 horsepower. (1909) 350 horsepower compound engine and surface condenser by Portland Co. replaced original plant. New screw propeller also fitted. (Late 1920s) Original Scotch boiler replaced by Almy Watertube model and new surface condenser. Requisitioned from commercial service, 1941. Transferred to U.S. Navy, 1942, renamed U.S.S. *Green Island*.	9 to 10

Official Number	Vessel Name(s)	Type	Tonnage (Gross & Net) Principal Dimensions (Length, b.p.; breadth; depth; in feet)	Year Built (Year Rebuilt)	Where Built (Where Rebuilt)	Engine Steamplant Particulars; Notes & Remarks	Crew
200852	*Maquoit*	screw propeller	77 gross, 43 net (108 gross, 52 net) 85.0′ x 20.5′ x 7.6′	1904 (1921)	South Portland, Maine; Portland Shipbuilding Co. (South Portland, Maine; as above)	Portland Co. upright 80″ x 124″ Scotch boiler and 10″ x 22″/14″ compound reciprocating engine rated at 250 horsepower. (1930) Scotch boiler replaced by Almy Watertube boiler.	8 to 9
203969	*Machigonne* b *Hook Mountain* c *Block Island* d U.S.S. *League Island* (YUB-20) e *Block Island* f *Yankee*	screw propeller	425 gross, 289 net 136.5′ x 29.0′ x 9.6′ (Not readmeasured; reconditioning and superstructure modifications)	1907 (1920) (1939) (1946 & 1948)	Philadelphia, Pa.; Neafie & Levy Ship & Engine Building Company (New York, N.Y. John W. Sullivan & Co.) (New London, Ct.; Thames Shipyard)	Triple-expansion reciprocating engine 11″ x 18″ x 32″/22″, steamed by single-end Scotch boiler of 13′ diam. and 10′9″ height. Rated 550 (indicated) horsepower. (Equipped with steam steering gear). (Circa 1929) Boiler conversion to oil-firing. Signal letters: K.V.W.T. (1907-33) K.J.M.W. (1933-58) (now supplanted by standard radio telephone call sign.)	14
16917	*Venture*	screw propeller (scow)	59 gross, 35 net 65.4′ x 22.1′ x 5.3′	1902	Pittston, Maine	Rated at 85 horsepower.	5
(*)	*Patent*	sidewheeler	200 tons Approx. 100′ length	1823	New York, N.Y.	High-pressure engine and copper boiler by Daniel Dod of Elizabethtown, N.J.	
(*)	*Flushing*	sidewheeler	107 & 53/95 tons 98′10″ x 17′4″ x 6′8″	1830	Brooklyn, N.Y.: Lawrence & Sneden	Low-pressure engine.	
24406	*Tyro*	screw propeller	22 tons	1860	Freeport, Maine		
(*)	*Harraseeket*	screw propeller	Unknown	1861 (?)	Freeport, Maine		
95811	*Haidee*	screw propeller	17.1 gross, 9.6 net 46.2′ x 14′ x 5.1′	1884 (1911)	South Freeport, Me. (Machias, Me.)	(1919) Boiler & compound reciprocating steam engine replaced by 48 horsepower gasoline engine (pilot-house controlled).	2 to 3 (later 1)
150414	*Phantom*	screw propeller	38.3 gross, 19.2 net 65′ x 15.3′ x 6.1′ (56 gross, 27 net; 66′ x 15.8′ x 7.4′)	1887 (circa 1902)	South Freeport, Me. (Eastport, Maine)	Unknown	3 to 4

Official Number	Vessel Name(s)	Type	Tonnage (Gross & Net) Principal Dimensions (Length, b.p.; breadth; depth; in feet)	Year Built (Year Rebuilt)	Where Built (Where Rebuilt)	Engine Steamplant Particulars; Notes & Remarks	Crew
92523	*Madeleine*	screw propeller	74.4 gross, 37.2 net 86.0' x 18.9' x 6.8'	1893	Cape Elizabeth, Maine; Nathan Dyer	Portland Company boiler and compound reciprocating engine.	5 to 7
145689	*Tremont*	screw propeller	81.24 gross, 64.34 net 80.5' x 21.6' x 4.8' (1907-Depth adm.as 6.2')	1895 (1907)	Brewer, Maine; Barbour Works		6; (1909) 8
161812	*Vivian*	screw propeller	11 gross, 7 net 40.8' x 9.5' x 4.7'	1898	Portland, Maine	Listed as steam yacht in inland passenger service, 1902; as gasoline yacht, 1904-08.	
127356	*Corinna*	screw propeller	45 gross, 33 net 64.1' x 15.6' x 6.2' (95 gross tons as rebuilt)	1899 (1913)	Portland, Maine (Castine, Maine)	Portland Co. boiler and 9" x 18"/12" compound reciprocating engine.	6
77042	*James T. Furber*	screw propeller	22.7 gross, 12.6 net 57.0' x 14.8' x 4.6'	1892	Kennebunk, Maine	Single vertical boiler of 125 lbs. p.s.i.; and two 7x7" surface condensing reciprocating engines. Rated at 30 estimated (combined) horsepower.	3
150297	*Percy V.* b *Anna Belle*	screw propeller	37.2 gross, 21.2 net 62.5' x 15.3' x 5.8' (61 gross, 41 net)	1883 (1909)	Bath, Maine (Castine, Maine)	Steel firetube boiler of 120 lbs. p.s.i. and keel-condensing 12x14" compound reciprocating engine. Rated at 40 horsepower. (1909) Repowered with larger compound engine, rated at 150 horsepower. Turned a 60" diameter propeller.	4
150818	*Pejepscot* a (unknown) c *Sea Gate* An error of omission in the MVUS Registers from 1894-98 finds this steamer listed in the 1899 Register under her second name of *Pejepscot*.	screw propeller	125 gross, 85 net 97.0' x 20.1' x 5.8'	1894	Newburgh, N.Y.	Two triple-expansion reciprocating engines; twin-screw. Rated at 250 horsepower (125 h.p. each engine.)	6
115776	*Samuel E. Spring* b *S.E. Spring*	sidewheeler	154.8 gross, 83.6 net 93.7' x 19.0' x 4.8'	1881 (1895)	East Deering, Maine (Boston, Mass.)	Portland Co. firebox-type (horizontal) 46" x 168" boiler, and 22" x 42" walking-beam engine.	6
85962	*Greenwood*	screw propeller	28.8 gross, 14.4 net 56.2' x 16.0' x 6.0'	1887	Portland, Maine; Nathan Dyer		

Official Number	Vessel Name(s)	Type	Tonnage (Gross & Net) Principal Dimensions (Length, b.p.; breadth; depth; in feet)	Year Built (Year Rebuilt)	Where Built (Where Rebuilt)	Engine Steamplant Particulars; Notes & Remarks	Crew
100286	*Isis*	sidewheeler (later screw propeller)	9 gross, 6.7 net 44.8' x 9.9' x 4.8' (11 gross, 8 net)	1881 (1887)	Thomaston, Maine (Portland, Maine)		4
77090	*Jeanette* b *Morris Block* c *Kingston*	screw propeller	73.6 gross, 42.8 net 80.5' x 19.6' x 5.4'	1893	Norwalk, Florida	Vertical boiler of 120 lbs. p.s.i. and 10-18x12" reciprocating compound (condensing) engine.	7
91869	*M.&M.* b *Stockton*	screw propeller	98 gross, 67 net 81.5' x 18.0' x 5.6'	1886	Thomaston, Maine		
100490	*Island Belle*	screw propeller	153.7 gross, 106.9 net 93.0' x 18.4' x 7.5'	1891	Buffalo, N.Y.	Scotch boiler and compound reciprocating engine, rated at 150 h.p. (1918) Converted by installation of American Whaley 14x20" 4-cylinder gasoline engine of 45 h.p.	7, later 3
107464	*Alice Howard* b *Utility*	screw propeller	77 gross, 45 net 73.1' x 19.6' x 6.2'	1899	Peaks Island, Maine	Portland Co. 73x114" vertical boiler and shop-built Howard compound reciprocating engine; rated at 24 horsepower. (1905) Original boiler replaced by Portland Co. 72x132" vertical type.	4 to 5
127563	*Comet*	screw propeller	35 gross, 23 net 54.6' x 17.3' x 6.1' (77 gross, 47 net) (74.6' x 22.0' x 6.1')	1901 (1907)	Peaks Island, Maine (Peaks Island, Maine)	Portland Co. 48x90" vertical fire-tube boiler of 150 lbs. p.s.i. and compound engine; rated at 100 horsepower, speed given as 10 mph.	3
211673	*Tourist*	screw propeller	33 gross, 28 net 58.4' x 16.2' x 5.6'	1913	Boothbay Harbor, Maine; Reed Bros. Shipyard	Upright boiler and compound reciprocating engine, rated at 150 h.p. (1925) Almy Watertube boiler replaced upright boiler. Speed: 12 knots.	2 to 4
212259	*Gurnet*	screw propeller	65 gross, 46 net 58.6' x 18' x 6.3'	1914	Boothbay Harbor, Maine; Reed Bros. Shipyard	Upright boiler and compound reciprocating engine, rated at 175 h.p. (1926) Converted to 4-cylinder Cooper-Bessemer diesel power, rated at 80 horsepower. (1933) First Bessemer diesel replaced by similar ex-Portland & Lewiston Interurban R.R. unit. (1948) Second Cooper-Bessemer powerplant replaced by new Cooper-Bessemer 4-cylinder diesel, rated at 514 r.p.m. and 110 horsepower.	2 to 4

Official Number	Vessel Name(s)	Type	Tonnage (Gross & Net) Principal Dimensions (Length, b.p.; breadth; depth; in feet)	Year Built (Year Rebuilt)	Where Built (Where Rebuilt)	Engine Steamplant Particulars; Notes & Remarks	Crew
201173	*Alpine*	gasoline screw propeller	17 gross, 11 net 51.0′ x 10.0′ x 3.9′	1904	South Freeport, Maine		2
92181	*Mary Jane* b *Neptune*	screw propeller	19 gross, 9 net 50.6′ x 14.6′ x 5.2′ (28 gross, 14 net) (49.8′ x 14.6′ x 6.4′) Note: Old-fashioned ornamental billet-head removed, for difference in length.	1890 (1917)	Noank, Connecticut (Portland, Maine)	Compound reciprocating engine steamed by upright firetube boiler. Rated at 150 horsepower.	1 to 3
222034 Later, Federally documented & Off. No. 222034	*Admiral*	screw propeller	13 gross, 9 net 38.0′ x 13.6′ x 4.0′ (44.0′ x 13.6′ x 4.0′)	1906 (1919)	Camden, N.J. (Portland, Maine)	Navy Standard (launch-type) compound reciprocating engine and boiler, rated at 65 horsepower. (1925) Steamplant replaced by Cooper-Bessemer 3-cylinder diesel engine, rated at 60 horsepower.	3
205213	*Sabino* a *Tourist*	screw propeller	24 gross, 9 net 45.2′ x 15.3′ x 5.4′ (overall dimensions: 57.25′ x 22.25′ w/max. draft of 6′4″, as recorded at Mystic Seaport)	1908 (a. 1922, b. 1929 & 1936, c. 1962 to 1967, d. 1976, e. 1977-78, f. 1991-92.)	East Boothbay, Maine; Irving Adams Yard (a. Bath, Maine; b. South Portland, Maine; c. Salisbury, Mass.; Corbin Yard; d., e., & f. Mystic Seaport, Conn.)	Scotch boiler and Paine compound reciprocating engine rated at 75 horsepower. (Circa 1940) Original boiler replaced by Almy Watertube type. Reboilered plant rated at 110 horsepower (estimated).	2 and later 3
130692	*Nellie G.*	screw propeller	9 gross, 6 net 36.8′ x 10.3′ x 3.5′	1895 (1938-39)	Woolwich, Maine (East Boothbay, Maine; Paul Luke)	Scotch boiler and compound reciprocating engine, rated variously as 18 (estimated) and 25 (nominal) horsepower. (1934) Steamplant replaced by a Lathrop 4-cylinder gasoline engine of 40 (indicated) horsepower. During World War II, a 45-horsepower 6-cylinder Lathrop gasoline engine replaced the smaller plant.	1 or 2
141377	*Louise* b *Longfellow*	screw propeller	27.6 gross, 21.3 net 59.5′ x 15.2′ x 4.5′ (Lengthened to 75.0′ and sponsoned)	1895 (circa 1899)	South Portland, Maine (Sebago Lake Station, and Bridgton, Maine)	Scotch boiler and compound reciprocating engine. Removed in 1901 and placed in new Lake steamer *Songo*.	

Official Number	Vessel Name(s)	Type	Tonnage (Gross & Net) Principal Dimensions (Length, b.p.; breadth; depth; in feet)	Year Built (Year Rebuilt)	Where Built (Where Rebuilt)	Engine Steamplant Particulars; Notes & Remarks	Crew
Undocumented	*Santa Maria* b *Hawthorne(?)*	screw propeller	27.6 gross, 21.3 net 59.5' x 15.2' x 4.5' (est. based on sister vessel *Louise*) (Lengthened to 75.0' and sponsoned)	1896 (circa 1899)	Westbrook (Portland), Maine (Sebago Lake Station, and Bridgton, Maine)	Scotch boiler and compound reciprocating engine. (If *Hawthorne*, engine and/or boiler went to new lake steamer *Goodridge* of 1913.)	
116600	*Sokokis*	screw propeller	15 gross, 10 net 58.2' x 12.4' x 4.1' (19″ deep draft)	1893 (189?)	Westbrook (Portland), Maine (Sebago Lake Station, and Bridgton, Maine)	Scotch boiler and two reciprocating engines; twin-screw. Hull sponsoned at Sebago Lake.	2
Undocumented	*We Two*	screw propeller	(Standard open steam launch model, circa 1895, no other data available.)				
93131	*Mineola*	screw propeller	295 gross, 107 net 121.0' x 26.0' x 9.6'	1901	St. George, Maine	Scotch boiler and triple-expansion reciprocating engine.	15
77364	*Jule*	screw propeller	19 gross, 11 net 50.7' x 12.3' x 4.5' (14 gross, 10 net)	1899 (1927)	Weymouth, Mass. (Boothbay Harbor, Maine)	Scotch boiler and compound reciprocating engine, rated at 8 horsepower. (1927) Converted by installation of 35 horsepower gasoline engine.	2 or 3
107760	*Alliquippa*	gasoline screw propeller	14 gross, 11 net 51.1' x 11.2' x 5.1'	1902	Bristol, Maine		2
Undocumented	*Pauline*	screw propeller	No data available.	Circa 1903			
200022	*Princess*	screw propeller	18 gross, 11 net 47.3' x 11.5' x 3.7'	1903	Portland, Maine		3

The Standard Bell Code in use on Casco Bay Steamers

One bell . . . . .Ahead slow
One bell and jingle . . . . .Ahead full
One bell . . . . .Slow
One bell . . . . .Stop
Two jingles . . . . .Normal steaming r.p.m.
Two bells . . . . .Slow astern
Two bells and jingle . . . . .Full astern
One bell . . . . .Stop (from any speed astern)

Fleeting Bygones—Other Steamboating Events Remembered

In this section are recorded other events, many lesser in importance, but certain of them of remarkable interest, and all deserving whatever part they can play to make this chronicle more complete, in its endeavor to be a truly definitive work. The entries have been arranged chronologically, either under the name of the steamer, with all relevant dates and events, or, in cases of a general operational event or accounting, by year and date or season of occurrence.

The entries under steamer headings were taken from an old notebook of observations, sightings, and other information gained over many years through conversations, reading and correspondence by Casco Bay Lines Purser Warren N. Graffam. These entries further illuminate the years 1897-99 covered in Part I, Chapter 2, and elsewhere.

Emita

Sept. 7, 1898   Reported broken propeller.

May 2, 1899   Reported on railway.

July 21, 1899   While entering Diamond Cove with government workmen, the lightning became so severe that Captain Prout decided to stop the boat and wait for it to pass. He reached for the bell pull just as lightning struck. It paralyzed his arm and it was necessary for one of the crew to take over the operation of the *Emita*.

Aug. 5, 1899   Reported [to have] new propeller.

Aug. 19, 1899   An early morning trip from the islands unshipped her rudder. *Forest Queen* took her in tow to Portland.

Forest Queen

Oct. 11, 1897   On Marine Railways, South Portland at time of fire in shipyard. Fireboat *Engine No. 7* [ex-*Chebeague*] under Capt. Gould put out the fire. Had it not been for her assistance, the whole yard would doubtless have been lost. On the railways at the time were *Forest Queen*, tug *William Woolley*, and several schooners.

July 2, 1898   Operating for Casco Bay Steamboat Co.; will make a round trip to Old Orchard Pier, leaving Portland at 2 p.m. arriving back at 7 p.m.

July 14, 1898   Making regular trips to Old Orchard Pier.

July 13, 1899   Takes picnic from State Street Wharf and South Portland.

Eldorado

Summer 1897   John Coughlin was Engineer.

Oct. 7, 1897   Hauled up for the winter on the west side of Custom House Wharf.

June 17, 1899   Fouls a cable in her propeller making landing at Fort McKinley, goes to railway.

Aug. 10, 1899   New searchlight used for first time. Worked fine.

Aug. 14, 1899   At 9:15 a.m., as she was going into the wharf at Long Island, she broke her crankshaft. Landing was made and passengers discharged. *Fannie G.* [tug and waterboat] came down and towed her to Portland.

Aug. 29, 1899   Broke crankshaft while making along Great Diamond shore. Tug *Belknap* towed her to wharf.

Pilgrim

Oct. 7, 1897   Hauled up for the winter on the west side of Custom House Wharf.

May 23, 1898   On railway.

July 29, 1898   Had to be towed in by *Eldorado* because of crankpin trouble.

July 31, 1898   Carried large crowds to Old Orchard Pier [Sunday trip].

Aug. 28, 1898   Capt. Oliver sick, Capt. Parsons relieves; running excursions to Old Orchard Pier.

Sept. 12, 1898   Hauled 90 passengers down the bay (strong northwest wind).

July 31, 1899   Canceled trip to Old Orchard Beach because of weather.

Sept. 17, 1899   Hauled 400 passengers to Bath.

Sept. 24, 1899   To make last excursion of the season at 2:15 p.m. [Sunday trip].

Josephine Hoey

July 18, 1899   Took picnic from Portland Pier to Basket Island.
Aug. 21, 1899   Mentioned as hauling one of the bands at the Sea Pageant off Peaks Island.

Mary W. Libby

Nov. 15, 1897   Mentioned as taking run (for double-ender *Elizabeth City*) for a while.
May 3, 1899   Reported taking place of *Elizabeth City*.
Aug. 3, 1899   Mentioned as hauled off for season.
Aug. 21, 1899   Mentioned as hauling one of the bands for the Sea Pageant off Peaks Island.
Aug. 29, 1899   Mentioned as taking run of *Eldorado* while she is repaired.

Merryconeag

July 13, 1897   While running to Rockland, turned back to Portland because of rough seas.
July 28, 1897   Brought a good load of passengers and freight to Portland from the Rockland run (stops).
Summer 1898   Chartered to run in Boston Harbor.

Sebascodegan

Summer 1897   Capt. Long was master.
July 22, 1897   Beat the *Pilgrim* in a race across the harbor.
July 31, 1897   Carried good crowds.
Oct. 2, 1897   Mentioned as tying up for the winter.
April 1898   Government took option for war service. Doing patrol duty during the spring.
Summer 1898   Chartered to run from Boston to Nantasket during the summer.
Sept. 9, 1898   Returns from filling a ten weeks contract in Massachusetts waters.
Sept. 12, 1898   On Orr's Island run.
Sept. 22, 1898   Maine Coast Navigation Co. negotiating with Harpswell Line for steamer *Sebascodegan* to replace *Salacia* on the Wiscasset and Boothbay run.

Aucocisco

July 7, 1897   Mentioned as taking largest crowd as yet carried; 250 in one group and 110 in another [besides regular passengers].
Oct. 2, 1897   Mentioned as the boat for winter operations on the Harpswell Line. Capt. Long to be master.
Oct. 3, 1897   Mentioned as hauling 100 excursionists [besides regular passengers].
April 1898   Government took option for war service.
July 1, 1898   Mentioned as making three round trips daily with Capt. Long and Capt. Bryan on Orr's Island run. Superintendent Daniels delays *Auco* for 12 minutes for late passengers.
Sept. 12, 1898   Went on railway.
Sept. 19, 1898   Completes annual overhaul.

Phantom

Nov. 12, 1897   Rough passage in Northeaster.
June 29, 1898   Doing service as patrol boat.

Madeleine

Summer 1897   Capt. Ben Seabury is master.
July 7, 1897   Mentioned as taking a group of 25 persons besides a large number of regular passengers to Town Landing.
July 15, 1897   Had a large picnic to Cousins Island.
Aug. 4, 1898   Broke rudder.
Sept. 10, 1898   To go out of service for season.
May 15, 1899   In operation for "Freeport & Brunswick Steamboat Company."

Tremont

May 30, 1899   Arrives to run for "Forest City Steamboat Co." on their Freeport run.

Percy V.

Nov. 3, 1897   Purchased in Bath by J.H. MacDonald, to start on the run to Small Point; to be a tri-weekly service for the present. She received the salute of every steamer in the harbor as Capt. Charles Howe took her on her trial run.

Nov. 10, 1897   Mentioned as good freight and passenger travel.

Nov. 12, 1897   Missed trip—Northeast gale.

July 24, 1899   On Small Point run—good freight and passengers.

Pejepscot

July 24, 1899   A new line of steamers between Portland and . . . [Small Point] under management of J.H. MacDonald. Steamer *Pejepscot* made two trips which were well patronized, both freight and passengers.

July 31, 1899   Carried good crowds.

Island Belle

July 10, 1897   Capt. John Berry as master.

Sept. 18, 1897   To tie up at Deake's Wharf for winter.

Aug. 24, 1898   Hauling workmen to Great Diamond.

Sept. 7, 1898   Discontinues service to Peaks Island. Landed at the Bay View Wharf during the time she was running to Peaks.

Alice Howard

June 14, 1899   Capt. Howard on *Alice Howard* and Capt. Joe Upton on *Mary W. Libby* started for Boston to carry passengers to [naval anchorage] warships for a week—Still laying at Cushing's Island (June 15th)—Thick weather forced them to turn back— Arrived in Boston after a rough trip on June 18th. *Alice Howard* had been launched at Peaks Island May 17, 1899. Built by Captain Howard. [Steamer *Princess* on shuttle line to Peaks.]

July 11, 1899   She broke a blade from propeller making Great Diamond. Ebb tide set her over.

July 20, 1899   Running Long Wharf to Great Diamond.

Aug. 3, 1899   To go to Bar Harbor to haul passengers to Admiral Sampson's fleet.

Sept. 19, 1899   In New York, where she will remain to carry passengers during the Dewey celebration. She came to New York from Philadelphia where she hauled 10,000 passengers in 9 days to the fleet during G.A.R. encampment.

Mary Jane

Sept. 14, 1899   Reported on railway.

The remainder of these entries are based on various sources, including notes and commentary by Warren Graffam.

Spring 1903   Steamer *Madeleine* was bereft of external "flush-to-rail" housing, allowing complete walk-around of open deck areas. Builder took careful notice of predecessor *Alice*, in quest of ideas, in modeling both *Chebeague* and *Madeleine*.
Nathan Dyer was no draftsman and, like most small shipwrights of his and earlier generations, built on basis of half-models. Method placed great emphasis on trial and error. Mr. Dyer's misfortune: to have developed fine steamboat designs largely through construction of less worthy (earlier) boats. Steamer *Madeleine* proved his advancement, which culminated in graceful Harpswell Line boats yet to follow.
Madeleine came out with unusual pilot house paintwork, consisting of white framework, offset by bright red center-paneling, yielding candy-stripe effect!

August 1903   *Aucocisco* substituted (or held route alone) for *Sebascodegan*.

and July 1904   Emergency timetable cancelled 5:45 a.m. and 10:40 a.m. trips from Portland to Orr's Island. *Auco* made trips at 8:45 a.m., 1:30 p.m. and 6 p.m. Return trips from Orr's Island to Portland (7:50 a.m. and 2 p.m. *cancelled*) were 5:30 a.m., 10:50 a.m. and 3:40 p.m.

Spring 1907   Rebuilding alterations to *Aucocisco*, made to update her as running mate of new *Machigonne*, included lengthening aft of main deckhouse; boat deck extended forward, once pilot house lifted from second deck; pilot house then pegged aloft and neat afterhouse added (ideal for overnight layover on Orr's Island line). New men's "smoker" built over old wheel house deck platform on second deck, and smokestack made taller with heightened whistle (to clear sounding range over wheelhouse structure).

July 22, 1909   (from the *Casco Bay Breeze*)
"If the C.B. & H. Lines does not pay a dividend this year, it will not be because of expensive operation of the boats, but by reason of the big fixed charges the company has assumed responsibilty for when they bought the equipment of the old Casco Bay company, sunk in debt as it was, and running a huge bluff in its dying throes."

Wayward Steamboats:
A Compendium of Prior or Later Histories of Island Steamers off Casco Bay

The following information consists of further historic notes and accounts of vessels in the text having either previous careers to Casco Bay operation, or later careers away from Calendar Islands environs:

Patent

(from *Steamboat Days* by Fred Erving Dayton)

Captain [Seward] Porter brought *Patent* to Portland, July 7, 1823, a low-sitting steamboat without hurricane deck, engine and boilers set in the hold, with a balance wheel that rose halfway above the main deck. The paddle shaft had a clutch to disconnect the paddle to aid in turning. Cabins were below deck. *Patent*. . . cost $20,000, and was capable of 10 miles' speed. . . . In the first trial the boiler blew its head, killing five persons including [engine builder] Mr. Dod.

This tragic explosion, on May 9, 1823, readily explains the *Patent*'s sudden availability for sale to Captain Porter in Maine, for a service well away from a locale which now shunned her presence. The same year, title passed to the Kennebec Steam Navigation Company, and the *Patent* ran Boston to Bath.

The *Patent* was the first regular steamboat to operate with overnight accommodations into Maine, or the northeast section of the United States.

Feb. 1828   Sold at Boston auction, again to bid by Captain Porter.
1828-30   Ran Boston to Portland.
1835   Last Maine operation, on Penobscot River. Tradition has it that *Patent* went to southern waters in 1835 and soon was wrecked by grounding at an undisclosed location.

Flushing

(from *History of the First Century of Steam Navigation* by Samuel Ward Stanton)

A new-comer in the harbor in 1830 was the steamboat *Flushing*, which ran between New York and Flushing and nearby Long Island Sound points and also to the Shrewsbury [River] that year and for many succeeding years. The first card of the new boat, dated June 10, 1830, read as follows: 'For Shrewsbury & Long Branch.—The superior new low pressure steam boat *Flushing*, Capt. Peck, built expressly to ply between Flushing, New York & Shrewsbury, will commence running on Saturday, 12th inst.'

Original owners of the *Flushing* were Curtis Peck, James P. Allaire, Saml. Leggett, Jacob Corlies and others.

Dec. 18, 1830   Advertised as running to Cold Spring, Oyster Bay and New Rochelle.
Winter 1831   Also used as a towboat around New York Harbor, assisting ships in or out.
Mar. 18, 1831   Started regular trips to Stamford, Greenwich, Rocky Point and Sawpitts.
1835   Hailed from Salem, New Jersey.
1838   Ran between Norwich and Sag Harbor.
1840   Connected at Lyme for New London and Norwich.
Dec. 17, 1856   Burned at Machias, Maine.

Emita

Spring 1880   Captain David H. Hitchcock, famed skipper of early Hudson River Day Line steamboats, also had become operator of short-line vessels. He had *Emita* built and put her in service between Albany and New Baltimore, about 14 miles down the river.

General Bartlett

Autumn 1883   Returned to the Merrimack River; at Newburyport until 1888, she was sold at New York for $10,000.

October 1888   Renamed *Atrato* by the trading agency of Campbell & Gardiner, bound to river service in South America. U.S. Registry was retained until 1891.

Verona

Autumn 1904   Sold to Hudson River parties and left Maine waters.

Nov. 27, 1907   Destroyed by fire at Highland Falls, New York. Last registered at Albany.

Sebascodegan (later *Commander*)

Autumn 1908   Sold to New York excursion line for Hudson River service. Altered by rebuilding to suit local trade. Main cabin extended aft, old pilot house dismantled in favor of larger one, new second deck cabin added, old smoke stack given tall outer jacket, and several lifeboats and rafts added. Renamed *Commander*. Joined other vessels, such as *Commodore* and *Atlantic*, on Hudson, with routine stops including West Point and Bear Mountain State Park. Also ran Battery to Coney Island and up East River.

1917   New York service ended due to World War I "anti-good times" feeling of populace. Idled, she was sold to southern businessmen from Beaufort, South Carolina, to link that port with Savannah, Georgia. Scheduled passenger and freight line; steamed across Port Royal Sound to Chechessee River, then via Skull Creek, May River and Calibogue Sound, Cooper River, Ramshorn Creek, New River, and both Walls and Field Cuts to Savannah River and city terminus. Ambitious route proved absurd. *Commander* at Savannah end when company folded; tied up idle until purchased by shipowner Joseph F. O'Brien and associates. Pressed into service ferrying workers from city proper to Terry Shipyard a few miles upriver.

Post WWI   *Commander*'s route expanded to other waylandings and considerable charter work included. Also stood in at intervals for Seaboard Railroad's cross-river ferry steamer. Cruise from city dock to Savannah Sugar Refining Corp. pier at Port Wentworth for $1.50 round trip fare was very popular. Docked each night at owner's private upriver landing at mansion Whitehall in idyllic "Old South" surroundings, and received careful attention at this period.

More on the post-1920 career of the *Sebascodegan* will be found in the Wayward Steamboats appendix of a future volume.

Machigonne

June 1913   Sold to Boston, Nahant & Pines Steamboat Co. for Revere (Point of Pines) and Nahant line. No change in appearance except added second set of forward gangways to cope with varied tidal stages at wharves.

1917-19   Requisitioned for U.S. Government service in Boston Harbor.

Oct. 2, 1917   Acquired for World War I service by U.S.Q.M.C. and given armament consisting of two one-pounder deck guns. Boston Harbor Islands Coast Artillery forts and Massachusetts Bay patrol service.

May 1919   Sold back to commercial use. Returned to private ownership in blighted condition.

More on the *Machigonne*'s career from 1920 will be found in the Wayward Steamboats appendix of a future volume. As with the *Sebascodegan*, this allows the reader to compare the later careers of these former Casco Bay steamers with those of their contemporaries still on the fleet rosters at Portland, Maine. All other steamers in this category have been covered similarly.

Haidee

Spring 1888   Sold to Machias owners for five-mile shorthaul passenger ferryage to and from Machiasport.

Autumn 1911   Encroaching automobile traffic forced *Haidee* into new role as towboat for local lumbering and general harbor work.

Spring 1919   Worn-out boiler and compound steam engine replaced by new gasoline engine.

Early 1920s   Still busy as carrier and freight boat for Booth Fisheries Sardine Co. of Machiasport.

1926   Abandoned.

Madeleine

Autumn 1899   Sold for Boston Harbor excursion service.

Spring 1903   Ownership again changed for Connecticut River passenger service out of Hartford.

Spring 1907   Acquired by Wilmington, North Carolina, interests for excursions and substitute ferry service on Cape Fear River. Primary run was Wilmington to downriver fishing resort town of Southport, passing between sprawling wilderness shore of Smith Island and Sunny Point, past tiny Battery Island across entrance bar and southerly to Southport wharf. Usually made a layover until late afternoon before returning daytrippers and beachgoers back to city. Also did fishing parties.

1910   Began off-season service as a coastwise freight boat, between Cape Fear River and points on or outside Pamlico Sound shore frontier.

June 10, 1912   Caught in violent line squalls on outside run with steam pressure down. Crew unable to build up steam to put her head to seas. Wallowing, shipped excess water, flooded hold and engine pit, and crew hastily abandoned her to founder 12 miles southeast of Cape Lookout Lightship, North Carolina. All aboard believed rescued from drifting tin liferaft.

Corinna

Spring 1909   Chartered to Devereux steamboat line at Castine for Bagaduce and Penobscot Bay runs.
Autumn 1911   Charter expired and *Corinna* returned to lay-up, purchased by former bankruptcy receiver, Thomas Skolfield, but remained unprofitably idle until placed up for auction.
Autumn 1912   Bid in by Captain Devereux of Castine and placed back in Penobscot operation.
Spring 1913   Rebuilt and modernized for all-weather service, with decked-over enclosed forecastle and flush-to-rail main deck house.
Sept. 12, 1915   Historically "lame duck" vessel caught fire, during layover at Captain Ben Arey's Brooksville wharf on Bagaduce River, and burned to the water's edge. Of the reported ten persons aboard, no lives were lost.

Percy V. (later *Anna Belle*)

The Kennebec Years 1883-97

1883   Built under sponsorship of the Fort Popham Summer Resort Association to replace irregular service of much smaller steamer *Creedmoor* of Eastern Steamboat Co.
June 12, 1883   Launched from C.B. Harrington Shipyard at Bath, for account of Popham Beach Hotel & Real Estate Co., at total cost of $7,000. Christened after Percy O. Vickery of Augusta, who had championed establishment of a summer resort at Popham.
June 29, 1883   Trials held after outfitting at George Moulton's riverfront machine works.
July 2, 1883   First commercial run, under Captain George H. Stacey of Parker Head, Purser/Mate James E. Perkins, 2nd Mate/deckhand Fred Hodgkins (both 16 years of age!) and Engineer Frank H. Lockery. Route consisted of stops along both banks of Kennebec, at Phippsburg Center, Hinckley's Landing at Georgetown, Parker Head, Cox's Head, and Popham Beach Landing close by imposing wooden Eureka Hotel. Schedule: one daily round trip, leaving Bath 8 a.m. and Popham 3 p.m., mid-May through early autumn, soon expanding to three daily round trips during July and August. 150-passenger capacity *Percy V.* became tidy profit maker.

1887   Vickery family gained full control of Bath-Popham Beach line and steamer. Status quo until *Percy V.* sold a decade later.
1888   Captain Stacey relieved by Captain James E. Perkins.
1897-98   Sale of *Percy V.* to James MacDonald of Portland (see Chapter 9).

The Penobscot Years 1903-19

1903-06   Operated in freight and passenger service between Rockport and West Penobscot Bay points.
1906   Became flagship of the Ellsworth & Swan's Island Line on Union River and across Blue Hill Bay.
1909   Purchased by Captain Benjamin R. Arey, repowered with large compound engine, and rebuilt with enlarged cabins, new pilot house and enclosed guard rails. Re-christened *Anna Belle* and registered at Castine for East Penobscot Bay and Bagaduce River trade.
1916   Sold to William A. Sanborn and Belfast registry for sporadic ferry and excursion work.
1918   Returned to Casco Bay under ownership of Captain Oscar Randall.

Pejepscot (later *Sea Gate*)

Winter 1902-03   Sold to New York interests for commuter service from Battery Park (lower Manhattan) to exclusive Sea Gate colony at west end of Coney Island. Renamed *Sea Gate*.
1905   Old stigma of costly operation caused resale to parties at Wilmington, North Carolina, on Cape Fear River. Used in passenger-excursion service to resort of Southport.
Spring 1907   Replaced by more economical former Falmouth Foreside steamer *Madeleine*. Returned to New York registry as freight boat.
1912   Purchased for bay and river freight service out of Brunswick, Georgia.
1923   Hauled up, stripped of fittings and steel hull scrapped.

Jeanette

Feb. 1905   Purchased from Salem, Massachusetts, ownership by the Johnston interests of Albany, New York, as replacement for *Augustus J. Phillips* on the Kingston-Poughkeepsie route. The one-time Howard steamer was renamed *Morris Block*.
1907   By this year, after another change of ownership, *Jeanette* had been renamed *Kingston*.
1923   Abandoned.

Alice Howard (later *Utility*)

1901   Sold to Portsmouth, Dover & York Street Railway Co. for its Piscataqua River crossing between Ceres Street ferry landing at Portsmouth and the large canopied ferry station at Badgers Island, Kittery. Also ran occasional special excursions to Appledore and Star Islands at Isles of Shoals; to Dover Point, New Castle, or Gerrish Island on the ocean side. Eventual improvements by new owners eliminated boiler and engine problems.

Jan. 1909   Chartered to Popham Beach Steamboat Co. as temporary replacement for *Eldorado* (former Casco Bay Line boat, destroyed by fire in December 1908) and inadequate *Jule*. Operated from Bath on Kennebec River route until relieved by the new *Virginia* in spring 1909.

Summer 1909   Resumed service at Portsmouth for Atlantic Shore Line Railway.

More on the *Alice Howard*'s career from 1920 will be found in the Wayward Steamboats appendix of a future volume.

Comet

Spring 1918   Sold to Captain Charles E. Pearsall of Yonkers, New York, for passenger ferry crossing between Yonkers and Alpine, New Jersey.

More on the *Comet*'s career from 1920 will be found in the Wayward Steamboats appendix of a future volume.

Sabino (ex-*Tourist*)

Spring 1908   Launched at W. Irving Adams shipyard, East Boothbay, for new St. John's Bay route extension of Damariscotta River Steamboat Co.; original name *Tourist*.

June 4, 1908   First trip from yard to South Bristol, under command of Capt. Elliot P. Gamage, line's founder and manager. Opened to public display. Acclaimed, except for "prosaic" name.

June 5, 1908   First revenue trip, connecting at South Bristol with *Newcastle* (sometimes *Bristol*), to Pemaquid Beach, Harbor, and Point, then to Christmas Cove (back shore wharf) and return.

Early spring 1913   Automobile and truck competition caused larger Damariscotta River steamers to be sold south. St. John's Bay extension abandoned to place *Tourist* on older main line, Damariscotta to South Bristol.

Autumn 1917   Line came under ownership of Captain LaForest E. "Foss" Ethridge of Bristol.

Summer 1918   Tragedy struck *Tourist* en route upriver to Damariscotta. Varied accounts conflict and contradict each other. Most popular are: (1) Capt. Ethridge, hurrying at speed toward Damariscotta wharf to beat incoming fog bank, finally rang down slow bell for maneuvering. Inexperienced (as temporary replacement for his ailing older brother that day) 19-year-old engineer, Everett Spear, was caught off guard. Reportedly up on deck, sitting on guard rail, he scurried to answer bell, hopped down into engine room, slipped on greasy deck plates and pitched forward, plunging one arm into crank pit. Rotating crank severed his lower arm. In shock, young Spear ran up on deck where no one could stop him from going overboard to drown in *Tourist*'s sternwake. Concern among passengers intensified as *Tourist* advanced too near town dock at speed. Skipper had swung wheel over hard, but *Tourist* careered sidewise into wharf, grazed and continued on past. Attempt to heave a spring line futile with too much headway.

(2) Engineer Spear (more plausibly) tried to free a suddenly jammed crankshaft after loss of a wrist pin. With no backing bell answered, *Tourist* carried too much headway. Unexpected shifting of shaft and disc-shaped eccentrics pinned Spear's hand and left him trapped below. *Tourist*, in any case, struck pilings, sprang free into the strong tiderace churning beneath the old arch-type river bridge, close by the wharf; sailed into bridge with jolting impact. Eight-knot river current forced steamer broadside, where upper deck canopy caught and held vessel long enough for passengers to evacuate safely over boat deck to bridge roadway. Finally, listed over sharply by current velocity and flooding tide, *Tourist* filled until fouled canopy tore away and steamer was swept under bridge and upriver, capsizing and sinking to river floor. Body of Everett Spear, sole victim, found in river nine days later, with one arm missing. Weeks later, *Tourist* righted by winching, partly raised and pumped out by small lighter. Beached stern-to in shallows of river bank.

Late spring 1919   Laid up at South Bristol wharf after reconditioning by "Foss" Ethridge for excursion work (scheduled freight and passenger line abandoned to motor vehicle competition), began seasonal operation in Boothbay Harbor area.

More on the *Sabino*'s career from 1920 until brought to Portland in 1927, and then her restoration away from Casco Bay, with later history to date, will be presented in the Wayward Steamboats appendix of a future volume.

Nellie G.

Autumn 1894   Laid down at Nathaniel Hansen yard on Woolwich shore of the Kennebec, to order of Capt. Amasa C. Williams and partner Charles Holbrook. Light towboat model, intended to tow logs to owners' lumber mill at Bowdoinham.

Early 1895 Launched as *Nellie G.*, christened in honor of Capt. Amasa's wife, Nellie (Gowell) Williams.

Winter and Holbrook and Williams landed contract for ferryage of freight spring 1902 and passengers between Boothbay Harbor village and exclusive summer resort colony at Squirrel Island. *Nellie G.* hauled off log-boom trade and rebuilt with passenger cabin and partial upper deck. Very successful on Squirrel Island line under command of Capt. Williams.

More on the post-1920 career of *Nellie G.* will be found in the Wayward Steamers appendix of a future volume for the years prior to her entry into Casco Bay service.

Island Belle

Autumn 1898 Sold to Eastern Steamship Co. by John Temple, to become largest Boothbay Division steamer to that time. Commanded by Capt. Naham W. Brewer of Southport in year-round operation.

Winter 1908-09 Became first steamboat in Kennebec River history to give uninterrupted winter service between Bath and Boothbay Harbor, despite severe ice conditions. Later served briefly between Boothbay Harbor and Wiscasset, but returned to Bath run. Daily trips were via Hell Gate on the Sasanoa River; waylandings at MacMahan Island, Five Islands, Isle of Springs, Southport; Capitol, Mouse and Squirrel Islands; and Ocean Point on Linekin Neck.

Summer 1911 Removed from active Eastern roster due to crankiness. Running mates *Wiwurna* and *Nahanada* proved able to handle traffic demands. Purchase offer by Baxter-controlled Island Ferry Co. at Portland, accepted by Eastern Steamship, brought ex-laker back to first home port on the Maine coast.

Alice

1904 Six years after leaving Casco Bay, career as a passenger steamer out of Eastport on Passamaquoddy and Cobscook Bays ended and she was converted to a fishing vessel. There was little life left in the old steamcraft, though, and *Alice* enjoyed scant success at fishing. She was beached and abandoned at Lubec in 1904.

Phantom

1899 The Passamaquoddy and Cobscook Bays passenger service was soon rid of her and *Phantom*'s final days were spent as a sardine carrier, slightly enlarged by conversion.

1908 During last months of 1908, abandoned at Eastport.

Vivian

1901 Beyond her brief sojourn in Casco Bay inner route service, little more is known of this former Portland, Freeport & Brunswick Line steamer, though she remained registered at Portland into the year 1901.

1902 Went to Boston registry as steam yacht, but also still listed as employed an "inland passenger" service. Though it might merely reflect another dubious entry or typographical error often found in MVUS Registers through the years, *Vivian* might actually have earned her later keep as a sightseeing yacht, both at Portland and Boston.

1904 The Lilliputian craft was converted to gasoline power.

1908 Last listed in the MVUS Register.

Tremont

1895 Registered at Bangor when launched, the *Tremont* remained enrolled there during her Casco Bay service. At this time, the steamer had an open deck with no forecastle cover or protection, but was still much more a suitable design for coastal islands work than the yacht-like light model competing boats such as *Vivian* and *Isis*.

1902-08 Registered at Castine.

1907 Sported a dignified decked-over forecastle, which was enclosed by sheathing in winter. She became more attractive as time went on.

1908 Returned to Penobscot River.

1908-12 Hailed from Bangor.

1914 By 1914, again Castine-registered and operated daily from this port, at the Bagaduce River entrance, across East and West Penobscot Bays to Belfast Harbor.

1921 After a relatively short career of 26 years, it was most likely a poor maintenance program which caught up with the still-graceful *Tremont*. She was listed as abandoned during the fiscal year ended June 30, 1921, her dismantled hulk beached on the Belfast waterfront close by that of another old Barbour-built steamer, the *Silver Star*. Both derelicts were eventually covered by landfill that provided an approach apron for construction of a new wharf on the site.

Bibliography

Army-Navy Publishers. *Pictorial History: The Harbor Defenses of Portland, 1941*. Atlanta: Army-Navy Publishers, 1941.

Baker, Wm. Avery. *A Maritime History of Bath, Maine and the Kennebec River Region*, Vols. I and II. Bath, Maine: Maine Research Society of Bath, 1973.

Bradlee, Francis B.C. *Some Account of Steam Navigation in New England*. Essex Institute, 1919.

Clifford, Harold B. *Charlie York: Maine Coast Fisherman*. Camden, Maine: International Marine Publishing Co., 1974.

Crowley and Lunt Publishing Co. *The Casco Bay Directory*. Portland, Maine: Crowley and Lunt, 1900-1940.

Cummings, O.R. *Trolleys to York Beach*. Bulletin No. 1, New England Electric Railway Historical Society, Inc. Manchester, N.H., 1965.

—— *Portland-Lewiston Interurban, Maine's Fast Electric Railroad*, Bulletin No. 3, New England Electric Railway Historical Society. Manchester, N.H., 1967.

Dayton, Fred Erving. *Steamboat Days*. 1925. Reprint. New York: Tudor Publishing Co., 1939.

Elwell, Edward H. *Elwell's Portland and Vicinity*. 1876 and 1881 editions. Facsimile reprint. Portland, Maine: Greater Portland Landmarks, Inc., 1975.

Goold, Nathan. *A History of Peaks Island and Its People—Also A Short History of House Island, Portland, Maine*. Portland, Maine: Lakeside Press, 1897.

—— *Looking Backward One Hundred Years—A Retrospect of Important Historical Events in Portland During the 19th Century*. Manuscript circa 1870s. Maine Historical Society Collection.

Goold, William. *Portland Sketches*, Vol. I. Bound manuscript 1872. Maine Historical Society Collection.

Goold, Hon. William. *When Portland Pier Was Built and How It Was Named*. Bound manuscript circa 1870s. Maine Historical Society Collection.

Hale, Robert and Agnes. *Cushings Island*. Baltimore: Waverly Press, 1971.

Jordan, William B., Jr. *A History of Cape Elizabeth, Maine*. Falmouth, Maine: House of Falmouth, Inc., 1965. Reprint. Bowie, Maryland: Heritage Books, Inc., 1987.

Lewis, Emanuel R. *Seacoast Fortifications of the United States: An Introductory History*. Washington: Smithsonian Institution, 1970.

Mitchell, C. Bradford (ed.). *Merchant Steam Vessels of the United States, 1790-1868: "The Lytle-Holdcamper List."* The Steamship Historical Society of America, 1975.

Morrison, John H. *History of American Steam Navigation*. 1903. Reprint. Stephen Daye Press, 1958.

Portland Directory, The. Selected editions, published annually. Maine Historical Society Collection.

Ross, Walter S. *The Last Hero: Charles A. Lindbergh*. New York: Harper & Row, Publishers, Inc., 1968.

Silverstone, Paul H. *U.S. Warships of World War I*. Garden City, N.Y.: Doubleday & Co., Inc., 1970.

Sinnett, Rev. Charles N. *Johnson Genealogy*. Concord, N.H.: Rumford Press, 1907.

Sinnett, Rev. Charles N. *Sinnett Genealogy*. Concord, N.H.: Rumford Press, 1910.

Stanton, Samuel Ward. *History of the First Century of Steam Navigation*. The Master, Mate and Pilot (periodical articles), 1911-12. New York Public Library Collection.

Sullivan, Robert F. *Shipwrecks and Nautical Lore of Boston Harbor: A Mariner's Chronicle of More Than 100 Shipwrecks, Heroic Rescues and Salvage Accounts, Treasure Tales, Island Legends, and Harbor Anecdotes*. Chester, Conn.: Globe Pequot Press, 1990.

Willard, Captain Benjamin J. *Life History and Adventures—Captain Ben's Book*. Portland, Maine: Lakeside Press, 1895.

Vessel registers:

Annual List of Vessels Registered, U.S. Customs District of Portland, Maine.

Merchant Vessels of the United States. Annual registers of the U.S. Treasury Department, Bureau of Customs and the U.S. Department of Transportation, 1868 to the present. Washington: U.S. Government Printing Office.

Collections:

The Peabody Museum of Salem, Salem, Mass.

The Joseph Conrad Library of the Seamens Church Institute of New York.

The Library of the Steamship Historical Society of America, University of Baltimore, Baltimore, Md.

The Library of the San Francisco Maritime Museum, San Francisco.

The Library of the Maine Maritime Museum, Bath, Maine.

The Jacksonville Free Public Library, Jacksonville, Fla.

Newspapers:

The Casco Bay Breeze. Weekly. South Harpswell and Portland, Maine, 1900-1917. Maine Historical Society Collection.

The Daily Eastern Argus. Portland, Maine. Microfilm files, Portland Public Library.

The Bath Times. Bath, Maine.

The Six Town Times. Weekly. Freeport, Maine, 1894-1904. Freeport Historical Society Collection.

The Portland Press Herald & Evening Express and predecessors. Portland, Maine.

The Lewiston Journal. Lewiston, Maine.

The Brunswick Record. Brunswick, Maine.

The Newburyport Daily News. Newburyport, Mass.

The Boston Herald. Boston, Mass.

The Maine Sunday Telegram and predecessor.

Periodicals:

Steamboat Bill. Journal of the Steamship Historical Society of America. Staten Island, New York, and Providence, R.I., 1940 to the present. The Peabody Museum of Salem and Author's Collections.

Down East. Camden, Maine.

Yankee. Dublin, N.H.

Parade

The New Yorker

The following list of authors and titles encountered during and since the research and writing of this book is offered for readers interested in a further accounting of Maine coast steamboat history. Although some works might not always be as accurate, factual, or complete as they could be, all are sure to add hours of reading entertainment and a nostalgic sense of the past. Exceptions are one biography of a celebrity who was a true fan of the *Aucocisco*, and one early 1900s novel which gave a continuing role throughout to the same steamer.

Ashley, Sally. *F.P.A.—The Life and Times of Franklin Pierce Adams*. New York: Beaufort Books, 1986.

Bosworth, R.S., Jr. (ed.). *Taskmasters of the Sea: The Story of Blount Marine Corporation, Warren, Rhode Island*. Barrington, R.I.: Barrington Times, 1961.

Cram, W. Bartlett. *Picture History of New England Passenger Vessels*. Hampden Highlands, Maine: Burntcoat Corporation, 1980.

Dingley, Robert Jordan, Walter M. Macdougall, Marion Reed Kimball, Grace Shaw Tolman, Maurice A. Richards, Herbert G. Jackson, Jr., Barbara A. Bruce, Harry Packard,and Harold T. Gilbert. *Maine Lakes Steamboat Album*. Camden, Maine: Down East Enterprise, Inc., 1976.

Dodge, David, Gainor R. Akin, and Maynard Bray. *Steamboat Sabino*. Mystic, Conn.: Mystic Seaport, Inc., 1974.

Driscoll, Jeremiah Timothy. *Crime Circles Manhattan*. New York: New York Marine Fuel Co., 1980.

Dunn, William. *Casco Bay Steamboat Album*. Camden, Maine: Down East Enterprise, Inc., 1969.

Favorite, Felix. *The Steamboat Era On Casco Bay*. Seattle, Washington: Favorite Creations, March 30, 1989 (rev. ed. Dec. 1, 1989).

Harding, R. Brewster. *Greetings From Maine—A Postcard Album*. Portland, Maine: Old Port Publishing Co., 1975.

Hauk, Z. William. *The Stone Sloops of Chebeague; And The Men Who Sailed Them—Also Some Chebeague Miscellany*. T-Wharf, Boston and Chebeague Island, Maine. Reprint. 6th ed. Freeport, Maine: Freeport Village Press, 1991.

Heiser, Ruth. *Harpswell's Steamboats*. The Harpswellian-1982. Freeport, Maine: Village Press, 1982.

Hill, Beth E. *The Evolution of Bailey's Island*. Bailey Island, Maine, and Concord, Mass.: self-published, 1992.

Humiston, Fred. *Windjammers and Walking Beams*. Portland, Maine: Blue Water Books, 1968.

Jones, Herbert G. *Isles of Casco Bay in Fact & Fancy*. Porter's Landing, Freeport, Maine: Bond Wheelwright Company, 1946.

—— *Sebago Lake Land*. Portland, Maine: Bowker Press, 1949.

Lang, Constance Rowe. *Kennebec & Boothbay Harbor Steamboat Album*. Camden, Maine: Down East Enterprise, Inc., 1971.

Long Island Historical Committee. *Long Island Long Ago*. Long Island Civic Association, n.d.

Millinger, Jim. *The Nellie G.s On Casco Bay*. Yarmouth, Maine: Yarmouth Printing & Graphics, 1993.

Moulton, John K. *Peaks Island: An Affectionate History*. Yarmouth, Maine: self-published, 1993.

Nicolls, William Jasper. *Brunhilda of Orr's Island*. Philadelphia: George W. Jacobs & Company, 1908.

Quinn, William P. *Shipwrecks Around Maine*. Orleans, Mass.: Lower Cape Publishing Co., 1983.

Richardson, John M. *Steamboat Lore of the Penobscot*. Reprint. Augusta, Maine: Kennebec Journal Print Shop, 1950.

Roberts, Franklin B. and John Gillespie. *The Boats We Rode—A Quarter Century Of New York's Excursion Boats And Ferries*. New York: Quadrant Press, Inc., 1974.

Ryan, Allie. *Penobscot Bay, Mount Desert & Eastport Steamboat Album*. Camden, Maine: Down East Enterprise, Inc., 1972.

Short, Vincent, and Edwin Sears. *Sail & Steam Along the Maine Coast*. Portland, Maine: Bond Wheelwright Company, 1955.

Snow, Richard F. *A History of Birch Island, Casco Bay, Maine*. Topsham, Maine: S'no Hill Publications, 1992.

South Portland History Committee. *History of South Portland, Maine*. South Portland, Maine: Brownie Press, Inc., 1992.

Stanley, Robert C. *Narrow Gauge—The Story of the Boston, Revere Beach & Lynn Railroad*. Cambridge, Mass.: Boston Street Railway Association, Inc., 1980.

Stevens, Jane, and James E. Perkins. *One Man's World: Popham Beach, Maine*. Porter's Landing, Freeport, Maine: Bond Wheelwright Company, 1974.

Taylor, William Leonhard. *A Productive Monopoly—The Effect of Railroad Control on New England Coastal Steamship Lines, 1870-1916*. Providence, R.I.: Brown University Press, 1970. An analytical economic study, unique among the selections listed here. A scholarly and meticulously researched work by the steamer *Sabino*'s last regular summertime engineer under Casco Bay Lines ownership.

Trefethen, Jessie B. *Trefethen—The Family and the Landing*. Portland, Maine: House of Falmouth, Inc., 1960.

Acknowledgments

This saga of Casco Bay steamboat days is the end product not only of extensive research, but of many personal interviews and informal dialogues. Much compiling, organizing, writing, rewriting, and endless editing, interrupted by many periods when it all had to be laid aside in favor of other pressing matters, have given the project a span of 25 years.

The first acknowledgment to make, therefore, is a spiritual one. My meditations, as I launched into the long writing process, were those of a career merchant mariner as well as an anxious-to-achieve writer. Composing and scribbling during the long off-watch hours of a 26-day Pacific crossing, for example, helped to create a work encompassing two large volumes in its original form, not to mention over 350 photographs collected for the publication. Although the cost in psychological terms has been great, God's grace has been sufficient.

There are many people to acknowledge and I'm very grateful to several who aided extensively but no longer walk among us. Noted marine photographer R. Loren Graham of Swampscott, Massachusetts, should head the list. Many of his photos taken while a summer cottager on Little Diamond Island illustrate these pages. A valued friend, he lent encouragement by the yard, and with authority as a founder of the Steamship Historical Society of America in 1935. For many years he served as its New England regional vice-president emeritus. Willis H. Ballard of Southwest Harbor, one-time purser for Casco Bay Lines and later the Eastern Steamship Lines, shared his memories with me as well as materials and photographs. Peter T. McLaughlin, part-owner and officer of Casco Bay Lines between 1958 and 1980, was more history-minded than most people realized, offering me the use of a large personal collection of memorabilia.

Others now passed on, but deserving of mention for their contributions, include former Casco Bay Lines freight agent Philip L. Sherry of Portland; Captain Carleton Morrill of South Portland; Herbert L. Jacobsen, general manager and last president of the old Casco Bay Lines steamboat fleet; Mr. and Mrs. Walter Randall of Stroudwater; and Mr. and Mrs. Philip J. Corbin of Salisbury, Massachusetts.

Given his all-consuming interest in the history of Casco Bay steam navigation, and a long career of island steamboating with Casco Bay Lines, it seems an eternal shame that Warren Graffam did not achieve that monumental definitive work, a book on Casco Bay steamboats, that he had consciously prepared for and planned to write for most of his life.

Warren N. Graffam. Hilda Cushing Dudley

Nothing remains to tell us exactly how far Warren Graffam went in transposing a tremendous collection of notes and photographs into anything like manuscript form, or if he really ever did steer all his Casco Bay steamboat memorabilia in that direction at all. A vast cumulative knowledge of the subject and a certain ability with prose would have stood him in good stead as a rightful author. As years passed, however, something went dreadfully wrong with his dream, and as a Portland school custodian in his later years, he became ever more reclusive until the day he died alone in an unkempt and cluttered State Street apartment.

Unfortunately, when the rooms of Warren's last home were cleaned up, much of his notebook, scrapbook, and photographic collection was carelessly mixed with the trash and trucked away. One itinerant laborer, seeing value in some of the collection boxes, made an unauthorized removal and soon sold them in two lots to prominent Portland waterfront figures, who were unaware of the circumstances involved. At any rate, the eventual rediscovery of these separated portions of surviving Graffam material finally made it possible to select and integrate the better photos and the contents of a single early journal into *Steamboat Yesterdays*, along with information gained in two research interviews with Warren in 1969 and 1970.

Thanks for their assistance must go as well to Captain Donald A. Crandall of Peaks Island; journalist Orville R. Cummings of Manchester, New Hampshire, who served as historian of the Seashore Trolley Museum at Kennebunkport; State of Maine rail transit historian Charles D. Heseltine of South Portland; Mrs. Frederick Wilson of Portland; marine engineer Frank E. Reilly of Pemaquid; Everett E. Clarke of Long Island; Robert and Grace Green of Orrs Island; Mr. and Mrs. Howard E. Mosely of South Portland; Mrs. George W. Salzer of Greenland, New Hampshire; Janet Taylor Scarponi of Portsmouth, New Hampshire; Kennebec River marine historian and author Jane W. Stevens of Popham Beach; Professor William B. Jordan, Jr. of Portland; and Professor Joel W. Eastman of South Portland.

I must also thank former Steamship Historical Society of America national president David Crockett of South Natick, Massachusetts; S.S.H.S.A. national and New York chapter officers Mr. and Mrs. James S. Wilson of Staten Island, New York; S.S.H.S.A. Southern New England chapter past chairman and national director William H. Ewen, Jr. of Providence, Rhode Island (especially for his excellent renderings of *Kennebec* and successive steamers of the Cook & Sands sidewheeler fleet); also William M. Rau of New City, New York, Editor-in-Chief of *Steamboat Bill*, the quarterly journal of the Steamship Historical Society of America; and S.S.H.S.A Librarian Laura Brown at the University of Baltimore, Baltimore, Maryland.

Thanks for their cooperation are extended to marine surveyor William Schell of Holbrook, Massachusetts; and Edward A. Langlois, former Maine Port Authority, Maine State Pier, and Casco Bay Lines general manager, who was a founder and longtime president of The Shipyard Society (officially known as the Society for the Preservation of the Historic World War II Contribution of the Workers of the Todd-Bath Iron and South Portland Shipbuilding Corporations). As such, Ed Langlois has been principal source of information on the Shipyard Ferries Company described herein.

A host of other personalities who shared their memories or contributed material are named in the text. My thanks and gratitude are extended to one and all, and no less to Mrs. E. Marie Estes, former director Gerald Morris, curator Thomas Gaffney and staff of the Maine Historical Society; the staffs of the Portland Public Library; the Peabody Museum of Salem, Massachusetts; the Staten Island Ferry Museum, Staten Island, New York; the Mariners Museum, Newport News, Virginia; the Maine Maritime Museum at Bath; the McArthur (Biddeford) Public Library; the Bangor Public Library; the Jacksonville (Florida) Free Public Library; and the Curtis Memorial Library, Brunswick.

The photos on pages 121 and 122 have been reproduced by special permission of the author, Jane Stevens, from the book *One Man's World: Popham Beach, Maine*, published by The Bond Wheelwright Company, Freeport, Maine.

Excerpts from Harold B. Clifford's *Charlie York: Maine Coast Fisherman*, have been reproduced with permission of The International Marine Publishing Division of McGraw-Hill, Inc.

Excerpts from "S.S. Aucocisco, A Salt Water Sound" by Esther R. Adams from the June 1956 issue of *Yankee Magazine* are reprinted with permission of Yankee, Inc., Dublin, New Hampshire. Esther's husband, Franklin P. Adams, one of the most influential journalists of the twentieth century, is also represented here. His poem "Maine Song at Sunrise" appears by courtesy of *The New Yorker* magazine. We know with certainty that an elderly "F.P.A.," one of Bailey Island's most notable summer residents, still possessed his biting wit and intended this light-hearted piece to be every bit as wry and plaintive as it sounded, once he had set it down with his trademark fountain pen and green ink.

A real debt of gratitude is owed Mrs. Hilda Cushing Dudley, owner of House Island and the Buccaneer Line, a gracious lady among the waterfront influentials of Portland Harbor. Thanks to her generosity and that of her son, Captain Harold "Hal" Cushing, Jr., of South Portland, the rare Warren Graffam collection of U.S.Q.M.C. steamer photographs, in addition to several other subjects, were made available to the author.

Finally, generous thanks are due Stewart P. Schneider of West Kingston, Rhode Island, and Bailey Island, as well as *Down East Magazine* of Rockport, Maine, for permission to quote extensively from the June 1966 article "Casco Bay Steamboats." A steamer fan and fellow Steamship Historical Society member, Stew played the organ at the Bailey Island Community Church wedding of the author's parents, as a teenager in 1940. He is now a professor of Library Science at the University of Rhode Island, and also travels frequently to lecture at New England state universities.

Index

Abenaki 42-43, 45, 47, 52, 67
Abner's Point 45, 70, 77, 94
Adams, E.L.O. 40
Adams, Esther Root 94-95
Adams, Franklin Pierce ("F.P.A.") 94
Alger, Horatio, Jr. 136
Andrews, R.S. 19
Archibald, Captain Isaac E. 50-51, 59, 66, 162-163, 165
Atlantic Wharf 18
Atwood, Harry 88
Bailey Island 43-45, 52-53, 55-58, 65, 67, 69, 70, 73, 77,
    79, 83, 93-94, 97, 99, 102
Bailey's Island Steamboat Wharf Co. 45, 55
Bailey, Florence 33
Bailey, Frank Linwood 79
Bailey, Henry 41, 56, 63, 67, 69, 77
Bailey, Jake 62
Bailey, Ralph 32, 75, 97, 99, 100, 141, 145, 150
Baker's Island 129
Baker, Captain Charles H. 120
Baker, Captain E.A. 72, 117, 118
Baker, Peleg 77
Bankruptcy of 1919 102
Barbour Works 34, 41
Barker, Captain Eugene A. 56, 59
Barker, Clark H. 20-21
Basin Cove, South Harpswell 59
Bass Point, Massachusetts 91
Bass Rock 45
Bates, Mr. and Mrs. Eben E. 61
Bath City Landing 34
Baxter, James Phinney 130
Bay Point 34
Beals Ledges Landing 67
Beard, Captain Ebenezer 14
Beck, Captain Charles H. 17
Bennett & Kerst 34, 51, 133
Bennett, Captain W.D. 34, 51
Bernstein, Levi and Abie 56
Berry, Captain John 41
Beyer, George W. 79
Biddeford, Maine 18
Birch Island 71-72
Birch Island Land Company 71
Birch Island Landing 71-73
Birchmont 71
Blue Hill Line 51
Boston and Marblehead Line 29
Bourne's Wharf 106
Boyce, John 151

Brackett's Landing 14, 17
Brown, George Winfield 140, 142
Brunswick & Portland Steamboat Company 71, 114, 117-118
Brunswick Telegraph 16
Bryan, Captain Ivan W. 49
Burnham's Wharf 41, 131
Burnham, George L. 115
Burnham, Mrs. Alice 41
Bustin's Island Landing 56, 110
Canada 97
Cape Ann 29
Cape Breton Island 30
Cape Cottage Landing 14, 17
Carter, J. Melvin 23
Carter, John 17
Casco Bay & Harpswell Lines 73, 75-77, 79, 80, 83-89, 93,
    95-96, 102-104, 106, 153, 155
Casco Bay Breeze 34-36, 54-56, 58-59, 61-62, 64-66,
    69-70, 76, 83, 85, 88, 94, 97, 114, 120, 162
Casco Bay Directory (published bi-annually) 53-54, 142
Casco Bay House 19
Casco Bay Lines (C.B.L.) 18-19, 27-28, 30-32, 34-37, 39,
    42, 47, 51, 54, 67, 73, 75, 77, 79, 81, 88, 91, 114, 137,
    145, 147, 149
Casco Bay Steamboat Company, The first 19, 21, 127, 130,
    149, 164
Casco Wharf 131
Catskill Lines, The 23
Central Landing (orig. Littlefield's Landing) 39-40, 65, 67
Central Wharf 58
Central Wharf Towboat Co. 39, 73
Chase, Captain Charles G. 21, 23
Chase, Captain Robert 106
Chebeague Island(s) 36, 43, 52-53, 70, 78, 87, 89
Clark's Island 40
Clarke, Charles B. (Portland Mayor) 104
Clay, Herbert (Eastern Steamship Lines Portland Agent) 104
Cleaves Landing 56
Cleaves, Captain Clinton 157
Cleaves, Captain George 157
Cliff Island Landing 67, 70, 77, 137
Clifford, Harold B. 52
Cod Ledges 16
Coffin, Dave 110
Coffin, Robert P. Tristram 72
Cohan, George M. 80
Commercial Wharf 39
Commonwealth Pier 91
Consolidation of 1907, The 75, 77, 86-88
Cook and Sands 16-17

Cook, Horatio G., Jr. 14-15, 17-18
Cook, William H., (engineer) 61, 66, 96, 99-100, 113, 123
Cousin's Island Landing 56, 63
Cousins Island 56, 63
Cox Ledge 73
Cox's Head 34
Crafts, Walter D. 43
Craig, Charles 106
Cramm, Harry L. 140
Crawford Plan (cottage colony) 72
Crockett, Captain Oscar 51
Cromwell Line 18
Cross, John 160
Crowley & Lunt, (publishers) 54
Cundy's Harbor 67, 69-70, 164
Cundy's Harbor Landing 67, 69
Cunningham & Banks Wharf 129
Curtis, John B. 17, 20-21, 30, 34, 40, 127
Cushing House 86
Cushing's Landing 56, 62, 67, 86, 144
Cushing('s) Island 15, 18-19, 23, 31
Custom House Wharf 20-21, 27, 30-33, 35, 40, 42, 54, 73,
    75-77, 79, 84, 89, 93, 97, 101, 103, 149
Daily Eastern Argus 44, 110
Daniels, Captain Bert 44, 47
Daniels, Isaiah 42, 44, 53-54
Davis, Alice Flynn 77, 80, 84, 88-89, 95-97
"Dead Ship of Harpswell, The" 13
Deer Island (Boston Harbor) 29, 91
Deer Island Thorofare 20
Deer Isle, Maine 20
Deering, Maine 17
DeHart, Kimber 102
Detroit, Michigan 28
Dewey, Admiral 62
Dewey, Henry P. 44
Diamond Cove Landing 16, 20
Diamond Island Landing (aka Farm Landing) 20
Diamond Island Roads 96
Diamond Island Transportation Co. 130-131
Diamond Island(s), The 18, 31, 77, 95, 104
Doughty's Landing 77
Doughty, Captain Warren 157
Doughty, Fred W. 57, 59
Doughty, George H. 41, 58, 65, 67, 86, 99
Douglas, Byron 31
Dow, Joseph 159
Dyer Yard 43, 47
Dyer, Nathan E. 34, 43-44, 47, 49, 50
Eastern Argus 13, 44, 102, 113, 131, 144, 150, 159

Eastern Dredging Co., The 23, 42, 64, 66
Eastern Steamship Co. 78
Edson, Captain Edward E. 144
Elwell, Edward H. 130
Evergreen Landing 18, 31, 86
Factory Island 19
Falmouth Foreside Steamboat Company, The 44, 114
Falmouth Foreside Transportation Company 155, 157
Farm Landing 130
Feeney, James 93
Feeney, Joseph 73, 86-87, 96
Fisher, Jr., Captain John A. 28-29
Flaherty, Thomas F. 165
Follansbee, Deacon 14
Foote, Francis M. 18-19
Foote, Lendall G. 18
Ford, John 80
Forest City Landing 17, 31, 86
Forest City Steamboat Company, The first 19-21
Forest City Steamboat Company, The second 18-19, 21, 23, 25, 88, 115, 127
Fort Preble 17
Foster's Point Landing 69
Fox Island & Rockland Steamboat Company, The 27
Foye, Captain James 32, 75
Franklin Wharf 18, 23, 25, 43
Freeport & Portland Steamboat Company 64, 119
Freeport Steamboat Co., The 109-110, 114
Freeport, Maine 13
Frenchman's Bay Steamboat Company, The 27
Frontier Steamboat Co., The 133
Furber, James T. 119
Gallovitch, Earl 80
Galt's Wharf 18
Garrison Cove 99
Garrison Point 73
Gates, Captain Wilbur 32, 93
George Russell Shipyard 42-43, 126
Georges Bank 13
Georges Island 29
Gibson, Montgomery S. 27
Gilliam, J.W. 62
Goding, Charles W.T. 27, 31, 33-37, 79, 84, 88-89, 103
Goldthwait, Captain Daniel 126
Goodridge, Captain Charles 160
Gosport 75
Gould, Tom 44
Graffam, Warren N. 96, 102, 115
Grand Trunk Terminal 53, 100
Great Chebeague Island 36, 39-42, 44, 50, 54, 56, 61, 65-67, 70, 75, 77-78, 86-87, 93, 96, 110, 157
Great Diamond Island 16, 31-32, 87, 89
Great Island 37, 47, 69
Green Island Passage 50-51, 67
Green Island Reef 50-51
Green, Robert 101
Greenwood Garden Steamboat Line 127, 129, 132
Griffin, John B. 20-21
Gurnet 35-36, 67, 70
Gurnet Bridge Landing 67, 69
Gurnet line 67, 70, 73, 76-77, 79, 81
Gurnet Point 137
Gurnet Steamboat Company 162

Guy Lawrence 37
Hale, Dr. Leon L. 165
Hamilton's Landing 56, 61, 65, 75, 157
Hamilton, Captain Alfred H. 56, 157
Hamilton, Captain Clifford S. 61, 63, 69, 73, 78, 81, 83, 87, 93, 102
Hamilton, Captain Walter W. 56
Hamilton, Mate Len 69
Hamilton, Mr. and Mrs. L.A. 61
Harpswell Center Landing 67, 72-73, 96
Harpswell Division 73
Harpswell Island Co. 40
Harpswell Steamboat Co. 34-36, 42-45, 47, 50-59, 61, 64-67, 69-70, 72-73, 77, 79, 81, 114, 121, 164
Harpswell, Maine 16-18, 39-42, 44, 54, 79, 100
Harpswellians 58
Haselton, Captain Joseph H. 159-160
Haselton, Captain Joseph H. Jr. 160
Haskell Island 71, 85, 98
Heseltine, Charles D. 159-160
Hill, Bessie A. 61
Hill, Captain Ernest 37, 75
Hill, Harry 66, 123
Hinckley's Landing 34
Hodgdon, Samuel 65
Hodgdon, Winfield 86-87
Hog Islands, The 18
Hope Island 36, 49, 53
Howard, Captain Charles W. 131, 135-139, 162-163, 166
Howard, Frank A. 137
Howe, Captain Charles 36, 75
Hudson River 23, 28, 79
Hunnewell's Point 17
Hurricane Island 27
Ingersoll, R.H. and associates 119
Inner Bay 56, 62, 64, 87, 95-96
Inner Bay Route Service 55-56, 64, 86-87, 106, 117
Inner Green Island 50
Isles of Shoals 75
Jenks Landing 44, 75
Johnson, Frederick C. 72
Johnson, J.H. 130
Johnson, Prudence 164
Johnson, Walter E. 115
Jones, William T. 15, 18
Jones (Wharf) Landing 18, 127, 129
Jordan, Edgar L. 54, 58, 73, 79
Kellogg, Elijah J. 122
Kennebec Steamboat Co. 20
Kennedy Line 149
Kennedy, Captain Walter 103-104, 142-143, 149
Kennedy, Captain William H. 149-151
Keough, John B. 165
Kerst, Daniel W. 34, 51
Kimball's Wharf 14
Kimball, Captain Nathaniel 17
King Edward VII 15
Knickerbocker Steam Towage Co. 66
Knowlton, Captain Charles Howard 17, 20-21, 127, 129, 131
Lake Erie 27-28, 30
Lake Huron 28
Lake Michigan 28
Lake Ontario 30

Lamoine, Maine 20
Lamy, John 62, 78
Land's End 77
Larrabee, Seth L. 130
Leeman, Elisha 52
Leighton, W.E. 70
Lenox, William 83
Lewiston, Maine 41
Libb family 18
Lincoln, President Abraham 17
Linscott, George 102
Liscomb, Captain John F. 25, 27
Little Chebeague Island 20, 39-40, 77, 87-88
Little Chebeague Landing 20, 41, 44, 50, 53, 67
Little Diamond Island 31-32, 77, 87
Little Mark Island 67
Littlefield Captain Manley 32, 56, 59, 61, 83
Littlefield's Landing 39, 40, 65, 67
Littlefield, George W. 61
Littlejohn Island 56, 63
Littlejohn's Island Landing 63
Locke, Walter (Superintendent) 87, 89, 95
Lond Island 18-20, 23, 28, 30-31, 34, 39-41, 44, 50, 52-53, 56, 61-62, 67, 70, 77, 81, 86-87, 95-96, 102, 137
Long, Captain James L. 41-42, 44, 47, 49, 54, 58, 61-62, 64, 66-67, 70-71, 81, 85-86, 89, 93
Longfellow, Henry Wadsworth 20
Lowell, Captain Granville 19, 40
Lower Goose Island 71
Luke, Paul 157
Lyford, S.L. 130
Lynn & Nahant Steamboat Company 29
MacDonald Steamboat Company 51, 66, 68, 70, 120, 123, 162
MacDonald, James H. 51, 121, 123
Mackerel Cove Landing 45, 69-70, 97, 150
Macomber, Captain Safford 30, 62
Madockawando Landing 113
Maine Steamship Company 61, 64
Mansfield's Landing 14
Mast Landing 106
Matthews, Captain Thomas 40
McCullum Bartley 80, 127
McMullen, William 98-99
McShane, Mr. (engineer-*Sebascodegan*) 55, 61
Merchants' Marine Railways 28-29, 32, 37, 67, 77, 83, 97
Mere Point Landing 56, 63, 65, 71, 104, 110, 118
Merriconeag Sound 36-37, 42, 71, 73, 85, 99
Merrill's Wharf 65
Merrimack River 23
Merriwell, Frank 17
Merryconeag (Merriconeag) Sound 36-37, 42, 71, 73, 85, 99
Metcalf, Captain Ernest Clifford 129-130
Millay, Edna St. Vincent 122
Mineral Spring Landing 43, 45, 52, 55, 65, 70
Morrill, Captain Carleton 99, 102
Morrill, Captain Charles B. 53-54, 57-59, 61-62, 64, 66, 70, 77-78, 81, 87, 93-95, 97-99, 102, 105
Morris Cummings & Co. 64
Morse Island 50
Morse, Frank B. 54
Munsey's Magazine 136
Neafie & Levy Ship & Engine Building Co. 67
New Meadows River 36, 66, 69-70, 106, 163

New Meadows Steamboat Company 70, 163
New York Harbor 19, 28, 58
Nichols, Master Chester 112
Nicolls, William Jasper (novelist) 78-79
Norton, Edward R. 114
Noyes, H.W. 130
Nubble'', ''The 45
O'Brien, Arthur 95
Old Orchard Steamboat Company 42, 125, 128
Old Stone Wharf (Hamilton's Landing) 56, 61, 65, 75
Oliver, Allie 19
Oliver, Captain Alfred S. 17-19, 30
Oliver, Frank 35
Orr's Island 42-44, 47, 50, 52-53, 62, 65, 69-70, 77, 93, 98-100, 151, 165
Orr's Island Division 61-62, 69-70, 76, 83, 87
Orr's Island Landing 42, 44, 62, 65, 67, 73, 98
Osborn, John E. 165
Outer Green Island 50
Oxnard Line 16
Oxnard, Captain William 17
Parsons, Captain Edward L. 30-31
Passamaquoddy Ferry & Navigation Co. 114
Pavilion House 14-19
Peaks Island 20, 23, 28, 30-36, 39, 59, 62, 64, 73, 77, 80, 86-87, 95-96, 102, 104, 131, 135-136, 166
Peaks Island Steamboat & Amusement Co. 135-136
Peaks Island Steamboat Company, The 17-19, 21, 145
Pease, Louis 14
Pennell's Wharf 115
Penobscot Bay 20, 27-28, 51, 59
Peoples Ferry Company 21, 44, 131, 142, 154, 165
Perkins, Captain James E. 35
Perry, Stephen C. 40
Phippsburg Center 34
Pinkham Island 42, 73, 100
Piscataqua River 135
Pleasant Cove Landing 20
Point Shirley Pier 25
Pollister, George A. 41
Ponce's Landing 20, 23, 86
Popham Beach Landing 35
Popham Beach Steamboat Company 34
Popham, Maine 34
Porter's Landing 13, 106, 114
Porter, Captain Seward 13-14, 106
Porter, Samuel 13
Portland & Cape Elizabeth Ferry Co., The 21
Portland & Harpswell Steamboat Company 40-41
Portland & Rockland Steamboat Company 50-51, 59, 66
Portland & Small Point Steamboat Co. 51, 121, 123
Portland company 34, 47, 49, 50, 55, 75, 80-81, 83, 102
Portland Express, The 49
Portland Harbor 14, 16-17, 20, 36-37, 39, 42, 47, 50-51, 65, 67
Portland Pier 35, 42, 44, 49, 51-53, 58, 62, 67, 69-70, 72, 75, 89, 110, 118, 121, 127, 159
Portland Shipbuilding Company 29, 45, 47, 49, 50, 55, 58, 67, 77, 83, 97
Portland, Freeport & Brunswick Steamboat Co., The 117
Portland, Little Chebeague & Harpswell Steamboat Co. 40, 42, 114

Portland, Maine 13-20, 23, 25, 27-31, 33-37, 39-44, 51-52, 54, 56, 58-59, 61-63, 65-66, 69-73, 75, 79-80, 84, 87, 93, 95, 97, 106, 113-114, 126-127
Portland-Boston Line 65
Potts Harbor 62, 71, 85, 99, 150
Presumpscot River Steamboat Company 159
Prince's Point 67
Prine & Daniels General Store 73, 99
Providence-Newport Block Island Line 91
Purington, William L. (Purser) 66, 70, 165
Quimby, Almond A. 165
Rackleff, James L. 126
Ram Island Light 67
Randall Line 140
Randall & MacAllister Company 16, 21
Randall, Captain George C. (''Cliff'') 51, 71, 136, 146, 154
Randall, Captain Oscar C. 96, 103, 106, 139-140, 145-146, 154, 163
Read, Lt. C.W. 16
Redman, Captain 40
Reed, Joseph B. 41
Ricker, Captain Stephen 39-40
Ricker, Harry 30, 93
Ricker, R. William 93
Rockland and Vinalhaven Steamboat Company 59, 66
Rogers, Sam 81
Root, Esther Sayles 79
Ross & Sturdivant 15
Roundie, Eddie 95
Rounds, Edgar E. 135, 137
Russell Shipyard 42-43
Saco River Towboat Company 126
Sands, Captain Cyrus F. 15, 17-19
Saugus River 91
Savannah Machine & Foundry Co. Shipyard 80
Sawyer, Charles 39
Sawyer, Harry E. 115
Sawyer, Lorell B. 49, 102
Schmader, Joseph 153
Schuyler, Peter 102
Scott's Landing 17-18, 23
Seabury, Captain Ben M. 112-115
Sebasco Landing 67, 69
Sebascodegan Island (Great) 37, 47
Sederly, Lt. Charles, Chief Engineer 59
Sherry, Philip L. 80
Sinnett, Captain Wm. Henry 52
Sinnett, David P. 45
Sinnett, E.E. Co. 55
Sinnett, Everett E. (''Rett'') 52, 165
Sinnett, Perley B. 52
Six Town Times 56, 112
Small, Alonzo (engineer) 56
Smith, E.G.P. 130
Snow's Arch Wharf 25
Soule, Captain Horace B. 110
South Freeport Division 55, 59, 63, 71-72
South Freeport Landing 56
South Harpswell-(North Landing) 58, 62, 65, 67, 70-71, 77, 85
South Harpswell-South Landing 36, 98
South Portland Marine Railways 28-29, 32, 37, 62, 67, 77, 83, 97, 99

Southwest Harbor, Maine 20
Sparrow, Charles A. 21, 23
Sprague, Captain Anthony 20
Sprague, Ralph B. 76, 83
St. George River 40
St. Lawrence River and Gulf of 30
Star Island (Isles of Shoals) 75
Star Line Steamboat Company, The 21, 25, 27-28, 87, 127
Steamboats, sidewheel 13-17, 30
Stockbridge, Captain Adelbert C. (''Bert'') 87, 96-97, 102
Stockbridge, Captain Earl 81, 93, 100, 155
Stockbridge, Mrs. Adelbert (Amy) 41
Stonington, Maine 20, 51
Storey Marine Railways 28-29, 32, 37, 62, 67, 77, 83, 97
Straits of Mackinac 28
Stroudwater Steamboat Company 161
Sturdivant, Cyrus 17
Sunset Landing 56
Swan's Island 87
Swett, Captain Oren R. 155, 157
Swett, Captain Paul V. 157
Swett, Sr. Captain Walter E. 155, 157
T-Wharf (Boston) 91
Taylor, Captain Prescott 62-65, 78, 157
Temple Bros. ''5-cent Line'', The 32, 64, 131
Temple Brothers Company 30, 64
Thompson, Captain Herbert 62, 81, 84, 97
Thompson, Joseph C. and Eugene 115
Thrumcap Islet 62, 79
Tinkham, A.W. 14
Tourist Steamboat Line, The 20-21, 40
Towboats, passenger 16-19, 23
Town Landing (Falmouth Foreside) 109, 155
Townsend, Captain Horace B. 106, 110
Trefethen family 18
Trefethen's Landing 23, 31, 33, 137
Trefethen, Walter S. 142
Trott's Landing 14
Turnip Island 77
U.S. Army Coast Artillery 32-33
U.S. Army Quartermaster Corps (U.S.Q.M.C.) 29
U.S. Government Patrol Vessel 99
U.S. Mail Service, contracts 43, 52, 93
U.S. Marshall sales 51
U.S. Steamboat Inspection Service 31, 61, 95
Union House 18-19
Union Steamboat Company, The 21, 23, 28, 87
Union Wharf 13-14
United States 13, 17
Upper Goose Island 71
Upper Goose Island cottage colony 71
Upton, Captain Joseph T. 61
Vinalhaven Island, Maine 27
Wadsworth, Wendall S. 117-118
Waite, Albert H. 113-114
Waldo Steamboat Company, The 41, 44, 113-114
Webber, Judson A. 50, 66
Webber, Mate Herbert 57, 59
Weeks Wharf Landing 13
Weeks, Captain Freeman N. 127
Weeman, Captain J.P. 106
Wesleyan University 70
West End Landing 56, 62, 67

West, George F. 40, 42, 54, 58, 72, 79
Westcott, George P. 40-42, 131
Western Landing 77, 86-87
White Star Line 95
White Star-Dominion Lines (British) 84
Whittier, John Greenleaf 13
Widgery's Wharf 161
Will's Strait 99
Willard, Captain Benjamin J. 20-21

Willard, Captain William 16
Willey, Captain O.E. 59
Williams Bros. & Island Evening Lines 152
Williams, Captain Harry 153
Williams, Fred 153
Wilson, President Woodrow 17
Winnegance Landing 69
Winslow & Co., J.S. 17
Winslow, Edward B. 147, 150

Wren, M.A. 121
Yankee Magazine 94
Yarmouth, Maine 42
York's Landing 43, 45, 52, 55, 65, 70
York, Captain Andrew J. 54
York, Charlie 52
York, Lendall M. 43, 56, 70, 165
York, Mertie 56

Vessel Index

A. J. Miller 19
Admiral 152, 153, 155, 157
Alice 41, 42, 43, 44, 65, 70, 113-114, 121
Alice Howard 112, 135-136
Allequippa 164
Alpine 139-140, 142
Anna Belle 145-146, 154
Antelope 14-15
Aucocisco 34-35, 41, 47, 49-56, 58, 61-62, 64-67, 69-70, 73, 75-79, 81, 83, 93-95, 99, 102-103, 105-106
Baltimore, U.S.S. 62
Brooklyn, U.S.S. 62
Cadet 21, 23, 25, 28-30, 91
Caleb Cushing 16
Carlotta 18
Casco 15-16
Catherine 51
Charles A. Warren 39, 66
Chase 18
Chebeague 42-45
Chesapeake 16, 18
Clinton 17
Comet 135-138, 140, 142
Comfort 16
Commander 80
Corinna 71-72, 116, 118
Cornelia H. 44
Dash 13
Dirigo 18
Eldorado 27, 29-32, 34, 81, 133
Elizebeth City 61, 113
Emita 21, 23, 25, 29-32, 36, 49, 75, 81, 87-88, 93, 102-103, 106, 113, 127
Emmeline 27
Engine No. 7 45
Experiment 14
Express 17-19, 21, 30
Falmouth 18
Favorite 15, 17
Florence 21, 23
Flushing 106
Forest City 18, 30, 129
Forest City 16, 18
Forest Queen 21, 25, 27-28, 30-33, 35-37, 75, 81, 84, 95, 102, 105-106, 113
Frederick N. Wilson 66

Gazelle 16-19, 21
Gen'l Lincoln 89
General Bartlett 21, 23
General Slocum 58
Gipsy Queen 17
Gordon 40-44, 54-55, 65, 70
Gov. Bodwell 27
Greenwood 127, 129
Guardian 30
Gurnet 106, 145-147, 152, 154
Haidee 55, 109-110
Harraseeket 106
Harriet Lane-USCGC 157
Hawthorne 161
Henrietta 39-42
Isis 112, 114, 116, 130-131
Island Belle 30, 32, 64, 131-132
Island Queen 17
James Sampson 47
James T. Furber 119
Jeanette 31, 130-133
Joseph Baker 19
Josephine Hoey 20-21, 116
Jule 163-164
Juliette 51
Kennebec 13-14
Lily 17
Longfellow 160
Lottie and May 120, 152
Louise 159-160
M. & M. 32, 131, 133
Machigonne 52, 61, 67-71, 73, 75-77, 81, 85-86, 89, 91, 93, 95, 152
Madeleine 66, 112-116
Magnet 17, 20-21, 40
Maine, U.S.S. 51
Maquoit 47, 55-56, 59, 61-66, 73, 75, 77-78, 83, 86-87, 95-96, 103, 105, 113, 157
Mary Jane 103, 104, 106, 149-152
Mary W. Libby 21, 75
Merryconeag 27, 34-36, 42-44, 47, 49, 50-52, 65, 75-77, 79, 81, 83, 87, 93, 97-101, 113, 121, 164
Mineola 50-51, 66, 162, 165
Minnehaha 20-21, 30, 40
Minnie 20
Montreal 18

Naos 53
Nellie G. 155, 157
Neptune 152
New York 20
North Land 129
Norumba 47
Norumbega 67
Patent 14
Pauline 166
Pejepscot (later Sea Gate) 51, 66, 68, 121, 123
Percy V. (later Anna Belle) 51, 66, 121-122, 125
Phantom 55, 109-114
Philomena 72
Pilgrim 27, 30-31, 33, 35-36, 75, 77, 81, 86, 93, 95, 103, 105, 133
Pioneer 27
Portland (steam tug) 73
Princess 166
Priscilla (fishing schooner) 91
Sabino 91, 154
Samuel E. Spring (later S.E. Spring) 42, 125-127, 129
Santa Maria 159-161
Sea Flower (later Gordon) 40
Sebascodegan 45, 47, 49-59, 61-62, 64-67, 69, 73, 75, 77-81, 137, 164
Sebascodegan-Woodbury 56-59
Sokokis 159-161, 166
Swampscott 59, 103-104, 106, 137, 154
Teazer 17
Tiger 16
Titantic 95
Tourist (of 1871) 17, 20-21, 40
Tourist (of 1913) 96, 103-104, 106, 139, 141, 144-146, 152, 154
Tremont 110, 115, 165
Tyro 106
Uncle Sam 16
Venture 27, 37, 75, 88-89, 103, 105
Verona 27, 34-35
Victory 157
Vivian 110, 114-115
Warrior 17
We Two 161, 166
Willard Clapp 19
Winter Harbor 113
Wm. H. Scott 39
Woodbury, Levi 57-58, 59
Yankee 91